Open an Online Business in 10 DAYS

Melissa Campanelli

Entrepreneur
MAGAZINE'S

Open an Online Business in 10 DAYS

E P
Entrepreneur
Press

Editorial director: Jere L. Calmes
Cover design: Desktop Miracles, Inc.
Composition and production: Eliot House Productions

This publication is designed to provide accurate and authoritative information in
regard to the subject matter covered. It is sold with the understanding that the publisher is not engaged in rendering legal, accounting, or other professional services. If
legal advice or other expert assistance is required, the services of a competent professional person should be sought.

Library of Congress Cataloging-in-Publication Data
    Campanelli, Melissa.
        Open an online business in 10 days/by Melissa Campanelli.
           p.   cm.
        Includes index.
        ISBN-13: 978-1-59918-084-7 (alk. paper)
        ISBN-10: 1-59918-084-7 (alk. paper)
           1. Electronic commerce. 2. New business enterprises. I. Title.
        HF5548.32.C3554 2007
        658.8'720681—dc22   2006037097

Printed in Canada
12 11 10 09 08 07   10 9 8 7 6 5 4 3 2 1

Contents

Chapter 22

eChat with Bruce Weinberg

Appendix

e-Chats

Online Business Resources

Riding the Web to Riches

C AN YOU REALLY OPEN AN ONLINE BUSINESS IN 10 days?

You betcha. While developing and growing an e-business may take a little longer, you really can get the basics up and running in 10 days.

So why even open an online business? Because the internet continues to offer a virtual universe of opportunity. While it may be more difficult to find the cheap funding that fueled the explosion of dotcom start-ups, driven entrepreneurs with good ideas are still devising ways to build solid businesses that harness the power of the internet to reach millions of people worldwide.

For every online business that flourishes, hundreds—maybe thousands—go bust. What does it take to build an online business that will grow and succeed? Read this book and you'll know, because in these pages you'll find recipes for success, road maps that pinpoint the hazards, and dozens of interviews with dotcom builders who have cashed in.

What separates the winners from the losers? Poor ideas, poor execution, poor marketing, and poor funding.

Worse, the competitive field has become crowded with companies that were online innovators and with traditional companies that reconfigured their operations to include an internet component. In some cases, launching a national, full-scale consumer-oriented site today may require more than $100 million to cover marketing, hardware, software, and staffing costs. Gulp! That's a big leap from the graduate school project days that gave rise to Yahoo!.

Web sites are still being launched every day—and making it to the big time—but now more than ever, they require a unique combination of customer insight, business understanding, technical know-how, financial resources, and entrepreneurial drive. The possibilities of success remain enticing, even when wallets are thin—if your ideas are smart and your execution is persistent. The one inescapable fact is this: It's war on the monitors, and more web sites will die than will survive. What will yours do?

The goal of this book is to give you the tools and knowledge you'll need to emerge among the victors. In these pages, you'll learn everything there is to know about starting—and running—your online business. You'll find the soup to nuts, the A to Z, of taking your idea through funding, building partnerships, launching, getting more funding, winning eyeballs, and laughing all the way to the bank.

We'll tell you what you need and where to get it. The first few chapters will cover everything you'll need to do to get your web site up and running—and this can really be done in ten days (or less). These chapters include the basics, such as writing a business plan and setting up your web site. The rest of the book will offer tools and tips related to how you can maintain your business and even watch it grow.

Throughout all of these chapters, the book also features interviews, called "e-Chats," with CEOs of big-budget name-brand sites—among them Drugstore.com, Netflix.com, eBags.com, and Newegg.com. Also, make sure to check out the Appendix, where we include e-Chats with smaller, yet still successful web merchants.

You'll also find three different kinds of tip boxes designed to hammer home key points:

- Smart Tip: bright ideas you want to remember
- Beware!: pitfalls and potholes you want to avoid
- Budget Watcher: money-saving ideas and practices

Here's the promise of this book: If you need to know it to do business online, you'll find it between these covers. Read on to find out how to make your internet dreams a reality.

The Internet Gold Rush

*T*HIS IS IT—YOUR CHANCE TO STRIKE IT VERY
rich because, suddenly, the internet has
changed all the rules. For a half century,
the big players in business, from IBM to Exxon,
dominated the game, leaving little room for
newcomers to move to the top of the heap. Then
in 1994, a little start-up named Netscape introduced a web browser—and the race for cash
was on. Amazon, eBay, Yahoo!, 1-800-Flowers
.com, Drugstore.com, and Priceline.com—today
they are million-dollar, and in some cases billion-
dollar, businesses, but where were they ten
years ago? Out of nowhere these companies,

and hundreds more, have emerged to challenge the gods of commerce. They are succeeding because the new rules favor small companies that are flexible, smart, tough, and ultra quick to react to changing market conditions.

Chew on these numbers: Online retail sales in the second quarter of 2006 were $49.3 billion, up 24.2 percent over the same quarter a year ago, according to the U.S. Census Bureau. Neither higher energy prices nor shrinking personal savings accounts are curbing consumer enthusiasm for online shopping. It is particularly impressive that the sales gains reported for the first half of 2006 come on top of strong online sales last year.

What's more, it's easier and less expensive than ever to get on the web today. For one, computer costs are continuing to fall, and computer chips are being paired in new ways to expand their capabilities. And, the free software movement born in the 1990s is arming a new generation of entrepreneurs with powerful development tools—at little or no cost. In addition, costs of high-speed internet access have been slashed.

The internet is for real, and in the 21st century; if you're not on it, you're not in business. That is today's reality byte.

A New Set of Rules

On the web, the advantage is yours—it belongs to the entrepreneur. Why? Consider Dell Computer Corporation. Dell long ago made the leap into full-steam web retailing. It yanked its merchandise out of retail stores and threw the dice, betting the company's future on direct sales (via catalogs and the web) to corporations and individuals. Its strategy worked. Today, *Fortune* magazine ranked Dell number 8 on its list of the most-admired companies in the United States in 2006.

The web is both a new distribution channel and a new way to do business. Don't miss either part of that statement. If you think of the web only as a relatively new channel—a different way to put products and services in front of customers—you'll miss the threat and the promise of the internet, which is that it will utterly change how you do business.

For one thing, the web is ruthless in the squeeze it puts on pricing. Fat and waste have to go, and good riddance, because many large companies (and too many small companies) have grown comfortably wealthy by exacting indefensible margins out of the retail process. No more. The web stomps margins flat, and to make profits, companies have to rethink where their dollars will be earned. Big companies (most of them) have responded to these new rules by shutting their eyes and praying the moment will pass. (Think of the big banks that treat customers terribly, pay laughable interest rates, and are forever hiking fees. Most are doomed to be dinosaurs.) All this is good news for you because it means you have a wide-open playing field before you.

Better still, the opportunities are unlimited. Would it be wise to go head-to-head against Yahoo! or Amazon? Not directly, because these companies are among the few internet businesses that can legitimately claim to have established major consumer brands. But the web is so young, and possibilities are everywhere. Want proof? Read on for a few amazing stories of internet success popping up where most people would least expect it.

SMART TIP
Always look for a niche the Big Boys have neglected—then exploit this opportunity swiftly, before the mega-companies come to their senses. And guess what: There always are such opportunities. Find yours and move fast!

Online Negotiations

Charles Brofman is an internet entrepreneur who has found success pairing fast-paced internet technology with the slow-paced process of settling insurance claims.

Brofman started Cybersettle Inc. (www.cybersettle.com) in 1996. Cybersettle is a White Plains, New York-based online dispute resolution company. Its web-based system facilitates high-speed, confidential claim settlements by matching offers and demands. Parties can settle disputes instantly, 24 hours a day, seven days a week via the internet, or by calling its customer service center during normal business hours.

SMART TIP

Just because your idea might seem a little out of the ordinary, don't quit if you're a believer. Charles Brofman didn't quit, and his Cybersettle is clearly a big winner in reinventing the way insurance claims are settled.

Why did Brofman, a seasoned trial attorney, start the company? "The courts today literally cannot handle the onslaught of litigation they face," he says. "As a result, people who are entitled to get compensated for their injuries have to wait long periods of time, and insurance companies that have an obligation to pay—and want to pay—have to wait a long period of time. Cybersettle really just came out of our frustration with this process, where everybody wants to settle, and we just can't get there because of the way the system has been set up."

Here's how Cybersettle works: An insurance company receives a statement of claim from a plaintiff's lawyer. When

THE E-COMMERCE QUIZ

Think you're ready to become a "Netpreneur"? Prove it. Before moving on to the next chapter, take this quiz. Answers are true or false.

1. I'm comfortable in a game in which tomorrow's rules are invented the day after tomorrow.

2. I see inefficiencies—waste and delay—in many current business practices.

3. I'm willing to delay this year's profits to potentially make more money next year.

4. I know how to size up customers I've never seen or talked with.

5. The 'net excites me—I like surfing around and seeing what's new.

6. I can live with thin margins.

7. Customer satisfaction is the most important thing a business can deliver.

8. I'm not afraid of battling Titans.

9. I see opportunity where others see risk.

10. I am willing to work harder and smarter than I ever could have imagined possible.

Scoring: Guess what—"true" is always the right answer for any netpreneur. But you knew that already because you're ready to compete on this merciless playing field.

the insurance adjuster reviews the case and is ready to settle, he then enters three offers into the computer. The plaintiff's lawyer is e-mailed, faxed, called, and sent a hard-copy letter saying that the insurer has made an offer. The lawyer then enters three demands. The Cybersettle main server compares the lawyer's first offer with the insurer's, and when the demand falls below the offer, the software splits the difference and settles the claim.

Brofman says the system mirrors the way the industry does business. "There's this bidding war that goes on," he says. "It's a numbers game. We just expanded the day—it now can go on 24 hours a day instead of eight hours a day."

Insurance companies like the service, which can be used in all 50 states and in Canada, because it helps them cut down on the more than $34 billion worth of claims administration they cope with every year. Claimants like it because they get paid far faster than they would if they wound their way through the legal system. And lawyers like it because they still get paid by their clients.

To date, Cybersettle has handled more than 100,000 transactions and has facilitated more than $1 billion in settlements, including bodily injury and other types of insurance claims. In addition, Cybersettle was awarded a U.S. patent for its Computerized Dispute Resolution System and Method. Cybersettle also has similar patent coverage in more than 15 other countries, and currently there are over a dozen countries where Cybersettle patents are pending approval.

Brofman says there are several reasons why his internet venture is successful. One is that his company has a "fabulous" investor, a strategic partner who understands his business. Another is that his business does what the internet was designed to do, and that is to conduct a transaction 24 hours a day, seven days a week. "If you are going to do something on the 'net," says Brofman, "you have to do something that the 'net was designed to do."

BEWARE
Venture capital funding, billions of dollars' worth, is out there—but be prepared for a grilling before any check is signed. Never forget that venture capitalists are in business to make money, lots of it, not to speculate on chancy business ideas.

Reaching Their Peak

Now, remember that just a few lines ago I advised against challenging Yahoo!. That only applies to Yahoo!'s own turf. If you're willing to expand your horizons a little, the sky's the limit. Consider Jim Holland and John Bresee, who in 1996 founded Backcountry.com, a Herber City, Utah-based online retailer of outdoor gear for skiing, kayaking, camping, and backpacking.

Holland, a two-time Olympic ski jumper and six-time national champion Nordic ski jumper, and Bresee, a former editor of *Powder* magazine, founded the company with the purpose of providing outdoor adventure gear to the hard-core recreational athlete.

"We developed the site ourselves and banked about $10,000 of our own money to get started, which we used for inventory," says Bresee. "We took a risk but knew there was an interest out there for what we were doing."

Backcountry.com now services tens of thousands of visitors daily via its world-class web site. As of June 2004, orders began shipping out of a new state-of-the-art 47,000-square-foot warehouse on California Avenue in Salt Lake City, Utah.

What's the company's secret to success? There's not one answer to that question, but one key decision the company made was to focus on a narrow niche—selling gear to hard-core sports enthusiasts—instead of competing with mass-market retailers such as REI that might sell the same items, but without the same knowledge.

Backcountry.com, for example, populates its call-center staff with hard-core skiers and trekkers who are out there using the equipment the site sells. Therefore, when a customer calls with a question, the staff can answer it using their own unique personal experience.

Excellent customer service, in fact, is the company's mantra. "We do things like put our phone number on every page of our

BEWARE

Not only can online catalogs be updated in seconds, but they must be! A sure way to frustrate electronic shoppers is to take them through the buying process only to annoy them at the last moment with a "Sorry, out of stock" message. Never do that. If merchandise is out of stock, clearly note that early in the buying process. Customers can accept inventory problems, but they'll never accept you wasting their time.

site because we want to make it as easy as possible for people to reach the company, as well as give people the opportunity to buy products from us if they feel uncomfortable about entering their credit card number into the site," says Bresee.

Other reasons for its success? Cost-effective online and word-of-mouth advertising that increases customer confidence in the site.

Sweet Dreams

Even when your dreams aren't so lofty, the internet can still save the day, as Barbara McCann found out. She and her husband, Jim, owned The Chocolate Vault, a store in Tecumseh, a village about 60 miles west of Detroit. They'd watched traffic—and customers—veer away from little towns, and they'd watched their cash flow dry to a trickle. Then Barbara McCann decided to give the internet a whirl.

On a skimpy budget—a few thousand dollars—she built her web site, www.chocolatevault.com, and then watched an amazing thing happen. "People from all over the country found us, and they started buying our chocolates!" she says.

McCann says the internet business has grown so much that she has decided to downsize by closing the retail store. She is also moving her internet business and home to another small town in southeastern Michigan and building a small factory type facility that allows the company more space. McCann doesn't have the money to buy major advertising space and instead puts all her energies into offering exceptional customer service. "We are trying to give our customers the kind of personal service online that they would receive if they walked into our store," she says.

McCann also says that most of her customers keep coming back because the site is easy to maneuver and understandable.

10 REASONS YOU SHOULD BE ONLINE

Need convincing that the web is the place for your business to be? It would be no sweat to list 25—even 50 to 100—reasons why you have to be online, but here are 10 to get you started:

1. It's cheap. There is no more inexpensive way to open a business than to launch a web site. While you could spend many millions of dollars getting started, low-budget web sites (started with as little as $100) remain viable businesses.

2. You cut your order fulfillment costs. Handling orders by phone is expensive. Ditto for mail orders. There's no more efficient—cheap, fast, accurate—way to process orders than via a web site.

3. Your catalog is always current. A print catalog can cost big bucks, and nobody wants to order a reprint just to change one price or to correct a few typos. A web site can be updated in minutes.

4. High printing and mailing costs are history. Your customers can download any information you want them to have from your web site. Sure, you'll still want to print some materials, but lots can be distributed via the web.

5. You cut staffing costs. A web site can be a low-manpower operation.

6. You can stay open 24 hours a day. And you'll still get your sleep because your site will be open even when your eyes are closed.

7. You're in front of a global audience. Ever think what you sell might be a big hit in Scotland or China, but feel clueless about how to penetrate foreign markets? The web is your answer because it's truly a borderless marketplace. Watch your site log, and you'll see visitors streaming in from Australia, New Zealand, Japan, Malaysia— wherever there are computers and phone lines.

8. There are no city permits and minimal hassles. This could change, but in most of the country, small web businesses can be run without permits and with little government involvement. As you expand and add employees, you'll start to bump into laws and regulations, but it certainly is nice to be able to kick off a business without first filling out reams of city and state forms.

9. There are no angry customers in your face. You can't ignore unhappy customers in any business; in fact, how well you deliver customer service will go far toward determining how successful you are. But at least with a web business, you'll never have to stand eyeball-to-eyeball with a screamer.

10. It's easy to get your message out. Between your web site and your smart use of e-mail, you'll have complete control over when and how your message goes out. You can't beat a web site for its immediacy, and when a site is done well, it's hard to top its ability to grab and hold the attention of potential customers.

You have other reasons for wanting a web business? Fair enough. The key is knowing your reasons, knowing the benefits of doing business online, and being persistent through the launch. This isn't always an easy road to take, but it's definitely a road that has transported many to riches, with much less upfront cash, hassle, and time required than for similar, offline businesses. And that's a tough value proposition to top.

Will The Chocolate Vault rise to the top and challenge the biggies in that space, such as Godiva? "Never," says McCann, who knows her budget and her ambition. But the miracle is that "the internet has been a lifesaver for us," she says. "We would've closed our shop without it."

Set the scale of your internet ambitions—dream large in the way of Charles Brofman, or dream on a more diminutive scale like the McCanns—because there is no "right" approach to the internet. Good, steady money can be earned by strictly local players who open on the internet and find a stream of global business pouring in. Or big bucks may be yours if you invent a new eBay or Monster.com.

Chapter 1 Summary
10 Things You Can Do Today

1. Meet a fabulous investor or strategic business partner who understands your business.

2. Develop a great business idea with a friend based on something you love.

3. Focus on a narrow niche instead of competing with mass-market retailers.

4. Train your staff to focus on excellent customer service.

5. Use cost-effective online and word-of-mouth advertising that increases customer confidence in the site.

6. Understand the power of the internet by using it to expand your reach.

7. Plan for your site to be easy to maneuver and understandable.

8. Hire local college students or interns and have them work part time to build up your business.

9. Be sure to update your online catalog regularly.

10. Set the scale of your internet ambitions—dream large.

Moving from a Brick-and-Mortar to an Online Store

*Y*OU HAVE A SUCCESSFUL BRICK-AND-MORTAR store. You are well respected in your neighborhood, and you have a loyal and growing clientele. So should you open an online store—in ten days, no less—and expand your universe? Should you close the store you already have? Should you expand to become a true multichannel retailer? Read on to find out.

Goodbye Brick-and-Mortar?

Should you shut down your brick-and-mortar store to focus exclusively on online retailing?

That's a question many small-business owners are chewing on. While there is a lot of buzz out there about the web and its many opportunities, the question that has to be asked is "Can the web and offline, traditional retailing coexist?"

E-tailer Sherry Rand has a definite opinion on the subject. "The smartest thing I've done in business is shutting down my store and going exclusively as an online retailer," she says. "Now I have a really neat business. I love it." Rand has an online store that sells one thing, and one thing only—gear for cheerleaders. You want pompoms in various styles and colors? You want megaphones for leading cheers? Then you should know about Pom Express (www.pomexpress.com), where Rand has conducted e-business for seven years since she shut the doors of her brick-and-mortar store.

"Online, I don't have to carry the great overhead of a store, and from a quaint town in North Hampton, New Hampshire, I'm selling globally," says Rand. "We get lots of orders from Europe, where cheerleading is really picking up." Rand, who was a cheerleader from fourth grade until she graduated from college, sold cheerleading supplies as a manufacturer's representative until she opened her own store. Now that she's operating solely on the web, she says, "This is a great niche. And on the internet, I can conduct business wherever I want to be."

Best of Both Worlds

Rand's arguments sound good—but are they good enough to persuade you to go purely online? The temptations are potent. Close a brick-and-mortar operation, go strictly cyber, and whoosh—you've distanced yourself from monthly rent payments and dealing face-to-face with grumpy customers, plus you've positioned your business to sell globally. At least that's what it seems like in theory. But can you count on it happening for you?

Probably not, says Jackie Goforth, a partner for Pricewatehouse-Coopers focusing on retail and e-commerce companies. While she says a great example of an industry that has shifted to online is antique and collectible retailing, "I would say for the average retailer, this is not the time to shut down your shop. I think we will find that retailers will use their online presence as a great complement to their stores. It may actually drive in traffic by allowing the customer to do some online browsing."

In addition, she says the appeal of being able to return merchandise purchased online at the local brick-and-mortar store gives shoppers confidence in their online purchases. "There still appears to be some fear that online purchases are difficult to return," she says. "The retailer who carries unique and exclusive merchandise could potentially tap into a much larger market by utilizing the web to reach a broad customer group."

You have to keep in mind, though, that for every dotcom that thrives, there are more that flop, says Mark Layton, an e-commerce expert. "Many dotcoms will become dot bombs—they'll fail," says Layton. "Online or offline, you need a sustainable business model. If you don't have that, you don't have a business."

Online Component

Experiencing second thoughts about burning the lease on your storefront and going strictly virtual? Consider Vino! (www.vino2u.com), the online complement to a Winter Park, Florida, wine store owned by Adam Chilvers. Built around the tasty proposition that all the wines it sells are rated 85 or higher by a prestigious publication (such as *Wine Spectator*), both the storefront (opened in November 1998) and the online store (launched a month later) are profitable, according to Chilvers. "Doing business on the web is a dream," he says. "The costs are very low."

But he has no intention of shutting down his brick-and-mortar store, for a flock of reasons. For starters, an online operation still needs some real-world warehousing for merchandise such as his, and the brick-and-mortar store provides that. But it's the second reason that is the clincher: "On the site we sell to many customers outside our area, but we also get many locals coming into our store with shopping lists they've printed out on the web," says Chilvers. For those customers, the combination of the web site and the store offers a great convenience—they hunt for wines they want online, at midnight or 6 A.M., and then they can get in and out of the brick-and-mortar store in a matter of minutes. "I'm happy with how the store and the web site are working together to build this business," says Chilvers. "It's a good combination for me."

Double Vision

Still, isn't this dual-channel strategy an unnecessary complication that forces an entrepreneur to focus on two distinctly different venues? The experts don't think so, and in fact, many point to it as the way to go forward into the next century. "There are tremendous advantages to be had by leveraging internet sales with a brick-and-mortar store," says Bart Weitz, a marketing professor at the University of Florida, Gainesville. Case in point: You can use the store to promote the web site, he says, and that means printing the web site address, or universal resource locator (URL) on bags, sales slips and advertising fliers. That can be a big step in overcoming the obstacle facing every dotcom today. "It's gotten very expensive to attract people to a site," says Weitz. "Stand-alone sites incur very high marketing expenses because they have to spend the money to get eyeballs."

"A [brick-and-mortar store] can be a billboard for your web site," says Bentley College e-commerce professor Bruce Weinberg, who points to clothier Gap as a for-instance. It already has massive brand awareness, and whenever a customer walks in—even walks by—a storefront, there's a reinforcement of the URL, www.gap.com. Your business might not be a Gap, but even so, says Weinberg, being in a physical location with signage and various advertising campaigns to promote the store will mean that you are also building awareness for a web site.

Another argument in favor of a dual-channel strategy: "Different consumers want different things," says Bill Gartner, the Sprio Professor of Entrepreneurial Leadership at Clemson

SMART TIP

What about returns? They are proving to be a real hassle in online retailing—both to e-tailers and to consumers— and that's where e-tailers with brick-and-mortar storefronts have a big advantage because consumers who want to return products can simply take them to the storefront. Smart e-tailers stress this perk, so if it's true for you, flaunt it!

University in Clemson, South Carolina. "Some customers want the kind of personal interaction that can only happen in a traditional retail setting. For others, it's simpler to log on to the internet. The smart, consumer-oriented business makes it easy to buy, no matter the customer's preferences."

Who's Minding the Store?

The biggest, most worrisome question is, "Isn't all retailing heading to the web anyway?" Just last year, that was the buzz, but nowadays—with more dotcoms struggling and few breaking through to profitability—a kind of cautious sobriety has taken hold. Explains PricewaterhouseCoopers' Goforth, "There are certain merchandise categories that'll be slow to succeed online—but I would anticipate it will follow the trends seen with the catalog industry. Unique products that are hard to find in stores and expensive for the brick-and-mortar retailer to stock will be the logical players online."

Some other types of businesses such as bookstores, consumer electronics sellers, and travel agencies are going to have a tough time prospering if they're not online. Margins are getting squeezed ever lower as multiple internet vendors and internet-savvy consumers create a situation with increasingly competitive pricing, and that means it will only get tougher to succeed in a brick-and-mortar context. But other types of businesses—from furniture sellers to clothiers—just may find the going stays smooth in brick-and-mortar stores.

"Some products are ideal for online; others just work better in a brick-and-mortar store, where customers want to test the look, feel, and fit," says Jonathan Palmer, a business professor at the College of William and Mary in Williamsburg, Virginia. Worried about being a merchandiser in an endangered category? Don't panic, says Goforth. "We heard that catalogs would put traditional retailers out of business, and it didn't happen. In

SMART TIP

A big consumer worry about e-tailers is that these cyberstorefronts are fly-by-night scams. When you have a brick-and-mortar storefront, you also have solidity in the minds of consumers. Don't hide it. Put up a photo of it on your web site. And definitely show the street address. Bingo—you are an established retailer. Consumer worries will vanish—and sales will start coming in.

FORTUNE-TELLING

Want an easy rule of thumb for assessing how your business might fare online? College of William and Mary business professor Jonathan Palmer shares the three factors that shed a green light on this decision:

1. You sell a product line that can be delivered economically and conveniently.

2. You have a desire to market to customers outside your own geographical location and a product with broad appeal.

3. There are significant economic advantages involved in going online.

Chew especially hard on points one and two because if they are on your side, the profits implied in the third point likely will follow.

A fourth decision factor just might be whether you can economically draw customers to your site. Chasing a mass market—and going belly-to-belly against Amazon, Drugstore.com, Priceline, and the like—means you had better bring a seven- or eight-figure advertising/marketing budget to the table to keep up with your competitors. But the good news is that there is still plenty of room for thinly-funded players who have targeted shrewd niches and a solid business plan. The experts agree: Those are tomorrow's dotcom success stories.

fact, some catalog retailers eventually backed into opening brick-and-mortar stores. Now we hear that the web will put B&Ms out of business, and that certainly has not happened. We may see e-tailers going for brick-and-mortar stores."

Paper-Based Sales

After opening your e-store, you can expand your reach by adding a catalog to the mix.

In fact, the tried-and-true catalog sent streaming through the mail along with all those bills, letters, and notices is still the top-rated method of garnering customers—and, of course, sales.

What's more, being a multimerchant can be good for your business. Research conducted in 2004 by comScore Networks for the U.S. Postal Service found that a business doubles its chances of making an online sale by mailing a catalog. Other findings from "The Multi-Channel Catalog Study" include:

SMART TIP
Want to learn more about multichannel retailing? Then see "e-Chat With GiftTee.com's Craig Bowen" and "e-Chat with RedWagons.com's Tony Roeder" in the Appendix.

- Catalog recipients account for 22 percent of traffic to a catalog company's web site and 37 percent of its e-commerce dollars.
- Catalog recipients make 16 percent more visits to that company's web site than those who do not receive a catalog.
- Catalog recipients view 22 percent more pages and spend 15 percent more time at the web site than those who do not receive a catalog.
- On average, the total amount spent on a web site by a catalog recipient is $39, more than twice the $18 spent by noncatalog consumers.

Catalogs also work well as a channel for e-tailers because they can easily leverage the web site's marketing, creative, infrastructure, and fulfillment systems and repurpose them for a catalog.

Chapter 2 Summary
10 Things You Can Do Today

1. Decide whether to shut your brick-and-mortar store, if you have one.

2. If you've decided not to shut your store down, use your online presence as a great complement to it.

3. Find a way to allow your customers to return merchandise purchased online at your local brick-and-mortar store.

4. Online or offline, make sure you have a sustainable business model.

5. Remember that the combination of a web site and a brick-and-mortar storefront offers great convenience to customers.

6. Use your brick-and-mortar store to promote your web site by doing things such as printing your URL on bags, sales slips, and advertising fliers.

7. Thinking of going solo on the internet? Try selling a unique product that is hard to find in stores and expensive for a brick-and-mortar retailer to stock.

8. Sell a product line that can be delivered economically and conveniently, and only open an online store if you have a desire to market to customers outside your own geographical location and sell a product with broad appeal.

9. After opening your e-store, plan to expand your reach by adding a catalog to the mix.

10. Keep in mind that being a multimerchant can be good for your business. In fact, one study found that a business doubles its chances of making an online sale by mailing a catalog.

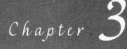

Getting Funding

S O WHY SHOULD YOU DO BUSINESS ONLINE? Because the internet enlarges your business's realm of possibilities. It allows you to communicate with anyone anywhere (or thousands of people at once) with e-mail. You can search for information from millions of sources on every subject under the sun. Advertising your product or service, showing potential customers your wares and allowing them to purchase immediately, doing test marketing, joining discussion groups with like-minded individuals, sourcing products, sending a monthly newsletter to customers, and linking with affiliated vendors are all part of what you can do with the web. So the question isn't "if" you should embrace it but "how."

Sounds Like a Plan

Within the first 10 days of planning to open your business, it is imperative that you write your e-business plan. Because you're exploring new territory, making decisions about technology and marketing, and establishing a new set of vendor relationships, a well-thought-out plan will guide you.

The first step in writing an e-business plan? Decide what kind of experience you want your online customers to have. Think not only about today but also about two and five years down the road. Your e-commerce plan starts with web site goals. Who are your target customers? What do they need? Are they getting information only, or can they buy products at your site? These key questions, asked and answered early, will determine how much time and money you'll need to develop and maintain an online presence.

Second, decide what products or services you will offer. How will you position and display them? Will you offer both online and offline purchasing? How will you handle shipping and returns? Additionally, don't overlook the customer's need to reach a live person.

As you explore the web for vendors to support your e-business, have a clear idea of how you want to handle the "back end" of the business. If you decide to sell online, you will need a shopping cart program, a means of handling credit card information, and a fulfillment process. (For more on this, see Chapter 5). You may decide, however, that your site is informational only and that you will continue to process transactions offline. These are all important business decisions.

Last and most important is your promotional strategy, which gets even more important when you think about the millions of web sites out there. Remember: The promotional strategy for your web site is no less important than the promotional strategy for your business as a whole.

"The web site should be viewed as an integral part of the marketing effort—as another 'front door,' if you will, into the business," says Frank Catalano, an Auburn, Washington, marketing strategy consultant and co-author of *Internet Marketing for Dummies* (IDG Books, 2000). "After all, the site is a way to distribute information, gather customer feedback, and even sell a product or service. Just promoting a web site without regard to overall business goals and other marketing efforts is pointless."

The Name Game

Once you've decided to have a web site, your first to-do item is to make a list of possible web site names. Then run, do not walk, to the nearest computer, log on to the internet, go to your favorite search engine, and type in "domain registration." You will find a list of companies such as www.network solutions.com, www.godaddy.com, and www.register.com that will guide you through domain registration. For a modest fee ($10 to $75), you can register a domain for a year. Register.com is particularly helpful because it tells you if the name you've chosen is taken, but it goes a step further by offering a list of alternative names that are still available. Let's say that you sell flowers and you would like to register your online name as www.flowers.com. A search shows that www.flowers.com is taken. Your next choice is www.buyflowers.com, but that's already spoken for as well. Register .com offers several alternatives, such as buyflowers.tv, www.buyflowers.cc, and buyflowers.ws.

How are these different? Because instead of the generic top-level domains (such as .com, .org, .net, or.gov), they include internet country code top-level domains from, respectively, the Polynesian island nation of Tuvalu, the Territory of Cocos (Keeling) islands, and Samoa.

These domain names have been marketed as an alternative to the more "crowded" generic top-level domains, where the selection of

SMART TIP

If you're serious about the success of your online business, then you need to find ways to give yourself every advantage you can over your competition. One way is to build a customized blueprint that outlines exactly how your business will succeed. Remember: The process of writing a business plan for your company can be a crucial step in getting your profits to where you want them to be.

unregistered domain names is much more limited. The .ws domain name has achieved some popularity because in this context it stands for "web site" or "world site" rather than the abbreviation for "Western Samoa," the nation's official name when two-letter country codes were standardized in the 1970s.

From the available names, choose one that is the easiest to spell and remember. Once you've chosen a name, prompts on the domain registration site will guide you through a simple registration procedure. You will generally be offered one-, two-, or three-year registration packages; choose based on whether you are completely happy with the name or think you'll want to switch in a year or so.

Why is domain name registration imperative? Because more than 11 million new domain names have been registered since the beginning of 2006. Everyone wants a catchy name, so registering yours ensures that no one else can use it as long as you maintain your registration. For a small investment, you can hold your place on the internet until you launch.

BEWARE

Can you "park" a domain name for free? When you park a domain, you reserve it but haven't yet mounted a site. Many outfits tout that they offer free parking, but that's not exactly true: You still have to pay the registration fee. Free parking only means they'll put up an "under construction" sign that anyone who hunts for your domain will find.

With your e-commerce name established, evaluate your initial advertising and office supplies budget, which should be part of your business plan. For example, make sure you've done everything you can do offline to tell people about your site before you go online, such as printing your web address on your business cards, brochures, letterhead, invoices, press releases, and advertisements. Stick it on other items, too—mouse pads, T-shirts, promotional key chains, and even the company van.

Catching Drop Catchers

Some e-tailers today who accidentally let their domain names expire are becoming victims of drop catchers—people who buy and sell web names that others let expire. Currently, there are hundreds of drop catchers that buy the names and resell them or use them for web sites loaded with advertisements.

WHAT'S IN A NAME?

What is a good domain name worth? Stories abound of names selling for seven figures or more, but proof of such transactions is hard to find. Nonetheless, if you think you have a zingy, salable name that you want to market, try Sedo.com (www.sedo.com), the leading marketplace for buying and selling domain names and web sites. The site claims to have more than one million domains for sale. How do you buy them? Sedo's model is an offer-counteroffer model. This means that you negotiate directly with the domain's owner until you both agree on a price. This system takes away the uncertainty of an auction model, reduces the potential for fraud, and gives you precise control over how much you pay. Also, try GoDaddy.com (godaddy.com), which recently announced that it had officially launched its internet auction site for domains, The Domain Name Aftermarket (tdnam.com). The new site offers customers four different ways to buy and sell domains. "Buy Now" enables customers to purchase domains at a single, set price. "Expired Domain Auctions" enables customers to bid on an expired domain, with the winning bidder receiving full ownership of the domain name after a two-week (post-auction) waiting period. "Offer/Counteroffer" allows users to extend an offer on any domain, with The Domain Name Aftermarket staff acting as an intermediary. And "7-Day Public Auction" permits sellers to set a minimum starting bid, with potential buyers placing increasingly higher bids.

"This has been going on since 1997, but over the past few years it has been growing as the number of registries has been increasing," says Jay Westerdal, CEO of Name Intelligence Inc. a Bellevue, Washington-based company that tracks the industry.

Industry experts say that roughly 200,000 expired domain names become available every day. While many are consciously discarded by their owners, others are mistakes.

So how do you protect yourself and make sure you do not become a victim? For starters, follow these tips from Warren Adelman, president/COO of Scottsdale, Arizona-based GoDaddy.com Inc., the largest domain registrar in the world with 12.9 million domains under management. The company

SMART TIP
For an inside look at how a web entrepreneur uses domain names, see " e-Chat with Thralow Inc.'s Daniel Thralow" in the Appendix.

sells domains to customers; it also runs a domain name auction, which allows people who have won names to put those names into the auction for sale. Expired names are also sold in that auction.

- *Make sure your contact information is up to date.* Why? Because renewal notices go to that contact information. "If you register a name for 12 months, at a certain point before the end of that year, we or other registries are going to communicate with you and let you know (via e-mail or direct mail) that your domain is going to expire in 90, 60, 30, 15, 7, 2 days, or 1 day," says Adelman. "So make sure your contact information, including your e-mail address and your physical mailing address, is up to date." Adelman also says that typically registrars give users a grace period after their registration expires—at GoDaddy.com it is 30 days—in which the users can still come back and renew their names. And even if a name totally expires and goes into an auction, "we don't reassign it until 30 days goes by," he says. "So that still gives a customer the opportunity to come back and say, 'Hey, I really meant to renew it.'"

- *Don't use a free e-mail account.* Adelman also suggests not using a free e-mail account for your contact information when registering for a domain name. "Oftentimes people will do this, and it's not an e-mail contact they necessarily use all the time, and oftentimes, with a free e-mail account, if you don't access them in 30 days, they go away," he says.

- *Take advantage of auto renew.* Most registries offer this service, which allows consumers or businesses that buy domain names for a year to automatically renew at the end of that year for an extra year by charging a particular credit card that they gave the registry. "If you do that, you won't have any chance of losing [your domain name]," says Adelman, who adds that you should also make sure you keep your payment information up to date. Adelman also suggests registering your domain name for more than one year; in most cases this will bring your costs down.

Borrowing Money

So now you have a domain name. What about getting funding for your business? And how much does it cost to start it?

"One of the beauties of starting an e-business today is that it doesn't take a lot of money to start it," says Rich Sloan, founder and head coach of StartupNation (www.startupnation.com), a leading provider of online content and community for entrepreneurs. "In fact the SBA statistics indicate that about $6,000 is what's required to start the average business today."

Sloan said most companies—and e-companies today—do the following: They bootstrap their business using their own money; they tap into their credit cards and home equity lines of credit; they get money from friends or family; or they get bank loans guaranteed by the Small Business Administration.

Each option has its challenges, and each should be treated in a professional manner, says Jeff Sloan, co-founder and the other head coach of StartupNation. For example, while the option of using friends and family for funding has the fewest contractual strings attached, "you should still draw up a contract to protect your friend's or family member's investment," he says.

Venture Capital Funding

Venture capitalists are individuals or companies with large amounts of capital to invest and they expect high returns. They typically only invest in established companies. Rich Sloan says you should only use venture capitalists if you already have a great track record in your field or as an entrepreneur, and if you have a business concept that will require a lot of money ($250,000 to $10s of millions) and will have a rapid growth curve. He also says that when getting funding from a venture capitalist (VC) firm, you must be willing to give up significant control over major decisions for your

SMART TIP
Want to see the definitive top-ten list for starting a business? Then see StartupNation's "Ten Steps to Open for Business," at www.startupnation.com/pages/start/10Steps.asp. It will give you a top-ten list covering everything you'll need to open a business.

company; have a "fast growth" company; and have an aggressive exit strategy to sell your business or do an initial public offering (IPO) within five to seven years. In short, he says "this does not describe how most people get funding when starting their own e-business."

If you decide to go the VC route, what should you do first? For starters, in your business plan you should pay close attention to the possible payday ahead (typically this is made vivid with charts that forecast revenue and profits). In short, an idea has to have the clear potential to be a major winner.

Why do VCs want big winners? Simple. They're realists who know that out of every ten ventures they fund, maybe eight will vanish without a trace; one will be a modest success; and that one home run will generate so much cash, it will make all the losses forgettable as it propels the firm deep into black ink. So don't be conservative. Think big.

SMART TIP

Practice, practice, practice. Before you go into any funding meetings, hone your presentation on your business; this can prove a lot more crucial than your business plan in the funding decision. Why? Investors invest in people who inspire them. Go in with a pitch that wows listeners, and you may walk out with a big check.

Next, think of the exit strategy. That's key. VCs don't invest to hold; they want a way to translate a business success into an economic success. Usually, that means the company gets bought by a big fish or it goes public. Either way, early investors want to know how they will get out of this deal before they go into it.

Once you have your plan in hand—with an exit strategy and a payday spelled out—you should look for every way possible to get it (and yourself) in front of VCs. It isn't easy. So often internet entrepreneurs complain, "I have a great business plan, and nobody will fund it." Maybe the plan is great, maybe it isn't, but step one in proving you've got what it takes to prosper in the rugged internet economy is finding a way to get in front of VCs.

You've tried and can't seem to land VC money? Take what cash you can from anybody, of course. Get the business afloat and then maybe VCs will come calling with cash in their

GOOD BUSINESS ADVICE

Want a source to tap for timely, practical information on how to start, manage, and expand your business? Try Kauffman eVenturing (www.eventuring.org), a web site from the Ewing Marion Kauffman Foundation, a Kansas City, Missouri-based private, nonpartisan foundation that works with partners to advance entrepreneurship in America.

Kauffman eVenturing offers a guide to entrepreneurs on the fast-paced journey toward high growth. The site has rich content, including new articles created by entrepreneurs exclusively for the site, and an indepth aggregation of existing information on the web on a wide array of subjects—from accessing capital to implementing successful recruiting strategies and competing in global markets. The site also features fresh material every day gathered through a link-blog that Kauffman has established to identify the latest information on different aspects of entrepreneurship from a wide variety of sources.

The Kauffman eVenturing site is organized around six subject areas—finance, human resources, sales and marketing, products/services, operations, and the entrepreneur (e.g., strategy, culture, leadership). New collections of articles are featured once a month, rotating among those subjects. The site is easy to search and navigate, so entrepreneurs can find the information they need quickly. Keywords in every article are "tagged" so that available information about a specific query can be assembled immediately.

hands. Even better, once your business is prospering, you can usually get much more favorable terms from VCs. The earlier they come in, the bigger piece of the company they want, which means second-stage VC financing may actually be more desirable. The moral: When the idea is good, the money will follow.

Angel Investing

Another alternative to venture capital funding is angel investors. These are individuals who invest in companies at an early stage in exchange

SMART TIP

It is not always easy to find VCs and angel investors because many choose to be anonymous for obvious reasons— if they weren't, they would always have people knocking at their door wanting to borrow money. The best way, however, to find them is to network. In short, talk to everyone you know, because you never know who they might know. In addition, keep in mind that the internet is also an infinite source of information.

for equity and the chance to help guide the company. In contrast, venture capitalists invest as a profession and generally on behalf of other investors.

Generally entrepreneurs are ready to approach angels when they have exhausted their friends and family but are not yet ready to approach venture capitalists for money.

Jeff Sloan says to approach angels if you are looking for large amounts ($25,000 to $1 million) of "smart money" because the people who provide this form of funding have already "made it big" in their own careers and can help guide you to do the same.

Sloan says there are several advantages working with angels: they not only invest money, but also provide mentoring and contacts; they are patient about their investment; and there are no monthly payments with this type of financing— angels make their money when you achieve your business's exit strategy.

The downside, he says, is that angels are difficult to find and require regular and thorough reporting, which can take up valuable time. In addition, as with VCs, "you are giving up equity in your company," says Sloan.

Legal Eagles

Covering your legal bases is perhaps one of the most important things to consider when starting up your business. If you don't pay enough attention to the legal aspects of your web business, you could end up in litigation, or lose valuable assets, such as your logo, brand, or site itself.

Why? Because unlike setting up shop in the real world, on the web all the assets you purchase, create, own, and operate to generate business and revenue consists of intellectual property rights, such as copyrights, trademarks, patents, and trade secrets. As a result, you will have to align yourself with a reputable lawyer, preferably one that understands intellectual property rights and the internet.

Before meeting with your lawyer, make sure you've registered your domain name, and ensured that it is not being used by anyone else. If it is, under trademark law, that company has superior rights to you, and if it discovers you are doing business under its name, it can sue.

The first time you meet with your lawyer you'll probably discuss the basics, such as who the founders of your company are and what type of company it is—and then delve into trademark issues, such as whether or not you've checked your trademark properly, and the importance of protecting it.

You should also get into copyright law, patent law, libel law, individual privacy law, and trade secret law. Trade secret law is particularly important for internet companies that have a new and valuable concept no other company has.

In general, the law states that everyone who has access to your ideas should agree in writing to a confidentiality agreement that says they will not disclose those ideas or use them themselves.

A good confidentiality agreement should be signed by all of your employees, an independent contractor, and even investors. The agreement should also be drafted in the very early stages of the start-up.

The legalities don't end there. Web companies using web development firms to develop their sites for them should be aware of ownership issues. In short, internet merchants need to make sure they own their web site—not the developer—and that they have the right to sue and make any changes to the site.

SMART TIP

How do you find a good lawyer? Use your contacts, or try FindLaw (www.findlaw.com), a web site that offers names not only of law firms (organized by region) that specialize in specific issues, but also of lawyers that cater to small businesses. You can also retrieve a large amount of legal information on the site that can help you run your e-business.

Chapter 3 Summary
10 Things You Can Do Today

1. Write your e-business plan.

2. The first step in writing an e-business plan is deciding what kind of experience you want your online customers to have.

3. The second step is deciding what products or services you will offer.

4. As you explore the web for vendors to support your e-business, have a clear idea of how you want to handle the "back end" of the business.

5. Plan your promotional strategy, which gets even more important when you think about the millions of web sites out there.

6. Once you've decided to have a web site, your first to-do item is to make a list of possible web site names. Then register your domain.

7. Make sure you've done everything you can do offline to tell people about your site before you go online, such as printing your web address on your business cards, brochures, letterhead, invoices, press releases, and advertisements.

8. Figure out how you will fund your business.

9. Before you go into any funding meetings, hone your presentation skills.

10. Make sure your legal bases are covered.

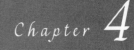

Dotcom Dreams?

REMEMBER THE WAVES OF GLUM NEWS OF internet hopes gone awry that washed over us in the year 2000? You'd be forgiven for thinking dotcom dreams are just another route to bankruptcy. And as we mentioned in the last chapter, don't think that venture capitalist will be knocking on your door, either.

You are probably not a richly funded dotcom nor do you need to sit around worrying about the day the VCs will show up at the door demanding some kind of return.

So why are we still talking about this? Because we can learn from other dotcoms' mistakes. Here

BUDGET WATCHER

When you start with little funding, do as small businesses have always done—operate on a shoestring. Dell Computers Inc., for instance, got its start in a dorm room. Apple Computer Inc. started in a garage. Your quarters needn't be that humble, but never, ever spend money you don't have to for the sake of "making an impression." If anything, it's the wrong impression you'll make because funders aren't looking to put money in the hands of CEOs who spend like drunken sailors. A little cheapness is always a good thing for a start-up.

is a quick look at some of the mistakes made by those dotcoms that have crashed and burned.

Bad Balance-Sheet Math

At no point did the companies that crashed and burned generate financial statements that indicated any reasonable relationship between income and expenses. Yet they spent wildly, renting expensive offices in Silicon Valley and what was then known as New York's Silicon Alley, hiring deep staffs (and often paying salaries upward of six figures for minor positions), and buying fantastic exposure in ads of every medium. No genuinely small start-up could afford these lush business habits for long. Sure, every start-up has a day or a week or a few months when income lags way behind outgo, but at least the math makes some kind of sense, and in the lean period, spending is lean, too. You do not need the ritzy office, the high-powered law firm, or the Stanford MBA employees, so you should be able to keep your expenses in some kind of rational alignment with income.

No Revenue Model

The core question that is supposed to be asked of dotcom start-ups is "What is your revenue model?" This is shorthand for "How do you envision bringing in income? What will be your revenue streams?" Potential investors will ask this, as will would-be employees, partners, and anybody considering a financial future with your dotcom. Strangely, however, when the question has been asked, the questioners have typically accepted formulaic answers. In the past, dotcoms have vaguely explained that their revenue model involved a mix of ad dollars and e-commerce, and in most cases, the answer was accepted. It was a mistake because, as the failed dotcoms proved, nobody had ever really put flesh on the revenue models.

Never open a business without understanding your revenue source. This seems so elemental, but in the heady days when vaporous businesses such as Yahoo! and eBay quickly snagged multibillion-dollar market caps, many people abandoned this axiom. Will your predictions be on target? Probably not. They may even be wildly wrong, but that doesn't mean they didn't serve a good purpose. Simply articulating realistic, workable revenue models is good discipline. In practice, businesses usually evolve in ways the founders did not anticipate—a fact that is all the more true on the wild and woolly internet—so early drafts of revenue models likely will get discarded, fast. But always know where, approximately, money will originate.

Incidentally, the unspoken revenue model of many dotcoms apparently had been additional rounds of funding—either from VCs or public markets—but, at the end of the day, those spigots will get turned off. Why? Read on.

No Clearly Defined Exit Strategy

Every well-conceived start-up comes equipped with an exit strategy for investors. This means how investors will get their money out of the business and when. Founders with hands-on roles in the business probably don't need to know their exit strategy, but angels and VCs want to know how and when they will get their money back. What are possible exit strategies?

- Going public: a prime choice for many dotcoms.
- Getting bought by a bigger fish: not as popular as going public, but attractive when public markets turn turbulent.
- Bringing in new investors to buy out others: another option but rarely used in the years of internet mania, probably because later-round investors have been unwilling to pay the inflated prices sought by early investors.

There is no saying which exit strategy is best, but what can be said is that no CEO needs anxious investors calling every few minutes to ask when they might cash out. And that happens all too often when there's been a lack of clarity—even realism—about the investment. This means that in early talks with investors (even if it's your folks who put up the money), you need to be honest about how you see them getting their money out and when. Be as pessimistic as possible. Sure, you might spook investors, but better to do it now than have them hassling you as you're trying to build the business.

Building Market Share to the Detriment of the Business

Market share is not God, although CEOs of the many failed dotcoms who pursued a strategy of building market share at any cost wanted you to believe otherwise. Look through the financial filings of many of the best-known dotcoms, and you'll see that a common practice is selling merchandise for less than these companies paid for it. Pay $300 to a wholesaler for handheld computers, and no matter how many you sell for $250, you won't do anything but go broke.

Yet a wacky mantra infected Silicon Valley that held that somehow, market share was the end-all. Sure, you will get market share when you sell items below cost because nobody can compete. But when pressures build and you have to tweak prices up to survive, how much of that precious market share will you lose? Lots, you can bet, which is why the only way to long-term survival is to price rationally to begin with. It makes sense to use loss-leader pricing on an item or two if that strategy generates orders that on a short-term horizon will produce profits. But it makes no sense whatsoever to consistently sell goods at below-cost prices. How can anybody wonder why so many dotcoms have nearly slid into extinction with such practices?

Ignoring Stakeholders

Who has a stake in your business? Investors, your community, your employees, management, and your vendors and customers. Long debates can explode around attempts to prioritize these stakeholders—whose stake is meatiest or weakest?—but probably the best strategy for most dotcoms is to assume that all stakeholders carry about equal weight (except for your community, which, in the case of an internet start-up, likely carries no weight at all).

To succeed, businesses want to satisfy all stakeholders. That doesn't mean all will get what they want (stakeholders quite commonly are in conflict with each other, and a management task is seeing that everybody gets enough to feel happy), but it does mean you need to stay aware of your stakeholders, those stockholders' wants, and what you're delivering. You will not last long if investors, employees, management, vendors, or customers get and stay cranky. Failed dotcoms often had little or no awareness that any stakeholders existed (at least any that were not on Wall Street), but stakeholders always exist and will always get their due.

Forgetting What Industry You're In

Guess what? Your online store is still a store, meaning you're competing in a retail universe. Yet CEOs of stumbling dotcoms talk as though they're in any industry but retail, throwing around terms like "new media," "content," and "consulting." Never fool yourself about your industry.

Having More Ego than Profits

Not only did many CEOs of defunct dotcoms forget what industry they were in, but some actually seemed to forget that they were in business at all and that the essence of a business is to make money from revenue—not from bedazzled stock market speculators and frenzied angel investors pouring cash into the till. The sad fact about many failed dotcoms is that they could have been successful—maybe not on the lavish

SMART TIP
You don't need a fancy business plan—it's probably a waste of time and money—but you do need to write down the basics of your business. As the business evolves, and as the fundamental assumptions change, take out the business plan and update it. Are you still on track to hit your targets?

scale hoped for by the founders, but profitable nonetheless. And they blew it by forgetting that in the end, business is business. While it might be fun to make it on the cover of a magazine, it's ultimately more fun to be on top of a steady stream of black ink (and it's no fun at all to manage a business that's dripping red ink).

The Message for You

Don't be discouraged by the stumblings of the name-brand dotcoms. They had it coming. That sounds cruel, but really, they did. You can avoid their mistakes and thereby create a very different outcome for your business.

Chapter 4 Summary
10 Things You Can Do Today

1. Operate on a shoestring.

2. Keep your expenses in some kind of rational alignment with income.

3. Make sure you have a clear vision about how you will bring in income

4. Never open a business without understanding your revenue source.

5. Be sure you have a clearly defined exit strategy.

6. Be sure to price your products properly.

7. Don't ignore stakeholders—stay aware of their wants, and what you're delivering.

8. Make sure to understand the industry you are in.

9. Make sure not to let your ego get the best of you.

10. Don't be discouraged by the stumblings of the name-brand dotcoms. Avoid their mistakes and create a very different outcome for your business.

Chapter 5

Web Site Building 101

WHILE THE IDEA OF SETTING UP A WEB SITE in 10 days or less may seem daunting at first, don't fret. The following chapter will show you just how easy it is.

Know Your Purpose

The starting point for putting up a web site is to determine what you want it to do—and know what it likely won't do. The bad news is that you won't get rich quick with a web site. Very few start-ups have achieved overnight success on the web—the most notable success being

Amazon.com. The web just isn't the fast track to Easy Street that too many commentators have depicted it to be.

Then why do it? Of course, persistence and ingenuity may eventually be rewarded with profits. But there are other sound reasons for putting up a web site. Even if your home page is little more than an electronic billboard for your company, it's still a powerful tool for building a business. On the web, for instance, "distance means nothing," says Jerry White, director of the Caruth Institute of Owner-Managed Business at Southern Methodist University in Dallas. A small business in the United States can use the web as a low-cost tool for reaching customers in other states, even other countries.

The clock, too, no longer matters. "On the web your business can be open 24 hours a day, seven days a week," says Gail Houck, a consultant and web strategist. Another reason for building a web presence: The web lets you serve customers in ways that would be unimaginable in a traditional retail environment. On the web, it's easy to offer far deeper product selection, for instance, and—with clear thinking on your side—prices typically can be driven down.

All good reasons? You bet, and you may have many more. Whatever your motivations, the single most important step you can take is this one: Define your goals and expectations. Do that, and the rest—including the mechanics of site design—will fall into place.

Where so many small businesses (and a few very large ones, too) go wrong is that they haven't taken this clarifying step. The resulting sites are fundamentally confusing because nobody ever took the time to specify their purpose. It's perfectly fine to erect a site that amounts to a company information brochure, but that site cannot be expected to function as a retail platform.

A Well-Thought-Out Site

A web page is a text document that usually includes formatting and links to other pages. This special formatting involves the use of tags, which are part of hypertext markup language (HTML) and are used to link one page, section, or image to another.

What makes a good web site? Before getting enmeshed in design details, get the big picture by writing a site outline. A well-thought-out site outline includes:

- Content
- Structure
- Design
- Navigation
- Credibility

An outline helps you get the most out of your e-commerce budget. You'll know whether you or someone in your company can do each piece or if you need outside help. That way, when you hire someone, it will be for only the parts of the job that you will need to have outsourced. Lillian Vernon, who founded the well-known catalog company Lillian Vernon Corp. in 1951, designed her original web site for a fraction of what her competitors spent. How? "It's a total misconception that you have to throw [big] dollars at an e-commerce solution," she says. You have to be a very careful shopper among vendors."

A detailed outline to prospective web designers makes the process more efficient.

- *Content.* The key to a successful site is content. Give site visitors lots of interesting information, incentives to visit and buy, and ways to contact you. Once your site is up and running, continually update and add fresh content to keep people coming back for more.
- *Structure.* Next, structure your site. Decide how many pages to have and how they will be linked to each other. Choose graphics and icons that enhance the content. Pictures of adorable children of different ages, for example, might work well if you're selling children's clothes, with pictures of toys and books that site visitors can click on to jump to other pages within your site where they can buy these items. At this point, organize the content into

a script. Your script is the numbered pages that outline the site's content and how pages flow from one to the next. Page 1 is your home page, the very first page that site visitors will see when they type in your web site address, or URL. Arrange all the icons depicting major content areas in the order you want them. Pages 2 through whatever correspond to each icon on your home page. Following our example of selling children's clothes, perhaps you'd start with the icon labeled "birth through one year" as page 2. Pages 3 through 12 might be all products and services pertaining to that age range. Page 13, then, would start with the icon from your home page labeled "one to three years."

Writing a script ensures your web site is chock-full of great content that is well organized. Write well, give site visitors something worthwhile for their time spent with you, and include lots of valuable information and regular opportunities to get more content. Whether you offer a free newsletter, a calendar of events, columns from experts, or book reviews, content and its structure becomes the backbone of your web site.

IMAGE BOOSTERS

When you play with images, you need specialty software that will let you change each image's size, resolution, and more. Good image-editing software will even let you edit photographs. There's a stain on your white shirt in that photo? Whoosh! An image editor will wipe away all such problems.

Such software used to be tricky to use and expensive and was mainly aimed at professionals working in graphics and photography. Nowadays, there's a boatload of good, cheap, easy-to-use programs. A top choice is Adobe Systems's Photoshop Elements (www.adobe.com), which costs $99.

- *Design.* With the content and structure in place, site design comes next. Whether you're using an outside designer or doing it yourself, concentrate on simplicity, readability, and consistency. Before you start using HTML tags right and left, remember what you want to accomplish.

  For example, if you have a pet products web site, you recognize that many pet owners have both dogs and cats. You want them to be able to shop and order in the way that's most comfortable for them. Perhaps they want to get their pet food order out of the way first, then shop for toys and fashion accessories. Maybe they prefer to shop for their cats, then focus on shopping for their doggie goodies. Cue them with graphics, colors, and fonts that make sense to you. Should all cat-related text and icons contain blue, while dog items are red? Should all food text and graphics be green, toys red, and accessories yellow? These subtle cues make all the difference in how visitors respond to your web site. Keep surfing the internet to research what combinations of fonts, colors, and graphics appeal to you, and incorporate pleasant and effective design elements into your site.

- *Navigation.* Make it easy and enjoyable for visitors to browse the site. Use no more than two or three links to major areas, never leave visitors at a dead end, and don't make them back up three or four links to get from one content area to another. For example, if you have a web site for convention planners, make it easy for visitors to link to city sites where they can find information about theaters, river cruises, museums, and the like so convention attendees can check out recreational activities on their own.

- *Credibility.* This is an issue that should not be lost in the bells and whistles of establishing a web site. Your site should reach out to every visitor, telling her why she should buy your product or

SMART TIP

Don't go crazy with colors— this is one of the biggest goofs of new web page designers. Stick with maybe two colors for fonts (words) and use a simple, basic color for the page background (white, off-white, and pale yellow are good choices). Always test your page on a laptop with a very cheap screen— don't assume surfers will have high-end monitors. If it doesn't look good on a small, cheap screen, it's bad page design.

your service. It should look very professional and give potential customers the same feeling of confidence that a phone call or face-to-face visit with you would. Remind the visitors that you do not exist only in cyberspace. Your company's full contact information—contact name, company name, street address, city, state, zip code, telephone, fax, and e-mail address—should appear on your home page.

Do-It-Yourself

As we mentioned above, you can build your own web site, thanks to the inexpensive, easy-to-use, and sophisticated e-commerce services available. These tools make it particularly easy to build a site in 10 days or less.

"If you're a one- to two-person firm, someone on your staff can design a web site, and you only sell a few products, then there really is no reason not to do it yourself, particularly with the out-of-the box solutions available nowadays," says John Jantsch, a marketing coach, author, and creator of the Duct Tape Marketing small-business marketing system based in Kansas City, Missouri. Jantsch, who built his own site, Ducttapemarketing.com, in 2001, says you can build a robust site for less than $150 per month, plus a few hundred dollars for software.

The best tool for creating web pages is Microsoft's Expression Web (www.microsoft.com), which costs $299. Microsoft Expression Web is a new version of Microsoft FrontPage. Other options are Adobe's Dreamweaver MX 8.0 (www.adobe.com) ($399) and AdobeGoLive CS (www.adobe.com) ($169). If you plan to have a large site—with more than a few pages—you also should have a contact management system, or a web application used for managing web sites and web content right from the get-go. To find a low-cost contact management tool, check the web.

Of course, you also might want to hire a web designer—especially if you plan to have a bigger site. The best way to find these folks? Networking.

ON FILE

You've created umpteen wonderful web pages, so now how do you get them onto your web site? You need another piece of software, a program that handles file transfer protocol (FTP). An FTP program lets you shift files from your computer to another computer via an internet connection, and that makes it an essential piece of any net toolkit.

FTP is built into many web page editors, but I find it faster and easier to use a specialty FTP program. For years I've relied on WS_FTP. Its newest version is WS_FTP Home 2006 ($39.95 from Ipswitch Inc., www.ipswitch.com). A free trial version is available for download.

An alternative is Cute FTP $59.99 for the home version, $89.99 for the professional version), available from GlobalSCAPE at www.cuteftp.com. Hunt for still others at CNET's downloads site—www.download.com. Type in FTP, and you'll be presented with dozens of applications that do this work.

Check out several applications and pick the one that works best for you—and know that even if you've never FTP'd, once you get into web site construction and maintenance, your FTP application will become one that's put to daily use.

A word of caution: FTP software generally seems tricky to use. That's because you need to specify things such as your user name and password and also correctly type everything in the right case (upper or lower). It can be a bit maddening to get an FTP program working right, but once you do, settings will be saved and future transfers will be no harder than making a few mouse clicks. For more tips, head to "FTP 101—A Beginner's Guide" at www.ftp planet.com/ftpresources/basics.htm. This is a helpful, free guide that should get you up and running in a matter of minutes. Oh, a vocabulary point: When you transfer a file to your web site, that's uploading. When you transfer a file from a web site to your computer, that's downloading. Keep those words straight, and all you read about FTP will suddenly make sharper sense.

After setting up your web site, you'll need a shopping cart software program or service, which allows you to take orders, calculate shipping and sales tax, and send order notifications. There are hundreds of

ALTERNATIVE CREDIT OPTIONS

In 2000, credit cards accounted for more than 90 percent of online payment volume—but by 2009, less than half that volume will come from credit cards, according to a May 2006 study from Celent Communications. The gradual shift away from credit card payments is due in large part to the lower costs for merchants in using alternative payment options.

"The model as it is today is unsustainable for credit cards to maintain their dominant presence because it is simply too costly for e-tailers," says Dan Schatt, an analyst at Celent in Boston. In addition, "There are large numbers of consumers that are sitting on the sidelines, not willing to make an online transaction today, because they fear their credit card information—or any information they leave with the merchant—will be misused."

Enter alternative online payment options. Besides eBay's PayPal another popular alternative option is Bill Me Later (www.bill-me-later.com), which offers an instantaneous credit line to consumers.

Here's a look at some other up-and-coming solutions:

- *PIN debit.* This option—which is just starting to appear on the internet—lets consumers use their PIN numbers to make secure debit purchases on the web.

- *Google Checkout.* Introduced by Google in the summer of 2006 as a PayPal competitor, the service is designed to serve as an electronic wallet that will enable consumers to buy products and services from online merchants without repeatedly entering the same personal and financial information at each store. Users with a Google account enter a credit card account number along with a few other details, and the company delivers the payments to any of the participating merchants, which must advertise on the search engine to participate.

- *ACH Consumer Push.* This innovative initiative from The Electronic Payments Association, or NACHA (www.nacha.org), is expected to launch in late 2007. It will allow for Automated Clearing House-based e-commerce transactions with the added security of authentication by consumers' online banks. During checkout, consumers will log in to their online bank to authenticate themselves, and the transaction will be secured by this authentication.

choices out there—a simple Google search will help you find the best one for your needs. These cost about $29 to $79 per month depending on the package you choose.

You'll also need a merchant account to accept credit cards and a gateway that allows you to process credit cards securely and in real time. Some companies offer both. There's a lot to choose from, so before you make a decision, search the web and ask around. In general, costs start at about $30 per month plus other fees, including transaction fees paid to your bank. (Some also have one-time setup fees that can run around $100.)

An even more inexpensive way to allow your customers to pay for your items is to use PayPal (www.paypal.com), an account-based system that lets anyone with an e-mail address securely send and receive online payments using their credit card or bank account.

PayPal is free, but the company charges 2.9 percent plus 30 cents for every transaction under $3,000. The company also has a product called PayPal Pro, which offers basic shopping cart functionality and costs $20 plus transaction fees.

The Taxing World of Online Sales Tax

If an online retailer has a physical presence, such as business offices or a warehouse in a particular state, it must collect sales tax from customers in that state. If a business does not have a physical presence in a state, it is not required to collect sales tax for sales from customers in that state.

This may change, however, because of the Streamlined Sales and Use Tax Agreement (SSUTA). Created in 2002 by the Streamlined Sales Tax Project, the SSUTA aims to make it easier for retailers doing business in multiple states to calculate, collect, and remit existing use tax. The SSUTA took effect on October 1, 2005, and 19 states have signed on.

While currently a voluntary program, if mandated by law, the SSUTA would require businesses to collect and remit sales

BUDGET WATCHER
Want to look up sales tax rates for free? Then visit www.Avalara.com and click to its free sales tax rate lookup, AvaRates NOW—a free, map-enhanced, rate look-up tool that provides accurate rates for any North American location in real time. Avalara is a provider of on-demand sales tax calculation service targeting small and midsized businesses.

tax for the 7,600 different sales tax jurisdictions in this country. It's hard to say whether the SSUTA will become mandatory. For several years, bills to make sales tax collection mandatory have been introduced in Congress—but none have ever been signed into law. Having 19 states sign on to allow voluntary collection, however, shows that the movement is gaining traction. What's more, several large, national retailers have negotiated with member states for amnesty deals in return for future collection of sales tax, and more are expected to follow. All this may get the attention of Congress.

To learn more about internet sales tax, visit the following web sites:

- The Sales Tax Institute (www.salestaxinstitute.com), which provides a range of services and links associated with sales tax.
- DavidHardesty.com, which provides news and feature articles about e-commerce taxation, including e-mail updates from e-commerce expert David Hardesty.
- Streamlined Sales Tax Governing Board Inc. (www.streamlined-salestax.org), which offers up-to-date information and news about the SSUTA.

SMART TIP

When updating pages, always go through your testing procedure as soon as you put up the changes. It's tempting to neglect this, but don't. I have often put up updated pages that, somehow, turned out to be bug-ridden. And never do page changes during your peak traffic periods! That's inviting calamity.

Testing, Testing

Gremlins often play tricks with web pages, and that's why no professional webmaster announces a new page to the public before testing it. Surf the web enough, and sooner or later you'll stumble into a test site mounted by a brand-name business that has put it online so that insiders can find the bugs before the public does. Do the same thorough testing before publicizing your page.

A crucial test: Make sure pages work equally well in Microsoft Internet Explorer, Netscape Communicator, or Mozilla's FireFox, another popular web browser. Ignore this advice at your own peril. Recently a business acquaintance implored me to look at his site, for which he had paid designers upward of $10,000. I logged in—and found only blank pages. Incredibly, the site had not been tested with Internet Explorer. When I checked the site with Netscape, it was indeed a spiffy piece of work, but not checking it with Explorer, the leading web browser, was simply nuts. If, in testing your own site, you find bugs, don't fret. Few pages get put up without at least some kinks, and a good place to start is to pinpoint things that show up on your screen offline but don't work online. The standard problem is that an image (or two, or three) isn't displaying, caused by a botched hyperlink. Strip down any web page to its essentials, and you'll find a little text interspersed with many hyperlinks, which are web directions to images and other files stored elsewhere. Put in the wrong hyperlink— and sometimes even web-authoring programs do it—and the online page will show up as a jumble.

This is when it's time to do a spot of dirty work with HTML code. Click "View/HTML," and a screen filled with gibberish will open. Hunt for the code pointing to the image or text that is not displaying. A good bet is that the link reads <img src="C:\Windows\temp\ bluediamond.gif"> or something like that. No link that includes directions to local drives will work online. The cure? Erase everything that comes before the image's name—the result will read <img src="blue diamond.gif">—and it will work exactly right online.

Follow the same drill with anything that's not displaying properly. HTML is intimidating at first glance—and at second glance, too. But tinker with it, and soon enough, all images and links will display the way you intended.

SMART TIP

Updating your web site regularly has a variety of benefits. They include:

- If you want to rank well in search results, it makes sense to post new content regularly.

- While customers may overlook an outdated printed piece, they expect your web site to be correct and updated at all times.

- Rounding out your site with timely, relevant information such as prices, hours of operation, and special offers can help users reach a buying decision.

Web Site Maintenance

A key part of maintaining your web site involves updating it with new content—which can mean anything from personnel changes to product

BUDGET WATCHER

Check your site for broken links, automatically and for free, with a stop at Keynote NetMechanic (www.net mechanic.com). Type in your URL, and—whoosh!—you will get a report on broken links and page load time, and even a freebie spell check. It can also give a free report on browser compatibility on the spot.

updates. Thanks to an array of new web-editing software and services on the market designed for novices, you can now take basic web site maintenance into your own hands. These tools give people with no web programming experience the ability to edit web pages as easily as they would a Word document.

Macromedia Contribute 3 from Adobe Systems (www .adobe.com) and Page Publisher from Interactivetools.com are two products worth a look, especially if you have a basic site that doesn't use any advanced programming. The tools used by web professionals to build sites, such as Dreamweaver and Microsoft Expression Web, which are mentioned on page 42, have become more intuitive. These products will meet your needs if you are comfortable with software and need a feature-packed tool for a more advanced site.

You can also try an online web site maintenance service such as Edit.com. This service gives you the ability to quickly and easily change text, links, images—and even add new pages. To use the service, which also offers personal support, sign up at Edit.com and schedule a 15-minute phone orientation. The cost? A one-time fee of $75 to make 15 of your web pages editable ($5 for each additional page), and a service plan that's either pay-as-you-go ($25 per day of use) or unlimited ($25 per month or $180 per year).

Another company offering a similar service is Editlet (www.edit-let.com). The standard offering costs $29 per month, but users can also pay quarterly ($78), twice a year ($148), or annually ($260).

A sure way to go wrong with a web site is to put it up and simply leave it there. To keep viewers coming back, a page needs regular updating. Basically, if your page is aging, or static, it tells the world that you just don't "get it."

How often does a site need updating? Probably once a month at a minimum. Updating takes time, but the investment is warranted.

Care to Dabble?

Want to dabble at e-tailing without a major money commitment? Take a look at Amazon's zShops (www.amazon.com). Think of zShops as auctions that don't involve bidding. There are no listing fees for selling at zShops, but zShops sellers must register for the Pro Merchant Subscription, which costs $39.99 per month for the maintainance of an unlimited number of items. A closing fee is assessed when your item sells. The fee is based on the sale price, and can be refunded if your transaction is unsuccessful. If your item sells for $0.01 to $25, Amazon.com collects a 5 percent closing fee. If your item sells for $25.01 to $1,000, Amazon.com collects $1.25 plus 2.5 percent of any amount greater than $25. If your item sells for $1,000.01 or more, Amazon.com collects $25.63 plus 1.25 percent of any amount greater than $1,000.

SMART TIP
Want to learn more about setting up your web site? See "e-Chat with BlueSuitMom.com Inc.'s Maria Bailey," "e-Chat With Fridgedoor Inc.'s Chris Gwynn," and "e-Chat With CarMD.com Corp.'s Keith Andreasen" in the Appendix.

THE 10 MOST DEADLY MISTAKES IN SITE DESIGN

Avoid these gaffes, and your site will be far better than much of the competition.

1. *Disabling the "back" button.* Evil site authors long ago figured out how to break a browser's back button so that when a user pushes it, one of several undesired things happens: There's an immediate redirect to an unwanted location, the browser stays put because the "back" button has been deactivated, or a new window pops up and overtakes the screen. Porno site authors are masters of this—their code is often so malicious that frequently the only way to break the cycle is to restart the computer. This trick has gained currency with other kinds of site builders. My advice: Never do it. All that's accomplished is that viewers get annoyed.

2. *Opening new windows.* Once upon a time, using multiple new frames to display content as a user clicked through a site was cool—a new thing in web design. Now

it only annoys viewers because it ties up system resources, slows computer response, and generally complicates a surfer's experience. Sure, it's easy to use this tool. But don't.

3. *Failing to put a phone number and address in a plainly seen location.* If you're selling, you need to offer viewers multiple ways to contact you. The smartest route is to put up a "Contact Us" button that leads to complete information—mailing address, and phone and fax numbers. Even if nobody ever calls, the very presence of this information comforts some viewers.

4. *Broken links.* Bad links—hyperlinks that do nothing when clicked—are the bane of any surfer. Test your site—and do it weekly—to ensure that all links work as promised.

5. *Slow server times.* Slow times are inexcusable with professional sites. It's an invitation to the visitor to click away. What's slow? There is no easy rule, but I'd say that any click should lead to something immediately happening. Maybe a new page or image will take a few seconds to come into view, but the process should at least start immediately.

6. *Outdated information.* Again, there's no excuse, but it's stunning how many site builders leave up pages that long ago ceased to be accurate. When information changes, update the appropriate pages immediately—and this means every bit of information, even tiny facts. As a small business, you cannot afford the loss of credibility that can come from having even one factual goof.

7. *Scrolling text and marquees.* It's an odd fact—Netscape and Microsoft Internet Explorer do not display pages identically, which is one way these site-design tools get easily messed up by browsers. They can also be maddening to the viewer who wants to know, now, what you're offering, but finds that the information keeps scrolling off the page. Use these tools in personal pages—they are fun and add liveliness to otherwise static pages—but put them aside when building business pages.

8. *Too many font styles and colors.* Pages ought to present a unified, consistent look, but novice site builders—entranced by having hundreds of fonts at their fingertips plus dozens of colors—frequently turn their pages into a garish mishmash. Use two

or three fonts and colors per page, maximum. The idea is to reassure viewers of your solidity and stability, not to convince them you are wildly artistic.

9. *Orphan pages.* Every page in your site needs a readily seen link back to the home page. Why? Sometimes users will forward a URL to friends, who may visit and may want more information. But if the page they get is a dead end, forget it. Always put a link to "Home" on every page, and that will quickly solve this problem.

10. *Using leading-edge technology.* Isn't this what the web is all about, especially since the number of Americans who have broadband at home has jumped from 60 million in March 2005 to 84 million in March 2006—a leap of 40 percent, according to a May 2006 report from the Pew Internet and American Life Project? Nope. Your pages need to be readable with a standard, plain-Jane browser, preferably last year's or older. State-of-the-art is cool for techno wizards but death for entrepreneurs.

Chapter 5 Summary
10 Things You Can Do Today

1. Know your purpose. The starting point for putting up a web site is to determine what you want it to do—and know what it likely won't do.

2. Before getting enmeshed in design details, get the big picture by writing a site outline including content, structure, design, navigation, and credibility.

3. Build your own web site with the inexpensive, easy-to-use, and sophisticated e-commerce services that are available.

4. After setting up your web site, invest in a shopping cart software program or service, which will allow you to take orders, calculate shipping and sales tax, and send order notifications.

5. You'll also need a merchant account to accept credit cards and a gateway that allows you to process credit cards securely and in real time. Some companies offer both.

6. An even more inexpensive way to allow your customers to pay for your items is to use PayPal (www.paypal.com), an account-based system that lets anyone with an e-mail address securely send and receive online payments using their credit card or bank account.

7. Understand the tax issues you'll be dealing with online.

8. Do not put up a web page without testing it first.

9. Remember to maintain your web site by updating it with new content—which can mean anything from personnel changes to product updates.

10. Avoid major gaffes—such as disabling the back button or having slow server times—and your site will be far better than much of the competition.

Hosting Your Site

CONGRATULATIONS. YOU'VE PUT EVERYTHING together and you actually have a web site that runs beautifully on your computer. Now how does it all get on the internet? You have two options. The first is to host it yourself on a computer that can be dedicated as a web server (or a computer that's permanently connected to the internet) and has a broadband internet connection. This will prove costly to set up and maintain, and will have limited capacity if you're at all successful in using your site for business. These factors make this option not such a good one.

The second option is to use a web hosting company, which stores and manages web sites for businesses, among other services. You may have already come into contact with such a company when you signed up for your domain name.

Many companies swear by some of the bigger names in web hosting, such as Network Solutions (www.networksolutions.com), Web.com (www.web.com), 1&1 Internet (www.1and1.com), Go Daddy.com (www.godaddy.com), Hostway (www.hostway.com), Verio (www.verio.com), iPower (www.ipower.com), Affinity internet (www.affinity.com), and Yahoo! (www.Yahoo.com).

Some companies, however, prefer local, small hosting providers, since they offer a direct contact—especially important if your site has an outage. Most of these companies also offer domain name services,

FREE HOSTED WEB SOLUTIONS

Microsoft and Google have launched beta versions of free hosted web solutions. In 2006, for example, Microsoft launched a version of Microsoft Office Live that provides small businesses with a basic package including their own domain name, web site, and e-mail accounts, for free. The company charges monthly fees, however, for more ramped-up packages.

Also, as of press time Google had begun offering a similar free solution called Google Apps for Your Domain, which allows small businesses to design and publish their own web sites (but they bring their own domain names), for free. The service also enables small businesses to offer private-labeled e-mail, instant messaging, and calendar tools to all of their users for free. It's all hosted by Google, so there's no hardware or software to install or maintain. Companies must submit a request to be a part of the beta.

Another option is OsCommerce (www.oscommerce.com) an Open Source e-commerce solution available for free under the GNU General Public Licenses. It features a rich set of out-of-the-box shopping cart functionality that allows you to setup, run, and maintain your online stores with minimum effort and with no costs, license fees, or limitations involved.

which we mentioned above, so you can sign up when you choose your name.

Whether you're buying from a large or small provider, basic hosting service—along with basics such as domain name registration and e-mail accounts—starts at about $10 per month.

Still not sure which host to choose? Log on to Compare Web Hosts (www.comparewebhosts.com), where you can compare hosts based on price. Other variables include amount of disk space allocated to you, number of e-mail services offered, customer service support availability, database support, and setup fees. For even more information, see CNET Editors' ISP Buying Guide at http://reviews.cnet.com, then click on "Internet Access," then "ISP Buying Guide" under the "Buying Advice" menu.

How much disk space do you need to store your web site? Generally, 1MB can hold several hundred text pages, though it holds fewer pages when images are included. Web hosts typically offer between 10MB and 35MB of free storage. The better web host contracts offer more than 100MB of disk space, and they should be adequate for most situations. If you're unsure how much disk space you need, check with your designer or computer consultant before you sign on a web server's dotted line.

Hosted Web Solutions

As opposed to a "do-it-yourself" (DIY) solution, which we covered in Chapter 5, many e-commerce entrepreneurs turn to the web hosting companies mentioned above to solve all of their e-commerce needs, such as handling credit card transactions, sending automatic e-mail messages to customers thanking them for their orders, and forwarding the order to them for shipping and handling. Of course entrepreneurs also count in these companies for domain registration and hosting.

In general, web hosting companies offer a combination of site-building tools, product catalog tools, content management tools, shopping cart technology, payment, shipping, and marketing strategies, tracking and reporting capabilities, domain registration, and hosting. eBay has entered this arena as well, offering a storefront solution, that is different from its eBay stores, called ProStores (www.prostores.com). The cost for all these plans starts at about $30 to $40 per month, plus setup fees ranging from free to $50 per month. Some companies also charge transaction fees. And, keep in mind, $40 will get you basic functionality; if you want more bells and whistles, you may have to spend a few hundred dollars per month.

Jacquelyn Tran, president and founder of Perfume Bay Inc., a Huntington Beach, California-based company that sells cosmetics, perfume, skin-care products, and home fragrances and candles on its web site Perfumebay.com (www.perfumebay.com), uses a full-featured e-commerce service from Yahoo!. Tran started Perfume Bay in 1999, and now offers more than 700 unique brands of perfume and thousands of other fragrance and beauty products from her Huntington Beach, California store and e-commerce site. Ninety-eight percent of Perfume Bay's $9 million-plus company revenue comes from 180,000 unique visitors who come to the site every month.

Yet during start-up, Tran knew nothing about the internet and hired a web designer to build her site. The customized site was expensive, however: It cost her $50,000. "This included advertising, a custom-built shopping cart—everything," says Tran. After a few years, Tran decided she needed a change. She learned about Yahoo! solutions (then called Yahoo! Stores), and signed on in the beginning of 2001. "The program was easy to use, fairly customizable with a lot of great features, and fully integrated," says Tran, 28. "This was very important to us, because we depend on having a really easy-to-navigate site."

Tran also found a web designer through Yahoo! to help set up the new site. (Yahoo!'s Merchant Solutions web site (www.smallbusiness .yahoo.com) offers a list of web designers who specialize in Yahoo! solutions.) Almost immediately after the new web site was set, Tran could see the difference: Quite simply, she says, "we just got more orders."

Yahoo!'s solution was not inexpensive—in fact, at the time, Tran chose the most expensive solution, and she still uses the most expensive one today: Yahoo! Merchant Professional, which costs $299.95 per month, plus a one-time $50 setup fee and a fee of 75 cents per transaction. Also, hiring a web designer generally costs about $2,000 to $10,000. Still, that's a lot less than it cost Tran to set up her customized site. "Looking back," says Tran, "I wish I went to Yahoo! first."

Yahoo! Small Business

Yahoo! Small Business is doing everything it can to help small businesses get up and running quickly.

In late 2006, the company introduced the first phase of a significant upgrade of its e-commerce platform, Yahoo! Merchant Solutions. The enhancements are part of Yahoo!'s "Open for Business" initiative, a multi-stage project focused on enabling merchants to more quickly and easily launch online retail businesses, and to help them become successful once they are open for business online. Currently, more than 40,000 online merchants, about one out of every eight online stores, use the Yahoo! e-commerce platform.

The enhancements include new "Design" and "Add Products" wizards that greatly streamline and accelerate the process for designing and setting up professional-looking online stores that are search-engine friendly.

The Design wizard features an intuitive interface that allows merchants to build an online store in minutes by choosing from a library of professionally designed store templates, or to create a more customized look by selecting from a range of color palettes and basic layouts. The Add Products wizard enables merchants to get an array of merchandise selections on display, and embedded with online purchasing capabilities, in a matter of a few mouse clicks. With clear, simple steps for setting up categories, and entering product descriptions, sizes, and prices, merchants can quickly show and sell their wares.

Yahoo! also recognizes that driving awareness and traffic to a small business online is critical to success. Web pages built with Yahoo! Merchant Solutions follow a standard coding so that search engines can easily read and index page content. In addition, each page has a static URL that can be customized to include a page keyword, which can help

WHAT TO LOOK FOR IN A HOSTED E-COMMERCE SOLUTION

Sebastian Moser, U.S. director of technical development at Chesterbrook, Pennsylvania-based 1&1 Internet, says you should make sure, before you sign on, that your hosted e-solution offers the following:

- *A full wizard-driven setup*. Most merchants setting up web sites aren't rocket scientists—they need a proper wizard-driven system that can take a merchant from start to finish in a fully operational, production-ready, e-commerce storefront.

- *Many templates*. One design template is not good enough. An e-commerce solution provider should have many different templates to meet the needs of varied customers and products.

- *SSL encryption*. The system should include the option of Secure Sockets Layer (SSL) encryption—a protocol for transmitting private documents via the internet. Having this means your customers can transmit their credit card and address information in an encrypted way to ensure security.

- *A database-driven system*. This allows a system to be integrated with a database of customer names, addresses, and e-mail addresses, enabling you to send out promotional e-mail messages.

- *Offers payment beyond PayPal*. PayPal serves the needs of a lot of e-tailers, but it isn't the only payment gateway and doesn't meet everyone's needs. The best hosted e-commerce vendors offer several payment gateways.

improve the store page ranking when shoppers search online for that keyword. Future enhancements in the "Open for Business" initiative will focus on payment methods, setting up tax rates, and shipping, and will be implemented early in 2007.

eBay

Before taking the plunge and starting a full-fledged web site, many companies test the waters by selling goods on eBay first. They have good reason: Today, the eBay community includes 157 million registered members from around the world. On an average day, millions of items are listed on eBay. "The most appealing and obvious reason a new business chooses eBay is the access to our enormous customer base," says Jim Griffith, dean of eBay Education at eBay.

To begin selling on eBay, you need to register and create a seller's account, then enter all the details about your item, including price, fixed price payment method, shipping cost, and a photo.

Griffith says listing an item is a five-step process that's easy to complete. But he suggests that before listing items, you research eBay to learn what the current market value is for the types of items you're selling, and what eBay sellers of similar items are doing on the site.

When you list an item on eBay, you're charged an insertion fee. The lowest insertion fee, for items with a starting price of under $1, is 20 cents, and the fee goes up to $4.80 for items that have a buying price of $500 or more. You are also charged a final value fee, which is a fee eBay charges when a listing ends. The fee is based on the "final value" of the item, which is the closing bid or sale price. Final value fees start at 5.25 percent of the closing value for items under $25.

Many e-tailers are also turning to eBay for their online storefront services—especially those who are already experimenting with eBay. eBay stores allow you to sell your fixed-price and auction items from a unique destination on eBay.

SMART TIP

Use web tools sparingly. Best advice: Introduce one, and only one. If it proves popular, leave it up and add a second. If users ignore it, put up another but take down the unloved tool. Always keep it simple, and you'll invariably do better.

You can build your own eBay store through an easy series of steps: Create customized categories, include your own logo or choose one of eBay's online images, and list item descriptions and policies.

Your eBay store is promoted to eBay users in several ways: All your listings contain an eBay store "red door" icon inviting buyers to visit your eBay Store; the eBay store icon is also attached to your user ID for extra visibility. Buyers are also driven to your store through the eBay store directory, designed to promote all stores. And you receive your own personalized eBay store web site address to distribute and promote.

How much does an eBay store cost? eBay offers three subscription fees, ranging from $15.95 per month to $499.95 per month.

One company that has made the most of its eBay store is Jeff Atchison Enterprises Inc., dba Dad's Toys. The Dardenne Prairie, Missouri-based

TOP 10 REASONS TO OPEN AN eBAY STORE

Want to open an eBay store? Proponents say you should since it will allow you to do the following:

1. Control and monitor your inventory

2. Showcase your merchandise

3. Get your own private search engine

4. Cross-promote your items on eBay

5. Reduce eBay selling fees

6. Become visible to search engines

7. Learn from store reports

8. Save time listing and relisting

9. Get marketing help from eBay

10. Improve your image

company, which started in 1999, sells high-end gadgets such as flat-screen TVs—many of them on eBay.

In 2002, founder and president Jeff Atchinson set up a basic eBay store. Why? "To add credibility to my listings," he says. "It shows people you are more of a permanent presence on eBay." It also allows Atchinson to keep all his listings organized on one web site that can be easily viewed by customers.

Advanced Tools and Tricks

Your site is up, so how do you make it special and filled with content that attracts visitors and keeps them coming back? That mission consumes site builders, both full-time professionals and part-timers, but if there is one fact we now know to be absolutely true, it is this: Simplicity is best.

Case in point: The web site for a luxury hotel chain based in India features a huge soundtrack of classical music, which is just annoying. Some sitar tracks—authentic Indian music—might make sense, but classical? It's bandwidth-hogging craziness. Resist the temptation to put something on your site just because you can. Never put up content that slows access to a page but doesn't demonstrably heighten user value.

What works? Content that gives users reasons to linger and absorb more of what you're offering. You'll find there are many ways to introduce this content, and you are going to have to exercise real discretion. Pick a few tools, try them out, monitor user responses, and then delete the ones that aren't proving valuable. Be ruthless and never forget that simple is better.

That understood, here are many tools for you to consider using to beef up your site. Just remember, this may be an all-you-can-eat buffet, but the more you put on your plate, the more discomfort your web site viewers will feel.

- *Polls*. Polls, where surfers register their opinion on an issue, are at the heart of the internet because this is interactivity in its most basic form. No matter what question you ask—"What's your favorite cocktail?" "Who's your favorite Beatle?"—surfers will want to register their point of view and see how others voted. AOL has long used polls as a staple on its pages. Learn from the masters and do likewise. Writing a poll from scratch is a tricky bit of coding, but free poll templates are readily available for insertion into your site. All you have to do is fill in the blanks in a template and copy and paste a bit of code into your site, and you're in business. Sources of such templates are plentiful, but a good one is from Freetools.com (http:freepolls.com).

- *CGI scripts*. These are easy-to-use scripts (prewritten code) that you simply pop into your page to create a guest book or the ability to track visitors. CGI (or Common Gateway Interface, a programming tool that lets many small applications run within a web environment) is one of the web's oldest resources. Newer, slicker ways to do much of what can be accomplished via CGI are plentiful, and a real plus is their price tag: Scripts put together by enthusiasts are free and available for anyone to use. Always test any CGI script thoroughly before going public with a page, however. In several cases, I simply haven't been able to get CGI scripts to work properly. Thousands of these free CGI scripts exist, and one of the best resources for finding the scripts you need is The CGI Resource Index (www.cgi.resourceindex.com). If you can't find the script you want here, it probably doesn't exist.

- *Chat rooms*. Wouldn't it be cool if your site had its own private, real-time chat room? It's both easy to put up and free from Dialogoo.com (www.dialogoo.com) or Bravenet.com (www.bravenet.com). All you need to do is add a few lines of HTML code to your web page, and in a matter of minutes you'll be able to get folks chatting. Before you do, however, mull on this: Empty chat rooms look very, very dumb. Will you have enough traffic to put people into a chat room on a regular basis? Do you want to monitor it? How frequently? Know that you won't be on call 24 hours a day, seven days a week—but the chat room will, theoretically, be available that often. My advice: For most small sites, this is a tool to avoid. Better by far is to set yourself up with an AOL Instant Messenger account (it's free, from www.aol.com) where visitors can fire off questions to you if you are online. This gives surfers an alternative to e-mail for finding information but doesn't expose you to the ridicule that comes with offering an unpopulated chat room. Do this in combination with providing a message board and surfer needs ought to be very adequately handled.

- *Guest books.* Sure, you could create a guest book using a CGI script, but probably the easier way is to insert some HTML code into your page—you can find it at Bravenet.com. Why would you want a guest book at all? It's a convenient way to collect more information about your visitors. And incidentally, surfers often like to look through guest books.

- *Weblogs (blog).* At its most basic, a blog is a frequently updated, timed, and dated online journal with a good dose of links involved. That may not sound like much to get excited about, but it has gone beyond fad to become a full-fledged internet phenomenon. The elements of interactivity, community, and collaboration will be key as growing businesses adopt blogs for customer relations, advertising, promotion, and even internal communications. Another plus: Adding a blog to your site may enable your site to do well in the search engines. Why? Blogs are frequently updated, and search engines are drawn toward content that is fresh and relevant.

- *RSS feeds.* Originally built to distribute syndicated news, RSS instant notification promises a host of other uses—including innovative marketing for your business. The fast-spreading internet standard lets you instantly publish or receive bits of text. While it's now used to show the latest news and blog updates, there's no limit to what it could be used for. Depending on whom you ask,

SMART TIP

If you plan to add a blog to your site, make sure you update it frequently. Why? Because blog readers want up-to-date content, and it may get your site higher in the search engines since search engines are drawn to content that is fresh and relevant.

RSS stands for Really Simple Syndication, Rich Site Summary, or RDF Site Summary. Created by Netscape as a simple way to swap news between consenting web sites, RSS is based on XML, the internet's master language, and comes in several variants. To see RSS in action, download and install an RSS reader (also known as an RSS aggregator) from the web. Open the reader, and you'll see a few sample RSS "feeds" with the latest headlines for each. Depending on the reader, the headlines may appear in your browser, in a separate application that looks much like an e-mail application, or within another application such as Microsoft Outlook. Simply click on a headline to bring up its associated web page. While this will appeal to the news junkie in you, RSS marketing skills may prove more powerful for your firm. In the simplest example, you could spiff up your web site by adding RSS feeds from news services or blogs that will intrigue site visitors. More strikingly, in the future, RSS may handle marketing tasks where e-mail now falls flat. For example, as with e-mail, visitors

RATING THE SHOPPING

E-tailers gain market share through user-generated product ratings/reviews. That was a key finding from a report titled "Retail Marketing: Driving Sales through Consumer-Created Content" from New York-based JupiterResearch, a division of JupiterKagan Inc.

The report found that the number of online buyers who cite customer ratings and reviews as the most useful shopping site feature has more than doubled from 2005 to 2006. In addition, survey respondents said user-generated ratings and reviews are now the second most important site feature behind search. Finally, the report found that 60 percent of online shoppers provide feedback about a shopping experience, and are more likely to give feedback about a positive experience than a negative one.

can sign up for marketing alerts (for instance, useful product news plus discount coupons). Unlike e-mail, visitors can rest assured that they can't be spammed. If you don't like what you're getting via RSS, just pull the plug.

- *News feeds, content, and more.* Big web sites build traffic by regularly changing content. Usually that means paying writers and other content creators big bucks to produce copy, but you don't need to spend that kind of money.

  There are plenty of legitimate ways to get new content without having to write it all yourself. If you have a special interest site, many of your readers may enjoy contributing occasional stories, just for the thrill of seeing their names in virtual print. Also, if you see an article you like somewhere on the internet, you may be able to get permission to reprint it.

  Many web site visitors also appreciate sites that offer a "tip of the day" and these people visit those sites on a daily basis, often in the morning, to glean the day's tip. Or they subscribe to a daily newsletter full of tips—and advertising.

- *Rich media.* Now that most of your customers have broadband, a great way to uprade your web site is to offer rich media features such as zoom, virtual e-catalogs, and dynamic color-swatching. What are the keys to using rich media? Make sure all your content is consistent and of the best quality; make sure your rich media vendor can scale to allow you to leverage your rich media across all products and pages, including the home page, thumbnail pages, product pages, shopping cart, and so on; and maximize your rich media investment by using dynamically served imagery to not only up-sell and cross-sell additional products, but also showcase items in your customers' shopping carts, on compare pages, in search results, and more.

- *Reviews.* What do customers think of your products? Let them tell other customers by posting their comments on your web site. As plenty of e-tailers have discovered, online reviews by happy customers carry more weight with other buyers than most other forms of marketing communication. A number of companies offer tools to help you get started: PowerReviews (www.powerreviews .com) offers a free outsourced solution. Bazaarvoice's (www.bazaar voice.com) hosted and managed solution, which starts at $2,000 per month, monitors reviews and updates them regularly. The Prospero CommunityCM platform (www.prospero.com) lets you manage online reviews yourself, for about $395 per month.

- *Gift tools*. Naturally, the end-of-year holiday season is a boon to e-tailers. But what about the rest of the year? The truth is, your customers purchase gifts year-round—and designing your site to appeal to gift buyers any month of the year will encourage additional sales. So how do you appeal to these gift buyers? You can start by making it easy for customers to purchase a gift. Add a gift suggestion section to your site (make sure to keep it updated), offer a gift registry service, sell gift certificates and gift cards/ messages, and offer gift wrap.

(For more on ways to make your site sticky, see Chapter 11.)

ADDING A SITE SEARCH TOOL

Should you add a search box to your site? Of course. In general, a web site search tool gives your visitors a chance to find something on your site by searching, much like the search engines such as Google. Because your site is focused on a particular area or topic, a site search tool will allow visitors to find the information quickly and without wading through hundreds of irrelevant results. It will keep them on your site, and will allow you to learn more about what your visitors are looking for.

Sites that benefit from search tools are those with valuable data in many pages, those that get many visitors arriving from search engines at pages deep within the site hierarchy, and growing sites that are adding new and valuable information.

Before adding a search box, think about where one would fit in your page design. Also, add meta keyword tags and descriptions to your pages, which will improve your look and feel when your page summaries are displayed by search engines.

If you are running a hosted site, ask your ISP what search services they provide. You may have to pay some additional fees for search tools. If they do not provide these tools, check with friends who have servers. A search engine does not have to reside on the local server.

For more information about site search tools, visit SearchTools.com (www.searchtools.com), a site that provides information, news, and advice about web site searching technology. It is maintained by Search Tools Consulting as a service to the web community.

Chapter 6 Summary
10 Things You Can Do Today

1. Decide if you will host your site yourself or use a web hosting company.

2. If you choose to use a web hosting company, consider using it to solve all of your e-commerce needs.

3. Do your research before choosing the right hosting solution for your e-commerce needs. Remember that Yahoo! Merchant Solutions is a good bet.

4. Make sure the hosting solution you choose offers features such as a full wizard-driven setup, many templates, a database-driven system, and payment beyond PayPal.

5. Before taking the plunge and starting a full-fledged web site, try testing the waters by selling goods on eBay first.

6. If you have success on eBay, think about turning to it for its online storefront services.

7. Think about adding content and other special features to your web site to keep visitors coming back.

8. Decide if you want to add polls, CGI scripts, chat rooms, guest books, blogs, RSS feeds, news feeds, rich media, reviews, or gift tools—or all of the above.

9. Remember that when adding content to your site, simplicity is best.

10. Think about adding a site search tool to your site.

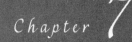

Managing Your Business

*Y*OU'VE DONE IT—YOU'VE OPENED YOUR BUSI-
ness in 10 days (or maybe less). Now it's
time to begin managing and ultimately
growing your site.

The next several chapters of this book will
include information to help you manage and
grow your business. You will learn how to fulfill
orders, keep track of customers, build traffic on
your site, use search-engine marketing and affiliate marketing, and offer the best customer service. You will also learn about some interesting
ways to grow your business, such as expanding
internationally and upgrading your site.

This chapter, in particular, will discuss a key part of managing your business: inventory, returns, and shipping. It's difficult to be successful in the e-commerce world without having a good handle on these elements. After all, we're talking about several things that are absolutely essential to your business: what you sell, how you get it to your customers—and what to do if they want to send it back. Here, we'll explore the ins and outs of managing your stock, and discover the secrets to efficient packing and shipping.

Inventory

You might think all there is to inventory control is buying merchandise. But just as with the groceries in your refrigerator and pantry, you have to know what to buy, when to buy it, and how much to buy. If you stock up on 40 loaves of sourdough sauerkraut raspberry bread because it's on sale and then discover that your family won't eat it, you've effectively mangled your monthly food budget and lost your customers. They're over next door, having supper with the Pinkelmans. On the other hand, if you come home with only two double chocolate macadamia dream cookies and you've got a family of five, you're going to be seriously understocked and you will, again, have lost your customers, who are down at the corner bakery ruining their dinners with somebody else's desserts.

Catch-22

Your inventory must serve two functions:

1. If you're working with a multiple-product line, it should provide your customers with a reasonable assortment of the products you offer.
2. It should cover the normal sales demands of your company.

Now we arrive at the Catch-22 of retail inventory operations. To accurately calculate basic stock, you must review actual sales during an appropriate time period, such as a full year of business. But you don't yet have previous sales and stocking figures to use as a guide. So you will have to use the information from your market research—and your intuition. Keep your ear to the ground and your eyes on your customers' buying habits. Maintain good records. Stockpile all this information in your brain's own inventory for future use.

Chocolate Zeppelins

Another factor you'll need to consider in calculating your basic stock is lead time, the length of time between when you reorder a product and when you receive it. Warning: math ahead. Let's say, for example, that you're selling chocolate zeppelins. You know that once you call and place your order, it will take four weeks for the vendor to deliver more zeppelins to you. This means your lead time is four weeks. So if you're selling 10 zeppelins a week, you'll need to reorder before your basic inventory level falls below 40 zeppelins.

If you wait until you're out of zeppelins, you'll also be out of luck, because you'll have to put all those lovely customer requests on backorder and risk losing sales and customers. You'll also lose cash flow. And then you can pronounce the word "lead" in "lead time" as "led," as in lead-headed. Or hearted.

One way you can protect yourself from inventory shortfalls is by incorporating a safety margin into your basic inventory figures. You can figure safety margins by anticipating external delays or problems. For instance, you might order extra quantities of seasonal merchandise that you know sells quickly, or, if you deal with a vendor located in a winter-blizzard zone, you could order extra products before shipping delays set in.

Nightmare on Inventory Street

A word of caution: Some mail order entrepreneurs get so excited about a new product that they order entirely too many items at one time. Excess inventory creates extra overhead, and that costs you money. Inventory that sits in your garage or warehouse doesn't generate sales or profits.

Newbie online order entrepreneurs sometimes add financial insult to injury by marking overstocks at reduced prices, hoping for a quick sale. This solves the overstock problem but plays havoc with your bottom line, because that product you've written into your financial plan as selling at $100 is now pulling in only $50. It's not holding up its share of the weight.

You may be tempted to bounce back from this Nightmare on Inventory Street by getting timid with your next orders. Don't do this, either. When you reduce normal reordering, you risk creating a stock shortage, and that's not healthy for your bottom line.

We've told you everything not to do, but what makes a good inventory plan? Try the following:

- Do as much research as you can before ordering so that you can order as realistically as possible.
- Order only what you feel confident will sell.
- Establish a realistic safety margin.

The Holiday Season

As an online maven, you'll probably find that your business is seasonal. The holidays, for example, are the busy season. For some e-tail companies, 50 percent of their business takes place right after Thanksgiving and through the holidays.

And there's more to a "good season" catalog than just higher numbers of orders. There are also price differences. Oftentimes, there might be higher-end products in a fall catalog versus a summer one—so you tend to make more money on your products at that time.

SMART TIP
Although most internet businesses have seasonal peaks and valleys, it pays to brainstorm ways to keep your customers buying during the lulls. Can you run a special sale or devise an off-season campaign to encourage purchases? Get creative!

Shipping and Handling

You've got your inventory squared away. Now you need to think about how you're going to get it to your customers. Fulfillment—speeding that package from your garage or warehouse to your customer's door—is perhaps the single most important thing you can do in your operation aside from effective marketing. Failure to provide prompt fulfillment will result in more complaints, cancellations, and nightmares than just about anything else in the mail order entrepreneur's world.

So exactly how will you get those packages to your customers? You've seen the TV commercials. Your main choices are the U.S. Postal Service (USPS), United Parcel Service (UPS), FedEx, and DHL, which has recently become a major competitor. Most online mavens use UPS for packages because it is generally cheaper than FedEx, is faster than the post office, and has better tracking capabilities.

PACKAGE TRACKING

Want to compare package rates and shipping time in one easy step? Then have a look at e-commerce solutions provider Webplus Inc.'s Shipping Sidekick (www.shippingsidekick.com). Using Shipping Sidekick you can compare the shipping rates of UPS, USPS, FedEx, and DHL. The service is important, especially since shipping rates can differ between shipping companies for any given package, often by $3 to $5 for small packages and much more for larger ones.

To use Shipping Sidekick, users enter their package weight, destination, and package characteristics once to retrieve the rates of shippers for all delivery speeds on one single screen. The difference between shipping rates allows users to choose the most cost-effective shipper for any given package. The company offers a 14-day free trial for the service, and then charges $14.95 a month.

Another solution to check out is RedRoller Inc.'s RedRoller.com (www.redroller.com). The free web-based, on-demand shipping solution provides side-by-side comparisons of major national and regional carriers. RedRoller shipping carriers include FedEx, DHL, the USPS, Eastern Connection, and Overnite Express.

SMART TIP

If your merchandise can't go out to the customer right away, send a postcard indicating that you've received the order and are processing it. This builds good customer relations and keeps your customer from worrying that you never got the order.

Of course, its smart business to offer your customers a choice of shipping services. You can tell them, for instance, that you can have their package out to them by USPS Priority Mail with an expected—but not guaranteed—delivery time of three business days. Then you can offer second-day service by UPS or overnight by FedEx at an extra cost. Give the customer options. This way people know you're working with them, in terms of both price and speed. What a great company!

Out of Your Hands

Understanding how the relationship between your business and shipping companies affects customers will go a long way toward keeping your shipping operations on an even keel. In short, your customers will hold you responsible for any delay in receiving their merchandise, even if the delay is caused by the shipping company. So be prepared to be sympathetic to complaining customers—and stern with the USPS, UPS, and FedEx.

Pass the Popcorn

There's a method to everything, including packing and shipping. Here's a list of smart tips that will help you help yourself and your customers:

- Take a tip from the box boy down at the supermarket. Place heavier or larger items on the bottom of the box and lighter ones on top.
- After you've got each piece of merchandise in the box, place a piece of cardboard on the very top. This way, if your customer gets carried away with his penknife while slicing open the box, he won't slash his brand-new goodies.
- Use shredded newspaper or actual (unbuttered!) popcorn instead of Styrofoam peanuts. Your customers will appreciate your concern for the environment, and if you get hungry while packing, you can eat your materials!
- Indicate which end of the box should be opened first or face up. Sometimes breakable merchandise will make an entire cross-country

trip in one piece, only to smash on the customer's floor because they opened it wrong side up.

- Make sure your shipping label is clearly visible to the deliverer. Some shipping companies will refuse to deliver a package if any part of the address is obscured or too small to read.

- Absolutely do not ship to a post office box. Most shipping firms cannot deliver to a post office box. Make sure your order takers ask for an actual street address.

- Include all invoices, receipts, thank-you letters, new catalogs, and other printed materials in one envelope with the customer's name on it, placed on top of the merchandise. This saves your customer the time and frustration of having to dig through packing materials to find these things.

- Reuse boxes. This is not only ecologically sound but also economically smart. When you reuse a box, make sure all old labels, addresses, and postage markings are covered up. Stick another label on top so the delivery man doesn't mix up for whom your package is intended.

- Design packing models so your shippers (and you) know how products fit into boxes, how merchandise is folded, stacked, or tissue-wrapped, and how packing materials are used. Weigh each packing model on a scale and make sure it doesn't go even one-eighth into the next pound. This cuts postage costs, reduces returns from damaged goods, and adds to your income by creating happy repeat customers.

SMART TIP

One way to lavish your customers with attention is to carefully package your merchandise. The UPS Package Lab is staffed entirely by engineers with four-year degrees in package engineering. (Bet you didn't know there was a degree in package engineering!) They'll design packing models and even special packing for your products—for a fee. For a price quote, contact UPS at (800) PICK-UPS.

Outsource Fulfillment

Should you outsource the fulfillment? In many cases, yes. One advantage of using a fulfillment outsourcer (especially one of the larger ones) is that it can buy shipping materials in large quantities in order to receive volume discounts. It can then pass the savings on to its clients. Another plus: When you outsource fulfillment, you don't have to run a large warehouse operation, and this in itself can be a big money-saver. (Remember: Buying large amounts of inventory and having that inventory sit is very ineffective and costly.) Perhaps the greatest advantage is that an outside fulfillment organization is likely to be automated. The contractor—who has invested millions of dollars to create a system that's highly accurate—keeps your costs down, speeds up your processing time, and lowers your inventory requirements. They can do this because they don't use a paper-based system in which an employee takes a piece of paper and walks through the warehouse picking out each product on the order. This approach is naturally prone to error, and a paper-based system's biggest failure is poor picking. A sophisticated fulfillment operation will have an automated system with bar code readers to ensure a higher degree of accuracy.

As you select a fulfillment service, here are some things to keep in mind:

- Fulfillment is connected with everything else in your operation. Select an outsourcer that understands the integration involved.
- Make sure you get periodic reports on everything that goes into and out of the fulfillment center.
- Your fulfillment contractor should be able to handle multiple sales channels. Regardless of where the orders originate, fulfillment should take place at the same speed and with the same level of efficiency across the board. Furthermore, you should be able to get a channel breakdown report.
- Find out about returns management. Can the fulfillment company handle returns to your satisfaction? Some providers can even take returned products and refurbish them for you.
- Some full-service fulfillment contractors also operate call centers, where they can take orders on your behalf and field customer service calls.

Many Happy Returns

One thing you will see as you expand your business into mail order is an increase in returns. It's part of the charted territory of mail order and retail. The reasons people return items are as varied as human nature:

- They change their minds.
- They order the wrong size or wrong color.
- They give gifts that aren't quite right (or are entirely wrong).
- They order so late that they no longer need the product by the time it arrives.
- They receive the wrong merchandise, or it arrives in less than pristine condition.

No matter what your customer's reason is, however, you will have to deal with it—preferably in a win-win manner. You should have a return policy already in place and clearly stated in all your advertising material. If you've decided on a no-return policy, you must spell it out in your advertising and/or catalog so that the customer already knows about it when ordering. If you've got a limited return policy, you must clearly write this out in your advertising and ordering materials.

Stick to your policy, but remember that you want to keep your customers happy. If bending the rules a bit might make the difference between a repeat customer and one who chooses never to use your company again, you know what to do.

Limited Return Policy

What's commonly included in a limited return policy? You might accept returns only on certain products, within a certain time period (say 30 days), with certain tags still attached, or (often in the case of CDs, DVDs, or software) with the product packaging unopened.

Think carefully about how you structure your return policy. More and more retail stores are allowing customers to try out products and then return them within 14 to 30 days. If you go for a policy like this,

HAPPY RETURNS, HAPPY CUSTOMERS

Want to make your customers happy? Then make your returns process easy. A survey commissioned in late 2005 by Newgistics Inc. (a returns management solutions provider based in Austin, Texas) and conducted by Harris Interactive shows that for the third year in a row an overwhelming number of U.S. adults who have shopped online or through catalogs (92 percent) are somewhat or very likely to shop with an online or catalog retailer if the returns process is convenient.

Conversely, 82 percent are not very or not at all likely to shop again with a direct retailer if the returns process is inconvenient.

In addition, 77 percent of U.S. adults report that returns policies and processes are important or very important when they are deciding to purchase a gift for someone else. The results also show that it is more important than ever for direct retailers to differentiate themselves by providing a clear and convenient returns process. In fact, 75 percent of adults who have ever shopped online or through catalogs say it is important or very important to know a direct retailer's returns policy before purchasing direct. In addition, most direct shoppers cite a convenient (71 percent) and visible (68 percent) returns policy as important or very important when deciding whether to shop with an online or catalog retailer for the first time. U.S. adults in general also report that they are somewhat or much more likely (61 percent) to shop with a retailer that offers customers the ability to create labels and track packages online than with one that does not.

The survey also reveals that retailers who recognize returns as a critical touch point for consumers can turn returns into a profitable component of the customer relationship process. According to the survey, half the adults reported they typically buy additional items when returning merchandise to a retailer, regardless of whether they ask for a refund or an exchange. Retailers that implement targeted promotions during the returns process can also improve customer loyalty and increase sales and multichannel purchasing. When returning merchandise purchased online or through a catalog, 88 percent of online or catalog shoppers are somewhat likely, likely, or very likely to take advantage of a discount on the next purchase.

A convenient returns process can also lead to greater operational efficiencies for the retailer by lessening the hassle of making returns and encouraging consumers to return merchandise to the retailer faster. More than four in five (85 percent) direct shoppers say they would return the merchandise purchased online or through a catalog more quickly if the returns process were convenient; this would get merchandise back into the hands of retailers more quickly, streamlining the restocking process. Retailers that implement a convenient returns policy may actually see more sales, more repeat customers, and better visibility.

you could be asking for a lot of unusable, returned stock. On the other hand, you can garner a reputation as a friendly, here-to-please company that customers will want to patronize.

And you can always offer those "test-driven" products at a discount, earning yourself happy customers of a slightly different bent. Also, check with your vendors; you may be able to send your returns back to them.

Processing Returns

Over the years, online mavens have adopted these tried-and-true methods of processing returns:

- Instruct customers to ship products back in the original packing materials within 30 days. This ensures that a) you won't receive returned merchandise years later, and b) you know the merchandise came from your company instead of somebody else's.
- Offer an exchange program in which the customer phones in their concern, and you immediately ship out a replacement product. When the customer receives the replacement, they put the damaged original into the same box the replacement came in, with the same packing materials, and send it back to you with shipping prepaid by you.

- Some companies such as Lands' End offer an open return policy. They'll take back anything for any reason any day of any year. You'll have to think carefully about whether you can financially handle a program like this.

Chapter 7 Summary
10 Things You Can Do Today

1. When managing inventory, do as much research as you can before ordering so that you can order as realistically as possible.

2. Order only what you believe you can sell.

3. Protect yourself from inventory shortfalls by incorporating a safety margin into your basic inventory figures.

4. Keep in mind that the holidays will most likely be your busy season, and prepare for it.

5. Brainstorm ways to keep your customers buying during the lulls.

6. Think about offering your customers a choice of shipping services.

7. Be prepared to be sympathetic to complaining customers—and stern with the USPS, UPS, and FedEx.

8. Make sure to package your products properly.

9. Have a fulfillment plan in place, and think about outsourcing fulfillment.

10. Decide on a returns policy and clearly state it in all your advertising material.

Knowing Your Customers

*K*NOW THY CUSTOMER. IF THERE'S A FIRST commandment of business, that's it. For those who run brick-and-mortar stores, knowing customers is easy. A traditional storefront owner can talk to customers, size up their clothing, hear how they form sentences, and in a matter of seconds know a lot about who's stopping in. But the question for companies doing business on the web is "How do we know customers when all they amount to is a wispy cybervisitor?"

This is a key issue because knowing your visitors can help you more precisely target your web site. Suddenly notice a flood of visitors from, say, Japan, and that could lead to a decision to edit certain sections of a web site to make them more friendly for those users. See that you're a hit on a particular college campus or in a government agency, and you can post a special deal just for those people. Observe that you're getting a lot of traffic from Puerto Rico, and that's a clear signal to market there. Not making an effort to get to know your customers makes as much sense as golfing in the dark.

Log Rolling

The good news: Every web site visitor leaves a trail that, when properly analyzed, will tell you the country of origin, the browser and platform used (such as Windows XP, Mac, Unix), the internet service provider, and more. This data is ordinarily collected by web hosting services in a "log file," but only hard-core techies could ever have the patience to scroll through a log because it contains a mind-numbing avalanche of details.

There are smarter ways to measure traffic.

Analyze This

If you're curious about your logs, go to your web hosting service and look for a directory called "Logs." Download the most recent file and

I SEE YOU

Most stats folders include a file that details the search phrases used by visitors in finding your site. Check it out regularly. Know what visitors want to find, and give them more of it.

have a look (any text editor should open the file). Your web hosting service probably provides—free of charge—a basic analysis of those logs. The log is run through interpretive software, and the output is tucked in a folder that's usually called "Stats." Open that folder and look at recent files.

What will you see? The date, followed by the time of day, amount of time spent on the web page, and the web page (or other web element, such as Java buttons) viewed.

The free stats file reports are good, but even better analysis is easy to come by when you use third-party software tools designed to dissect log files and automatically produce spiffy, usable reports that will tell you not only which countries are producing visitors but also their ISPs and more. The products and services today also allow you to do things such as web site optimization, which allows you to track how people behave on your site and then, using that information, optimize it in the best way possible.

Top choices among traffic-analysis tools and services include:

- *WebTrends 7 On Demand and WebTrends 7 Software.* This software or service allows retailers to discover and optimize different areas of their sites, conversion scenarios, and web marketing initiatives, and allows the user to generate reports that track results. For more information, visit www.webtrends.com.
- *NetTracker Professional.* NetTracker Professional includes clickstream analysis, custom reporting, content analysis, campaign reporting, and more. For more information, visit www.unica.com.
- *HitBox Professional.* This self-service solution requires no hardware or software and provides real-time web site visitor analysis to help improve your online business. Get hundreds of reports, including how visitors are getting to your site, what pages they look at, and whether your site is gaining in popularity. All the data is collected in real time and made available on demand through a convenient web browser interface. For more information, visit www.websidestory.com.

Also, Google offers a free web analytics service that measures the effectiveness of web sites and online marketing campaigns.

Google Analytics allows customers of its AdWords service (Google's pay-per-click program where webmasters can create their own ads and choose keywords) to see exactly how visitors interact with their web site and how their advertising campaigns are faring. The hosted service is

ABCS OF A/B TESTING

Not long ago, A/B testing was solely available to large companies—it was time-consuming, was expensive, and required heavy information technology (IT) intervention. Times have changed: Many companies now offer hosted testing and optimization services at prices within reach of smaller businesses.

That's good news for e-tailers seeking to improve their sites. A/B testing (also known as A/B split testing) allows you to test two different versions of your web site. You can measure how customers respond to both versions and then optimize the site based on that information. Kefta (www.kefta.com), Optimost (www.optimost.com), and Offermatica (www.offer matica.com) are three leading companies that offer A/B testing; services run about $10,000 per month.

To be effective, A/B testing should be ongoing—your "best" page will change over time, so it's important to continue testing. For additional A/B testing tips, we asked Matthew Roche, CEO of Offermatica. Here are his suggestions:

- Run tests on the registration or shopping cart page. "Improving these areas generally provides the greatest impact on the bottom line," says Roche.

- For big impact, focus on big elements. "Small changes to small elements nearly always yield small results," says Roche. Instead of testing text color, font size, or font type, focus on big elements such as product, pricing, primary copy, images, offers, and calls-to-action.

- Test heavily trafficked campaigns in a time frame of two weeks or less. Says Roche, "This creates better answers fast."

available in English and 16 other languages, and uses technology from San Diego-based Urchin, which Google acquired in March of 2005.

Web site owners can see exactly where visitors come from, which links on the site are getting the most traffic, which pages visitors are viewing, how long people stay on the site, which products on merchant sites are being sold, and where people give up in multistep checkout processes.

Marketers can also use the service to track banner, e-mail, nonpaid, and paid search advertising campaigns from other ad service providers. That service is free even if companies do not advertise with AdWords, as long as their users do not view more than five million web pages in a given month. For more information visit www.google.com/analytics.

Which one should you choose? Well, you can't go wrong with Google's free service. But you can also try downloading a trial version of WebTrends 7 software or service. In addition, NetTracker offers personalized one-on-one NetTracker demos for business professionals. Put them through their paces and see what you like best. Also, before deciding to buy, ask yourself if you really need this level of analysis. Many low-traffic sites don't, and for them, the free stats files provided by the server may be sufficient. When traffic increases to the point where you need more fine-tuned analysis, buy a sophisticated tool— but certainly wait until the traffic increases to more than 100 visitors daily.

Getting to Know You

Logs provide a step toward knowing your customer, but more can be done. Here, the big guys can clue you in on strategies you can use.

Survey Says

Many e-tailers today offer discount coupons, with strings attached. If you answer some multiple-choice questions, you can earn a credit good on any item sold by the e-tailer. Through highly specific questions about its competitors and its own product offerings, prices, and service, the e-tailer picks up valuable insight into the thinking of a customer and its competition. Wow!

Strip this down, and what the e-tailer is doing is taking its customers' e-mail addresses, firing off a survey, and, to sweeten the pot and up the percentage of respondents, offering a discount to those who answer the survey. The discount isn't hefty enough to obliterate margins; it's exactly what it seems to be—a small "thank you."

Don't wait: Do a survey right now. Keep it short, and offer a tangible reward. You don't have Amazon's many millions of people to survey, so randomly choose 10 or 100 customers. Then—and this is crucial—read every answer that comes in. If you want to find out ways to run your business better, look at it as customers do.

Companies that offer easy-to-use online survey tools include SurveyMonkey (www.surveymonkey.com), Question Pro (www.question pro.com), and Zoomerang (http://zommerang.com).

To get the best results from online surveys, make sure you send out questionnaires at the point of service, when the interaction is fresh in the customer's mind. And even if you ask the questions at the right time, remember that posing the wrong questions can skew results.

Going to the Polls

What tools should you use besides e-mail? Online polls can be tailored to serve many ends, and you'll find many variations. For example, visit Sparklit (www. sparklit.com). Here you'll find a free option that lets you sign up for advertising-supported web polls, or for $9.95 per month plus $5 per month per poll, you can receive "Gold Web Polls," including advanced features, improved integration, and no advertising. You can also try Pollwizard (www.pollwizard.com), which offers free polling.

These tools may cost you next to nothing, but, used intelligently, they can be powerful. "Free Polling on Your Site, Setup in Five Minutes," shouts Pollwizard on its front page, and these resources live up to that promise. How good will the data you collect be? As good as the polls you create and as good as the tools you use for analyzing your responses.

Don't just put up a poll as a plaything for visitors. Sometimes that's useful—polls are fun and we all like completing them, at least when they're short (never go over 10 questions in a poll—five or fewer questions is ideal). But the real payoffs come when you carefully construct polls to target highly specific concerns. Do customers like your web site's speed? Your product selection? Pricing? Ask them, and watch out—they'll love telling you their answers. Big corporations pay megabucks to marketing wizards to examine customers and their motivations, but the truth is, you can get most of the payoffs from this work, free of charge, just by using the tools that are readily at hand.

And one last thing: Read and respond to as much customer e-mail as possible, because it, too, is a real window to customers and their motivations. Strangely, many small businesses, when asked, will mumble and admit that they don't read e-mail and certainly don't respond to it, but there is no faster way to make yourself obsolete than to stay aloof from customers. Sure, nine customers will write with complaints for every one who has good things to say about you, but read it, absorb it—and stay alert to trends. If one person complains about your packaging materials, big deal. If 10 do and you only sent out 12 orders last week, you have a problem—and the great thing is that now you also have the opportunity to fix it.

Private Eyes

Now that you're excited about gathering information on your customers, know this: It all has to be done gently, respectfully, and cautiously. That's because a very sensitive topic these days is web site snooping. And sensitivities are increasing as more users realize exactly how detailed a trail they leave behind when visiting web sites.

There is a remedy, however, one that will let you gather the information you need while also reassuring visitors. It's simple: Develop a privacy policy. If you don't, this lack just may cost you big bucks.

Why? Because by not winning trust—and by not safeguarding visitor privacy—you just may be inadvertently pushing would-be customers toward the exits before the cash register rings.

Too Close for Comfort

In America, proof of consumers' sensitivity to this issue can be found in the public relations nightmares suffered several years back by RealPlayer, Alexa, and numerous other internet companies that were found to surreptitiously collect information on users. The companies claimed no harm was done—that the information (mainly pertaining to a user's viewing habits) was collected so that user needs might better be served—but for a time, dark clouds hung over many internet companies as users fretted about invasion of privacy.

Privacy is not a concern only for the paranoid, either. Everything from your internet address to your computer's name is readily known by sites you visit. Also revealed is your e-mail address, so this can get very personal, very quickly.

Why do web sites want this information in the first place? Mainly because it's a marketer's dream. In an era when "knowing thy customer" is seen as a path to riches, it's hard to resist collecting vast stores of customer data that tumble into your lap when you create a web site. Know where a visitor has been before—which sites he's visited earlier in this internet session, for instance—and you can use that insight into the surfer's interests to tweak offerings to more closely match the surfer's wants.

That's so tempting that some sites dramatically up the ante by overtly collecting more detailed and personal information from visitors. Usually that occurs in tandem with an offer the visitor accepts. This is common, and experienced web surfers have come to expect a trade-off of personal information for freebies—except the savviest surfers long ago stopped giving out accurate information. Many maintain a separate e-mail box just for use in connection with freebies and simply lie when filling out the forms.

Another dose of bad news is that, in some cases, information collected in your "cookies" has been transmitted to third-party sites—and that can strike fear in just about everybody. A cookie, theoretically, is a bit of information about you that's written to your hard drive while you are visiting a web site that will let that web site identify you as a repeat visitor in the future. This is how some sites greet you with "Welcome Back, Fragonard" (or whatever your name is) when you return. Cookies, their architects argue, save users time and make the surfing process more efficient. Who could complain? Well, there have been instances where those cookies have been visible to other sites—and that's a scary thought indeed.

GET LOST

Never assume your online activities are private. With court orders in hand, law enforcement can track virtually all surfers in a matter of minutes. That may be no big deal to most of us, but if you're doing stuff you want kept private, think about it. One way to avoid the scrutiny is to head to a public internet cafe and pay cash for a surfing session. You might do that simply to keep competitors from knowing you're checking out their sites.

Another option: Go to Anonymizer (www.anonymizer.com) and purchase Anonymous Surfing, which allows anonymous surfing, starting at $29.95 per year.

A last privacy breach is that wherever you go on the internet, you leave a trail. Very good hackers can hide their trails, but 99.9 percent of us leave tracks that are easy to follow. That is no big deal to most of us. But it means that your feeling of anonymity on the net is a false one: Your movements can be cataloged and associated with you.

Added up, the situation is this: Experienced surfers do their best to mock the system, while comparative newcomers—fearing privacy violations—avoid making purchases to protect their identities. This is not good for you, and it's not good for web users, either, because it is limiting their use of the medium.

Confidence Boosters

What should you do to reassure visitors? As a rule, mainline web sites explain their privacy policy. At the Entrepre neur.com site, for instance, there is a link at the bottom of the front page that says "Privacy Policy." Click it, and you are delivered to a clear, concise statement of what information is collected from visitors, what's done with it, and whether it's made available to other companies. (The answer in this case is no—"Any information collected about you will never be sold or rented to any third party for any purpose," says the Entre preneur.com statement.)

Most other leading U.S. sites you'll visit will explain their privacy policy somewhere on their sites in much the same way. They may vary in how easy it is to find the link and how clear the statement is, but poke around and you'll probably find a policy.

Another trend: privacy promises made by third parties, such as the Better Business Bureau Privacy Program (www.bbb online.org/privacy) and TRUSTe (www. truste.com). Program mechanics vary a bit, but the essence is that a business site

SMART TIP

Not getting the response you thought you would from an e-marketing campaign? Check with your ISP to make sure it isn't blocking your e-mail via its spam filters. What do these filters look for? Use of large or colored fonts and ALL CAPS; use of words such as "free," "special," or "click here"; language in a subject line that says something such as "urgent assistance needed"; and incorrect or dated date stamps. Some ISPs will also block based on volume. If they see an IP address that is blasting a bunch of e-mail messages, they may block it or shut it down to investigate. The message won't get to anyone on the list, and you might not find out for days.

meets certain basic privacy requirements, pays a fee, and then gets to display a button on the web site touting that it fulfills the program's requirements. Some users grumble that these programs don't truly guarantee privacy so much as they promise disclosure of what happens to information surfers reveal, but nearly everybody agrees that such programs are a step in the right direction. Should you join? Since the cheapest TRUSTe membership started at $849 annually at a recent look, it may not be the shrewdest use of sparse cash in a start-up. My advice: Keep the money in your pocket and look for do-it-yourself tactics to up visitor security.

In general, you should post a link to your privacy policy in a prominent place on your site. In that policy, be clear, simple, and direct. A good strategy is to say: "We sell no information that we collect about you. Never. To anybody." Don't ask questions about visitors' children—unless

SPAM ALERT

The ability to reach millions of people instantly has proved too seductive for some unscrupulous and shortsighted people. These are the advertisers who spread spam on the internet.

"Spam" is the internet term for utterly undifferentiated advertising that's sent to millions of people daily, offering instant riches, high-quality sex talk, lucrative investment opportunities, and other suckers-only come-ons.

The problem is so prevalent that the Controlling the Assault of Non-Solicited Pornography and Marketing Act (or Can-Spam act of 2003) was passed into law and went into effect in 2004. The law requires commercial e-mail messages to be labeled and to include opt-out instructions as well as the sender's physical address. It also prohibits the use of deceptive subject lines and false headers.

So, follow the law—don't spam. Your customers will thank you for it. (For more on spam and e-mailing, see Chapter 11.)

there's a compelling and obvious reason to do so. And if you offer visitors free sign-up to e-mail newsletters or sales notices, be quick to remove anybody who asks not to be on the list—preferably on the very day you receive the request. Users grumble a lot about spam, and an easy way to win visitor confidence is to promptly remove anybody from any list upon request.

Winning—and keeping—visitor trust isn't, and shouldn't be, rocket science. Lots of the same hurdles were overcome years ago by direct mail and catalog sellers. In the case of the internet, plenty of credit card issuers, including American Express and Citibank, are working overtime to encourage their cardholders to make online purchases with the full assurance that the card will protect them from fraud. And in probably the broadest, most objective look at internet privacy issues, the Federal

DSL DANGERS

Are you using high-speed internet access via a cable modem or always-on DSL? If you are, you're enjoying the best web access around, but you also are exposing yourself to invasion by hackers.

Theoretically, a hacker could penetrate your system when you are connected to the internet with a dial-up connection, but the likelihood is not high. Why? Usually when you're connected you are sitting at the computer. If suddenly you were to see that you were opening Quicken financial files—and in fact you were not—you'd know a hacker was there, and poof, you'd shut down. End of threat.

Always-on connections raise different worries. Maybe 20 hours a day your computer is sitting there, open to invasion. But antidotes are plentiful. A popular one is Norton Internet Security (www.symantec.com). It costs less than $70, installs in minutes, and protects your system against intruders. Plenty of other packages are available. Whatever you use, if you have high-speed access, get software to protect the privacy of your computer. It's an ounce of prevention that can save many pounds of tears.

Trade Commission (FTC)—a lead government agency in the e-commerce arena—has argued that there is no need for government intervention to offer more assurances of privacy and that, on balance, the industry is doing a satisfactory job. For most site operators, this means don't screw up, and you'll be able to develop trust on the part of visitors. And once they trust you, they will buy. (For more on privacy, see Chapter 19.)

Chapter 8 Summary
10 Things You Can Do Today

1. Make sure you know your customers.

2. A good way to know your customers is to track your web site visitors by going to your web hosting service and looking for a directory called "Logs."

3. Remember that while these file reports are good, you can get an even better analysis by using third-party software tools.

4. Respond to all e-mail the same day—and offer answers that are truly responsive to what the customers are writing about.

5. Try A/B testing, which allows you to test two different versions of your web site. A host of companies now offer hosted testing and optimization services at prices within reach of smaller businesses.

6. Learn about your customers by experimenting with surveys. But keep them short, and offer a tangible reward.

7. Try online polls, which can be tailored to serve many ends.

8. Now that you're gathering information on your customers, know this: It all has to be done gently, respectfully, and cautiously.

9. Reassure visitors by openly explaining your privacy policy.

10. Follow the law—don't spam. Your customers will thank you for it.

Chapter 9

The Scoop on Business-to-Business e-Commerce

*E*NTREPRENEURS USED TO DREAM OF STARTING the next McDonald's, or maybe inventing a new widget that everybody would need, putting them on the fast track to wealth so immense it could scarcely be counted. Today, of course, the dream is to come up with the new Amazon.com or Yahoo!—but that might be the wrong dream.

Isn't this book all about launching the Next Big Thing? Nope. It's about building businesses on the internet. Nowadays, a very good argument can be made that there's a smarter

SMART TIP

If it can be sold by phone or by mail, it can be sold, probably better, on the web. E-commerce may never completely replace face-to-face selling (who wants to rent an office space over the web?), but it sure will take a huge bite out of telemarketing and direct-mail sales.

way to go than scouting around for the idea that will spawn a new Amazon.

The Many Faces of B2B

Just who is making it in B2B e-commerce? Sure winners have yet to emerge, but lately the web is filled with enticing players that illustrate the breadth of this marketplace. That's because B2B e-commerce offers diverse opportunities, with some players seeking to establish themselves as marketplaces where buyers and sellers meet to do deals, while others are positioning themselves to provide services and products to business customers in a wholly new, web-based way. The bottom line: B2B e-commerce entrepreneurs are limited only by

IN THE KNOW

What industry do you know, and know well? Substantial expertise is needed to create a viable B2B. What industries have you worked in? Which ones interest you enough that you'll enjoy the long hours of research you'll need to put in?

Ironically, you could probably pick any industry and do well—if it truly interests you and your ideas are good. That's because just about every industry will go through massive structural changes in the next decade as the underlying business processes are impacted by the internet. Savvy entrepreneurs need to be watching for the turf where their ideas can make a difference.

Marketing glitz doesn't go as far in a B2B context as does getting down to the nuts and bolts of what you have to offer businesses that will positively affect their bottom lines. Business executives tend to be more cold-blooded about these things, so show them where they will save time and money, and they will follow you.

their own imaginations. There are plenty of possibilities in this exploding space.

Want concrete examples of how businesses on the web are serving other businesses? Read on for a sampling of the strategies B2B web sites are pursuing.

Liquidation.com

The success of eBay, online discount retailers such as Amazon.com, and other brick-and-mortar discount shops has proven that consumers and businesses want high-end products but want to pay less than high-end prices. As the market for less-than-new items grows for both consumers and business purchasers, those with an entrepreneurial heart are eager to capitalize on selling to these markets.

The challenge is where to find this type of inventory for prices low enough to make a profit on the resale.

Washington, DC-based Liquidity Services Inc. (LSI) has created a business that helps organizations shed unwanted inventory through online auction marketplaces and has amassed more than 400,000 registered buyers of wholesale and surplus goods.

LSI provides a consistent flow of new and used assets including overstock, consumer returns, refurbished items, and seasonal items on its online auction marketplaces www.liquidation.com, www.govliquidation.com, and www.liquibiz.com.

The merchandise comes from LSI's contracts with Fortune 500 companies, public sector agencies, top retailers, manufacturers, wholesalers, and distributors to sell surplus inventory and assets.

Buyers often resell the merchandise as individual units or in multiple quantities to small retail chains, through eBay, to small businesses, and even in export markets.

"Our business model is very simple and transparent for both sellers and buyers," says Bill Angrick, chairman and CEO of Liquidity Services Inc. "Not only do we convert surplus assets to cash for large and medium-sized organizations, but we enable buyers with easy access to find and purchase this inventory through secure online marketplaces." Angrick says it is also common for a new business to purchase computers, office equipment, and other necessary items for running a business that are costly in the retail market.

The LSI marketplaces offer buyers a total solution to source inventory in bulk through an online auction process. Liquidation.com, Gov liquidation.com and Liquibiz.com have hundreds of auctions to bid on at any given time in more than 600 categories including consumer electronics, computers and networking equipment, clothing and accessories, and general merchandise.

To bid on auctions, wholesale buyers register for free on the sites and can start bidding on posted auctions. All auctions start with a low opening bid (typically $100) with no reserve so the marketplace decides the final price for each lot. Each auction lasts two to five business days and includes detailed descriptions, manifests, and photographs of items. Buyers can sign up for e-mail newsletters and alerts to be notified when new auctions are posted for specific items, in a certain demographic area, or in a general category.

In addition, LSI has contracts with UPS and other domestic and international shippers that reduce shipping costs by as much as 40 percent. This means that buyers are able to resell the merchandise at more competitive prices while still maintaining a profit margin.

Liquidation.com also allows buyers the opportunity to arrange their own shipping for inventory that is stored in Liquidity Services Inc.'s warehouses located in Dallas, Texas and Cranberry, New Jersey, according to Angrick.

Dedicated to providing excellent customer service, LSI offers a Buyer Relations team that is available to assist buyers throughout the buying process by answering questions about the inventory, managing the shipping procedures, and discussing payment options.

On the seller side, LSI offers a full range of services including reconciliation of surplus, auction creation, marketing to current and potential buyers, buyer assistance, payment arrangements, and complete and transparent tracking.

"The overall goal of our asset remarketing activities is to provide a solution that maximizes the recovery value of surplus property," says Angrick. "We have over 400,000 registered buyers that consistently use our marketplaces to source bulk and wholesale inventory, which ensures a competitive market price on the surplus inventory we handle for our sellers. Our buyers have confidence bidding on these items and know that they will receive winning purchases in an easy and trusted manner."

According to Angrick, sellers can obtain 20 to 200 percent higher recovery using LSI's marketplaces, as well as save significant time, resources, and costs associated with traditional liquidation options.

In June 2004, LSI launched its Advertising Solutions Division that includes its goWholesale and Wholesale411 search portals for small businesses and the wholesale industry.

The sites, www.gowholesale.com and www.wholesale411.com, enable the nearly 460,000 middle market wholesale buyers and sellers in the United States to find, buy, and sell everything wholesale. Together, the sites generate more than two million business searches per month for wholesale goods and business services.

"Through our search portals, we provide the $2 trillion wholesale economy with the most comprehensive offering of online advertising services and the largest online business community serving the industry," says Angrick.

The key elements of goWholesale's and Wholesale411's offerings are pay-per-click keyword search advertising and online resources specific to the wholesale business community such as organic web listings, wholesale auctions, and wholesale classified ads. goWholesale and Wholesale411 also provide business users significant industry related content such as blogs, tradeshow information, news feeds, directory listings, and community forums.

Angrick says LSI has more than 1,500 pay-per-click business advertisers and over 8,000 active members in its wholesale community forum.

With more than $100 billion of surplus assets in the United States per year, LSI has focused on bringing the organizations economies of scale in technology, buyers, product sales knowledge, compliance expertise, and value added services to maximize revenues and reduce overall costs, says Angrick. In the past five years, LSI has stayed true to this focus and has grown from a raw start-up to a global market leader within the surplus asset disposition industry. LSI went public in February with an IPO of 7.7 million shares. Also, LSI announced that in its fiscal second quarter, which ended March 31, 2006, it had record revenue of $37.1 million and net income of $1.9 million.

Elance.com

Elance (www.elance.com), based in Mountain View, California, runs a highly successful online marketplace. The Elance Marketplace is used by small and midsized businesses to outsource projects across 100 service categories—from web site development to logo and graphic design, bookkeeping to administrative support—through a large, global pool of service providers that bid and pitch for business.

Using the Marketplace, buyers post projects and then qualified service providers with the relevant skills bid on these projects. Buyers determine the service providers that are best for their projects by reviewing proposals, experience, and project portfolios, as well as feedback on each supplier aggregated by Elance from previous buyers. Buyers can also browse service provider descriptions and, if they find service providers they would like to work with, simply invite them to bid on their particular project.

Typically, buyers create a shortlist of service providers, narrowing their choices to two or three, and begin a dialogue with them through the Marketplace. When comfortable with their selections, buyers award the projects to the selected service providers. Once a project is accepted, buyers and service providers use the Marketplace's online work space and message boards to manage their projects and, upon completion, use the system to securely pay their providers online.

While buyers post projects for free, service providers pay a subscription fee to Elance to gain access to the buyer network. Additionally, Elance collects a small fee from the service providers once projects have been completed and they have been paid. Prices are extremely competitive due to the strength of the supplier network and nature of the bidding process.

To make the purchase of services even simpler, Elance recently introduced packages for popular projects, such as logo development, brochure creation, and web site design. These packages are fixed-price, fixed-scope projects that are guaranteed by Elance and merchandised like traditional products. Elance also draws on its extensive network of service providers that participate in the Marketplace to fulfill these projects. These packages both encourage first-time buyers to get started and take the guesswork out of scoping and buying services.

The Elance Marketplace continues to grow, particularly as small and midsized businesses are seeing the benefits of outsourcing their projects, and service providers look for additional channels to market their services. Today, more than 100,000 small and midsized businesses post projects through the Marketplace and over 75 percent of these buyers return with additional projects, a testament to the value of the marketplace and the quality of the service providers therein.

"The Elance Marketplace is the top spot for accessing high quality, affordable service providers across the broadest number of service categories," says Elance president and CEO Fabio Rosati. "We enable small and midsized businesses to source their projects at a fraction of the cost of what they would pay at 'retail' rates. And recently, we celebrated with our first service provider to cross a key milestone—$1 million in revenue derived from projects entirely through the Marketplace."

Based on the success of the Marketplace, Elance brought its vision for services and contractor management to the enterprise in 2002. The Elance Services and Contractor Management Solution is designed to streamline and automate the process of finding, buying, and managing services and has been adopted by leading companies including American Express, BP, FedEx, GE, and Motorola.

Today, Elance is the most widely used application for services and contractor management. More than 200,000 employees are using Elance to find, evaluate, buy, manage, and pay for external services and contractors from more than 2,000 suppliers across 50-plus services categories, including contingent labor, information technology, consulting, call-center operations, operations, maintenance, and facilities.

Bulbs.com

Steve Rothschild is passionate about bulbs—lightbulbs, that is. He sometimes even closes his e-mail messages with "Have a Bright Day!" Perhaps that's why his privately held company Bulbs.com (www.bulbs.com) is thriving. What is Bulbs.com? "We are a B2B e-commerce company that specializes in lighting and drives sales through direct marketing," says Rothschild, founder and CEO of Bulbs.com. "We are pursuing a share of the $12 billion domestic commercial/industrial lighting market." The company has a straightforward business model in which customers—85 percent of which are businesses—order lightbulbs directly from the company's web site.

Bulbs.com has distribution agreements with Philips Lighting and a host of other manufacturers.

Since its launch in August 1999, Bulbs.com has received orders from more than 31,000 companies and more than 90,000 of those companies, locations, and 65 percent of its business clients have reordered. Major customers include Central Parking Systems, Samsonite Stores, Best

Western, Work 'n Gear, Perfumania, House of Blues, Verizon Wireless, and Leath Furniture, as well as the U.S. Military and the National Park Service.

Why did Rothschild decide to set up a web site that sold lightbulbs? "I was searching for my next opportunity, which I knew was going to be e-commerce related, and I knew that for it be successful, I had to find a product that would be identifiable via the web, had to be replaced on a regular basis, and its cost-to-freight ratio had to be viable," says Rothschild. "Lightbulbs was the obvious choice for me." Rothschild also says there was a need for this business in the marketplace.

Bulbs.com has raised debt and equity financing from investors including Arbor Partners LLC, Hexagon Investments, the Ralph Wilson Equity Fund, and management. The business, which grows at an annual rate of more than 50 percent, is "break-even and cash-flow-neutral," says Rothschild. "Our intentional reinvestment for growth has temporarily kept us from being profitable."

As these examples show, there are many small B2B web companies thriving despite the current economy. Some traditional B2C companies are also entering the B2B e-commerce fray. Consider eBay. At any given time, there are approximately 55 million items available on eBay worldwide, and approximately 5 million items are added per day. To make business buying easier for small- to medium-sized businesses (SMBs), eBay has created a section on its site called eBay Business (http://pages.ebay.com/businessmarketplace/index.html). The business-oriented site brings together all eBay's business and industry listings under one easy-to-browse web destination and currently features more than 500,000 product listings, focusing heavily on office technology products, such as computers and networking devices, as well as wholesale lots of consumer goods and services, such as insurance and shipping.

SMART TIP

No medium has ever been as fast at moving time-sensitive merchandise as the web. If a product will rot or become terribly dated if it doesn't sell fast, the web is the best sales agent there could be. What, besides produce, can you think of that's extremely time-sensitive? Come up with possibilities, and then search Yahoo! to see if that niche already has players. Maybe you'll hit upon a real gusher of a new B2B play.

SMART TIP

The best news about B2B e-commerce? Launching a B2B site is significantly less expensive than trying to create a winning consumer site. Usually it's cheaper to target an audience and pursue it in B2B. If you have narrowed down a business niche and know how to cost-effectively target it, a B2B site can gain traction fast and on a minimal budget.

A Slam Dunk?

Hold on, however, because the sailing for new B2B entrants won't be entirely smooth. In key respects, the bar may be higher in B2B e-commerce than it is in B2C, and the requirements for succeeding will likely be stiffer. "B2B is different from B2C," says John J. Sviokla, vice chairman of Diamond-Cluster International Inc., a global management firm that helps companies develop and implement growth strategies. "To succeed in this space, you will need deep domain knowledge." You don't need to know much about farming to successfully peddle peaches to consumers, but to build an exchange for farmers, you have to grasp the fundamental issues in that industry. Lack that, and there will be no trust on the part of your target audience.

Another hitch: B2B involves long selling cycles, and before big deals are nailed down, you'll probably need to do face-to-face selling. It is one thing to buy a $10 book with a mouse click. It's an entirely different matter to buy $100,000 worth of coffee mugs.

And there are times when a B2B model doesn't work. Consider Winery Exchange (www.wineryexchange.com), which was founded by Peter Byck in 1999 in Novato, California. The company now offers private-label wine brands for large, global wine retailers and creates and delivers strategic information to assist wineries and spirits companies in building, growing, and managing their brands.

When it started, however, its web site allowed suppliers of wine, grapes, equipment, and services to sell their wares in bulk to wine growers, wineries, and retailers in a secure, user-friendly environment. "We are not trading online anymore," says Byck. "That didn't really work because there are a lot of relationships in the business, and people want to deal with people when they are buying these products. Also, some exchange models may work, but if you are trading bulk wine and grapes, it's just not a big enough industry with enough buyers and sellers to make a big business."

The company switched its focus to the private-label wine brand and strategic information sides of the business "At the end of the day, you have to go where the growth and opportunities are," says Byck. "There were demands for those products, so we followed those paths."

Some analysts are somewhat suspicious of pure-play B2B e-commerce companies in general (these "pure plays" are purely online—they don't sell out of storefronts). But not everyone agrees. Many experts believe that it is indeed a great time to be in B2B e-commerce if you are a small company because with the technology and services available, you can appear to have the resources of a bigger company. And you can reach buyers from all over the country—and the world.

SMART TIP

Want to read some B2B e-commerce success stories? Then see "e-Chat with Corporate Toners Inc.'s Kapil Juneja" and "e-Chat with VenturePoint LLC's Karen Torbett" in the Appendix.

Chapter 9 Summary
10 Things You Can Do Today

1. Think about entering the world of business-to-business e-commerce, which can offer diverse opportunities.

2. Remember that substantial expertise is needed to create a viable B2B.

3. If you plan to target businesses, forget the marketing glitz and instead explain how you can help businesses save time and money.

4. Stick with a simple business model for the best chance of success.

5. Before choosing a particular product or service to sell to businesses, make sure there is a need for it in the marketplace.

6. Are you already selling to consumers? Think about whether or not you can expand to reach businesses.

7. Remember that the bar may be higher in B2B e-commerce than it is in B2C, and the requirements for succeeding will likely be stiffer.

8. Keep in mind that B2B involves long selling cycles, and that you'll need to do face-to-face selling before big deals are nailed down; make sure you are ready.

9. Don't be discouraged if you find that the B2B model doesn't work for you. Simply try something else.

10. Keep in mind that it's cheaper to target an audience and pursue it in the B2B world than in the B2C world, especially if you've narrowed down your business niche and know how to cost-effectively target it.

Chapter 10

e-Chat with Drugstore.com Inc.'s Dawn Lepore

*H*ERE IS THE FIRST OF SEVERAL E-CHATS WITH heads of successful e-commerce firms.

Drugstore.com Inc.

Dawn Lepore, president, CEO, chairman of the board

Location: Bellevue, Washington

Year started: 1998

Drugstore.com (www.drugstore.com) has been one of the most popular sites on the web today—and is continuing to be—thanks to its recently appointed president, CEO, and chairman of the board, Dawn Lepore.

After a 21-year career at discount brokerage Charles Schwab, Lepore—who had risen to vice chairman of technology, operations, and administration and in her early years was also responsible for moving Schwab onto the internet—moved with her family in October 2004 from the San Francisco Bay area to Bellevue, Washington to run Drugstore.com. Listen up as Lepore explains what prompted her to take the plunge into heading up Drugstore.com and what she believes it will take to succeed in the online drugstore space.

Melissa Campanelli: Why did you join Drugstore.com?

Dawn Lepore: I love retail businesses, and I am a firm believer that the internet is at the beginning of its evolution. I believe in what Drugstore.com is offering, which can make a difference in customers' lives. Also, the company is not a technology company but technology plays a huge role and that was attractive to me. And I met so many happy customers and really loved the passion of the employees—so the combination of that, along with the investors and the board members, all made it a great opportunity from my perspective.

Campanelli: Can you elaborate on how Drugstore.com can make a difference in a customer's life?

Lepore: There are two pieces to this. One is that you can't pick up a newspaper today without hearing about affordable prescriptions for Americans, and of course we all know that many people are going outside of the country and buying things from pharmacies that maybe are less regulated and there might be some kind of risk associated with that. We, however, offer very, very great prices on many of our generic prescriptions—and on our brands we are 15 to 20 percent below retail because we have less overhead because we are not operating a lot of drug stores—we just operate through our web site.

Another way Drugstore.com can make a difference in a customer's life is our breadth of product. We focus on both men and women, but our demographic happens to be predominantly female and I have very young children, so I know what it's like when it's 10 o'clock at night before you really have time to think about doing the errands you need to do for your family or for yourself. I've heard from so many women who sit down at 10 o'clock at night, log on to the site, and get the diapers for their children, their shampoo and favorite face cream, and their husband's favorite products all at one sitting. They just love the convenience and they love the service and they love the breadth of our offering.

Campanelli: How big is the drugstore category? How big will it become?

Lepore: This market is huge, although I'm not sure anybody knows exactly what it is. I think it is probably close to around $300 billion, but I still think the internet penetration in this category is very low—definitely below 5 percent—so there is a lot of upside there for us.

Campanelli: What's your major competition?

Lepore: Competition is a lot about people's habits, such as stopping at the drugstore on their way home from work. We have to continually remind them to come online. It does take time to change customer behavior, but I think we are at the beginning of the trend of people moving these types of purchases online and that we will be the beneficiary of that.

Besides the brick-and-mortar stores, we also compete with some niche players, in different categories like Sephora [a makeup company] or MotherNature.com [an online retailer that primarily sells vitamins]. But what our customers tell us they love about us is that they can get the Maybelline mascara next the to Philosophy face cream next to vitamins. You can't do that at Sephora, you can't do that at MotherNature.com, and you can't do that in almost any other place. We are unique in that capability and I think it's a good differentiator.

Campanelli: Hasn't the online drugstore space taken off more slowly than many expected?

Lepore: I do think this category is a little bit slower to adapt online, and I think that it has to do with the fact that it takes a while to change customer behavior. You know why? Because it is just so darn convenient because there are so many brick-and-mortar stores out there. But the problem is, people don't like the customer experience in a brick-and-mortar store, and they can't find all the products they want. Another thing: Sometimes people run out of their shampoo or deodorant or toothpaste. And what we need to do is train people to order a few days before they are going to run out. So it is definitely changing customer behavior, and customer behavior takes a while to change.

Campanelli: Do you think it will grow?

Lepore: I do think the online drugstore space will grow, but I think it will take time. E-commerce in general is growing at 25 or 30 percent a year, and so just looking at that alone shows me that we have potential for growth.

Campanelli: How will you beat competitors?

Lepore: It's the breadth of product, our prices—which are very, very competitive—our offers, and our free shipping if you spend $49. We also have special offers where you can get free shipping when you spend $25. And it's our convenience, service, and customer experience. We make it very easy for our customers to order and reorder. For example, we will send you your list and you just click on what you want. It's all of these things, really, that add to our competitive advantage.

Campanelli: Where will your profits come from—prescription drugs or other merchandise?

SMART TIP

How do you persuade wary consumers to buy? For Drugstore.com, the answer is information—and that's an area where the internet can excel. For example, Drugstore.com's web site has customer reviews. Here, people can write reviews about products they use and post them on the site. Dawn Lepore says that customers really love reading the reviews and learning what people have to say about specific products before making a purchase. And keep in mind that on the web, an e-tailer can offer this kind of information at very little cost, while gaining a leg up on traditional retailers.

Lepore: Our over-the-counter [OTC] category—which includes items like shampoo and deodorant, for example—is our fastest-growing and highest-margin category. That's where most of our profitably comes from. The prescription part of our business makes up about 40 percent and is a lower margin category, and while it is not growing quite as fast, it is important. Certainly our customers appreciate the fact that we carry prescriptions. Within OTC we have segments that are growing very nicely. Beauty, for example, which includes makeup, face creams, and hair dryers, is growing the fastest right now.

Campanelli: Critics say online drugstores will sell drugs to kids—is this a worry?

Lepore: We absolutely have to have a valid prescription—we verify the prescriptions with doctors—so there is no way that you can get a drug that you don't have a valid prescription for. We take lots of information, and we do insurance claims, etc. And then, from a quality perspective, we check and double-check, and triple-check those prescriptions going out of our distribution center. We are very, very confident in the quality and the legality of our prescription business.

Campanelli: In your opinion, what will e-commerce look like in a few years?

Lepore: I definitely think e-commerce's growth will continue, and there are certain categories where that growth will accelerate. I think people will do more and more on the internet, and I think there will be a number of new business models that will continue to emerge.

SMART TIP

Closely scan your product sales reports—and don't be thrown for a loop if there are a few surprises in the mix. Audiences you never expected can find you on the web. When you see unanticipated sales trends, however, react fast—that's a key edge of the web over other kinds of retailing. Adjust product mix to meet customer needs, and redo pages to point to what customers are looking for.

Chapter 10 Summary
10 Things You Can Do Today

1. When setting up you site, remember a key thought from Dawn Lepore says: Technology is only part of your business. Don't focus solely on the technology, and remember that you will be selling things to people.

2. Think about selling a product that you are passionate about and that you truly believe can change a person's life.

3. By operating a web site, you might be able to offer lower retail prices than your brick-and-mortar competitors do because you'll have less overhead. So plan accordingly.

4. People love the convenience of the web—in many cases that's why they use it—so build your site around that concept.

5. If you are not selling a niche product, try offering your customers a wide variety of merchandise.

6. Think about offering special promotions, such as those where your customers can get free shipping if they spend a certain amount of money.

7. Figure out ways to make it easy for your customers to order and reorder.

8. Try adding a feature that allows customers to write reviews about products they use and then post those reviews on the site.

9. Make sure you closely scan your product sales reports and adjust your product mix to meet customer needs.

10. After scanning your report, think about redoing pages to point to what customers are looking for.

Chapter 11

Web Site Traffic Builders

*I*N ORDER TO KEEP YOUR E-COMMERCE BUSI-
ness growing, you've got to get people to
visit your web site—and keep them coming back. Sounds easy, right? Especially since
you've got a great product or service to sell, and
you've followed our plan up until now. But
here's the bad news: There are currently more
than three billion web pages. Wow! Just 20
years ago, the web didn't exist. Now every
business needs a web site—but just because you
build it doesn't mean a soul will ever visit.
"Putting up a web site is just like opening an
antiques store down a country road," says

Larry Chase, publisher of *Web Digest for Marketers*, a weekly e-mail newsletter that delivers short reviews of marketing-oriented web sites. "Unless you tack up signs on better-traveled routes, you won't get any visitors." What's more, traditional marketing campaigns don't necessarily produce results for web sites, warns Mark DiMassimo, CEO of DiMassimo Brand Advertising, an agency that has handled many dotcom clients. A case in point: "Generally, television advertising for dotcoms, although expensive, has been very ineffective," says DiMassimo, whose agency at one time surveyed consumers and discovered that only 6 percent of heavy web users said they had ever visited a site due to a TV ad. "Offline advertising hasn't always worked as well as the dotcoms have hoped."

Baiting Your Hook

What will lure visitors to a site? Although heavily funded internet companies can make seven- and eight-figure deals to buy prime advertising real estate on the major internet portals and online services such as Yahoo! and AOL, you're likely to be priced out of that race. So winning visitors becomes a matter of creative, persistent marketing. And the good news is that it's still the little things that will bring plenty of traffic your way.

There are fundamental steps that too many businesses neglect. For instance? "You should always put your URL and a reason to visit your web site on your business cards," says Chase. "I call this cyberbait. For example, you should mention what people will get when they visit the site, such as a newsletter or a list of 'Top 10 Tips' or something. That substantially increases visitors and eventually customers or subscribers."

A few years ago, Chase says, "You could get away with just putting a URL on your business card, because the novelty of that URL was enough to draw people to the site. Nowadays it's just like putting up a

SNAZZY SIGNATURES

Nearly every e-mail program offers the ability to include a signature that goes out with each e-mail. Think of a signature—"sig" in techspeak—as a teaser, a fast ad for your web site. How do you create a signature? In Microsoft Outlook, for example, go to "Tools/Options/Mail Format/Signatures." Some advice: Short is better than long with signatures. Rarely should you use more than six short lines, and three or four are better.

What to include? If your web site sells foreign language tapes, for instance, you might use this sig:

> John Smith
> President, TapesRUs.com
> "Learn Languages by Tape"
> www.tapesrus.com

Once you've set it up, that signature will appear on every e-mail you send out (unless you override the default). If you send out 20 e-mails in a day, that's 20 repetitions of a fast ad message. It's one of the internet's best marketing bargains.

---

fax number. People are not going to fax you just to see how your fax machine works." An e-mail signature—the bit of text you put at the end of your posts identifying who you are—is also an especially powerful and absolutely free tool. Create a signature with a link to your web site in it and have it automatically attached to every one of your outgoing e-mails. If your e-mail recipients click on the link, they'll be taken to your site. It only takes a few seconds to create an e-mail signature, and it'll bring in visitors to your site every day.

Another low-cost traffic builder: Get active in appropriate online discussion groups and chats, and, where appropriate, give out your URL.

There are two types of online discussion groups. The first type is an e-mail-based discussion list. In the internet parlance of the past, this type of group was also known as listserv, after the type of software that makes it work. Essentially, a member of the group sends correspondence to a central group e-mail address, where software redistributes the message to everyone else in the group. When other members reply, those messages also get sent to the same central e-mail address for the group—starting the process of message redistribution all over again.

The second type of online discussion group is a web-based group. In this system, members of the group respond to messages listed on a web site.

In both systems, a discussion on a particular topic is known as a "thread" and the individual messages making up the thread are known as "posts."

To write a post that talks about something outside of the subject of the thread is known as "going off-topic." It is the job of the "moderator"—a member of the group that reviews all posts—to make sure everyone stays "on-topic" and the dis-cussions run smoothly.

Remember: When marketing via online discussion groups, it is important to use online discussion etiquette. For example, do not post messages at random to any groups, ever. If you want to announce the availability of your new site or resource, contact the mod-erator privately and get permission first. Basically, the moderator's job is to screen everything for the other list members. If the moderator says your message is OK, it is likely everyone else on the list will be recep-tive as well.

When answering a question in a group, it is OK to reference your own web site or other online resources you control as long as you dis-close any personal interest in the web site or resource.

It is always advisable to put a link to what you are promoting in your e-mail signature—that's the bit of text you put at the end of your posts identifying who you are. It is also all right to disagree with a fel-low group member's point of view, but never let your statements turn into personal attacks—that is a fast way to get you disliked by the group, and even banned by the moderator.

When replying to a person's message, only quote the relevant parts of that message in your reply. Do not send the whole message back to the list. As the thread progresses, the posts get too hard to follow unless you edit out the extraneous information.

In general, keep this tip in mind: Don't post commercial messages to news groups that have rules against these types of messages.

So how do you find online discussion groups? For e-mail-based discussion groups, try http://groups.yahoo.com, www.tile.net/lists, or http://lists.topica.com. For web-based discussion groups formed by private parties and usually hosted on their private web sites, try www .forumhaven.com, www.boardtracker.com, or http://search.big-boards .com. There are also public discussions that occur in an area of the internet known as the Usenet Newsgroups. These are primarily web-based today, and they can be found at http://groups.google.com.

The Most Bang for Your Buck

Another big-time traffic builder for any web site that retails is posting items for sale on the major auction sites, such as eBay, Yahoo!, and Amazon. Those sites let you identify yourself to viewers, and a few dollars spent on putting out merchandise to bid may just bring in lots of traffic from surfers seeking more information. Many small e-tailers tell me their entire advertising budget consists of less than $100 monthly spent on eBay, but they nonetheless are seeing traffic counts above 500 daily, with most of those viewers coming via eBay. My advice: Put up a few items for bid on each of the leading auction sites and then track traffic. Even if you sell the auctioned goods at no profit, the traffic jams your site may experience could well justify your efforts.

Classified ads offer more possibilities for traffic generation on the cheap. Check out Yahoo!, for example. Classified ads there are relatively low-cost and vary depending on what you are selling. Listing is simple—just follow the steps at the site—and, again, you can insert your URL so readers who want more information can get it with a click. There are also many web sites that let you run ads for free. The best way to find these is to search the web.

For my money, classified ads—at least the freebies—represent one of the very top ways to generate no-cost traffic. And classified ads are becoming a major online advertising category. JupiterResearch, a division of Jupitermedia Corporation, said in 2005 that online classified advertising would grow at nearly 10 percent, reaching $4.1 billion in 2010.

When it comes to offline advertising, expert opinion is mixed. Some pros advocate big investments in traditional media, while others tell you to fish where the fish are, and that means advertising online to promote an online store. I split the difference here, and my advice is to incorporate your URL prominently into all offline advertising you're doing—never overlook a chance to plug your web site—but don't launch an offline campaign for an online-only property. Sure, many of the big guys, such as Priceline.com (www.priceline.com) and Over stock.com (www.overstock.com) extensively advertise in offline media, but these are businesses with heavy venture capital backing and the dollars to experiment with. When money is tighter, go where you know you'll find surfers—and that means hunting online.

A Direct Approach

For many businesses, direct mail—good old e-mail—may be the surest and certainly the cheapest tool for building traffic. And it gets results: Customized e-mail can generate response rates upward of 6 percent— sometimes as high as 30 percent.

What's more, according to a Direct Marketing Association-commissioned consumer survey conducted in February 2005, 44 million adults in the United States had made a purchase in response to an e-mail in the preceding 12 months (up 5.1 percent from a similar survey in 2004), generating $37.6 billion in sales.

News Flash

What's the best way to get people to respond to e-mail? First, follow the law.

In 2004, the Controlling the Assault of Non-Solicited Pornography and Marketing Act (or Can-Spam act of 2003) was signed into law. The law requires commercial e-mail messages to be labeled and to include opt-out instructions as well as the sender's physical address. It also prohibits the use of deceptive subject lines and false headers. (For more information on this subject, see Chapter 8). A good way to get folks to opt-in to your e-mail list—which of course they will have the option of opting out of—is to offer a free monthly e-mail newsletter.

About what? Content is wide open, but effective newsletters usually mix news about trends in your field with tips and updates on sales or special pricing. Whatever you do, keep it short. How short? Six hundred words is probably the maximum length. Another key: Include hyperlinks so that interested readers can, with a single mouse click, go directly to your site and find out more about a topic of interest.

How often should you mail? Often enough to build a relationship with your readers, but not so frequently that you become a pest. Monthly, most experts say, works for most mailing lists, but every other week is also OK for some businesses.

Daily updates are a big mistake, and weekly ones are probably ill-advised, too. The reason: Recipients will ask to be deleted from the list or, worse, they'll simply delete each of your e-mails, unread, as soon as they come in. I am on a couple of lists whose daily incoming e-mail goes straight into the trash, unopened. Don't make that mistake.

Some mailing list drawbacks: Maintaining a list can be time-consuming. Worse, most ISPs put limits on the size of outgoing mailings (a maximum of 50 recipients is common) to keep spammers away, so mailing to a large list can be an aggravation involving the use of many small lists.

SMART TIP

Don't want to take on the task of producing a regular e-mail newsletter? Contact a local college or university. There you'll find plenty of students in communications or journalism departments who would be glad to write up your newsletter for a small monthly fee. But make sure you give the student plenty of direction—it still has to be your newsletter.

MANAGING YOUR DATA

Using e-mail services is not the only way to go when sending out e-mail marketing messages. Some small e-tailers swear by FileMaker Pro 8 database software to manage and execute their e-mail marketing efforts. The software includes an e-mail campaign management solution that allows you to deploy e-mail marketing from within the system to targeted customer groups easily. The software is especially great for monthly newsletters and staying in touch with your customers and prospects. FileMaker Pro 8 also lets you track e-mail campaigns by printing individualized bar codes or promotional codes in e-mails and then placing detailed notes in each customer's file so you can create reports on current and past campaigns. Best of all, FileMaker Pro 8 starts at only $299, which is a good deal. For more information, visit www.filemaker.com.

Special Delivery

A solution to common mailing hassles is to use a mailing service. Three good choices? Topica (www.topica.com), Constant Contact (www.constantcontact.com), and ExactTarget (www.exattarget.com). These services maintain mailing lists and, on your schedule, send out the mailings you provide.

A lot of the grunt work involved in mailings is handled by these services, which leaves you free to focus on the fun part: your message. Keep it simple, keep it sharp, and always use e-mail to drive traffic to your site. Don't make the big mistake of trying to cram your web site's entire message into every e-mail. Nobody has the patience for that. E-mail should stick to "headline news," with the full story residing on your web site. (For more e-mail best practices, see sidebar, "Best Practices for Successful Delivery of E-Mail Marketing Communications.")

Is your list succeeding? There's no reason to guess at the answer. Just track site traffic for a few days before a mailing and a few days afterward. Effective e-mail ought to produce a sharp upward spike in

BEST PRACTICES FOR SUCCESSFUL
DELIVERY OF E-MAIL MARKETING COMMUNICATIONS

In a report titled "E-mail Delivery Best Practices for Marketers and List Owners," the Direct Marketing Association offers some practical advice for marketers on how to be more successful at reaching current and potential customers or donors through focused e-mail messages.

The best practices are intended to improve the likelihood of permission-based e-mail being delivered to the inbox and read by the intended recipient. Some of the broad recommendations from the e-mail best practices include suggestions that e-mail marketers do the following:

- Encourage customers and prospects to add the marketer's legitimate sending address to their personal "approved list/address book" and provide up-front instructions on how to do so in registration pages. Benefits vary by mailbox provider, but may include special icon designation and full image content/link rendering. Being an "approved" sender yields higher response rates and generates fewer complaints and blocking issues.

- Carefully consider the content and presentation of marketing messages, as recipients are increasingly labeling as spam any e-mail communication that is not relevant or that looks suspicious. In addition, marketers are encouraged to create messages that strike a balance between images and system text, as many mailbox providers now routinely "hide" images in default settings.

- Follow established protocols such as authentication and whitelisting criteria to ensure that e-mail messages "pass muster" with mailbox providers. A growing number of ISPs use spam-filtering software to eliminate spam. This technology uses algorithms to determine whether incoming messages qualify as junk e-mail and filters them out before they get to an end-user's inbox. In addition, marketers should register for all mailbox provider feedback loops. In general, marketers should aim to keep complaint rates (total complaints divided by total delivered e-mail) below 0.1 percent to avoid temporary or long-term blocks.

- Adopt good list-hygiene and monitoring practices that help facilitate message delivery. Monitoring campaign delivery and open and click-through rates is essential, as a low open rate or high bounce rate may indicate a delivery issue.

- Educate consumers and other stakeholders about anti-spam tools, technologies, laws, and industry programs developed to separate legitimate communications from fraudulent messaging.

visitors. How big a spike? That answer hinges on your usual traffic, the size of your list, and your personal goals. A good target, though, is the 6 percent response rate.

If you don't see an increase in traffic, take a hard look at what you're mailing. Is it succinct? Focused? Does it encourage readers to click through for more information? If not, odds are you need to hone your message to encourage recipients to click through.

Another possible reason for less-than-desirable results: Your mailing list is bad. Send a vegan mailing to a list of self-proclaimed steak lovers, and you're knocking on the wrong door.

The best way to build a targeted mailing list is to make it simple for site visitors to sign up to receive it. This way visitors can show they are interested in your message—enough to indicate they want to hear more from you. Those are the folks who should be stimulated by your e-mail newsletter to click through for more information, at least sometimes. Keep working on both your newsletter and your list, and it will happen for you, too.

Stick It to Me

"Sticky" is the dream that keeps web site builders going. When your site is sticky, visitors hang around, and that means they're reading and

WHAT'S IN A DAY?

What's the best day to send an e-mail marketing message? Try Friday, according to a January 2006 report from e-mail marketing agency eROI titled "Q4 2005 E-Mail Statistics." The study found Friday to be the best day to send e-mail because it showed a tendency for higher open and click rates on Friday.

Why are the rates higher on Fridays? E-mail volume may have some correlation to open and click rates. Excluding the weekends, fewer e-mails were sent on Friday than any other day of the week. The highest volume fell on Monday, with 23.3 million messages. On Friday, the firm's clients sent an average 16.3 million.

buying—and you can bet that every minute a surfer sticks to your site translates into greater brand awareness for you. Whether you also have a store in a mall or your site is stand-alone, sticky is the Holy Grail—but making your site sticky doesn't have to be that elusive. When the information—the content—is there, people will stick to your site.

For a measuring stick, just look at the following statistics: Nielsen//NetRatings (www.nielsen-netratings.com), a firm that offers internet audience measurement and analysis, published a chart called "Top 25 Stickiest Brands" for June 2006 that measured, among other things, how many hours people spent on different web sites during that month. The number one site that month? PokerStars.com, which had people spending more than nine hours on its site. In second place was FanFiction.Net, a web site that allows writers and readers a place to post and read stories, review stories, and communicate with other authors and readers through forums and chat rooms. On this site, people spent more than seven hours that month. In third place was AOL, where people spent more than five hours. So what do the winning sites have in common? Good content—especially in the case of PokerStars.com, where people actually play poker on the site—and a site that is easy to navigate. Of course, content is a lot easier to say than it is to deliver. The following are concrete building blocks for making any site stickier:

- *Fast loading time.* Surfers are impatient. Force them to watch a stagnant screen as dense images or fancy Java applets load, and they will be out of there before your cool bells and whistles ever come into sight. It's tempting to use these gizmos—you might think they will increase your visitor stays because just watching them load eats up minutes—but in most cases, forget it. When you force surfers to wait until meaningful stuff happens, they won't. They will simply leave—often in a huff—and that means they won't be bookmarking your site for future visits.

  Keep in mind, however, that more and more people are using broadband services, such as cable modems or DSL, to access the internet, which means they can get a faster connection. But it's still important that you don't overload your site with too much "stuff."

- *Good copy.* "The web is still about text, words," says Motley Fool co-founder David Gardner, and he's spot on. You're not a writer?

CHEAP TRICKS

Want more pointers about traffic building and promotion on the cheap? Read *Cheap Web Tricks! Build and Promote a Successful Web Site without Spending a Dime* (McGraw-Hill) by Anne Martinez. While the book was published in 2003, there are plenty of good tips inside that are still relevant today. Or do a quick Google search for things like "How to Drive Traffic to Your Web Site, Cheaply." You'll be surprised at how much information pops up. Understand, however, that there are no magic formulas. No-money promotion can work if you work at it, and that means consistent, solid effort. Do that, and you'll see the results in a rising daily visitor count.

That doesn't necessarily matter—not when you stick to your field of expertise. Are you a criminal lawyer? Put up a list of the "10 Dumbest Mistakes Defendants Make." An accountant could do likewise. An electrician could put up a list of dangerous goofs made by do-it-yourselfers. Think snappy and useful, and try to provide info readers can't easily find at thousands of other web sites.

- *Loyalty programs.* Another way to get targeted customers coming back for more is by using online incentive marketing, such as setting up loyalty programs on your site. Acquiring customers isn't as easy as it used to be—so if you have regular customers, it is wise to do something to keep them coming back for more. There are numerous programs out there. You could do something as simple as offering customers the ability to earn gifts—such as T-shirts emblazoned with your logo—if they buy enough merchandise on your site. Or you could go with the most popular option, known as a frequent-buyer or points program. This choice gives customers the opportunity to receive discounts or points toward the purchase of merchandise by buying products on your site. The more your customers spend—which can also mean the more times they come back to your site—the bigger the discounts or the more points they receive.

- *Easy navigation.* Every pro webmaster has a few "favorite" awful sites that offer great content but that nobody will ever see because they are too hard to find. Simplicity has to be a byword for any site builder, because the price of boring or confusing a visitor is that surfer's quick exit. (For more information on how to keep your site sticky, see Chapter 5.)

BEWARE
While encouraging more frequent shopping with a loyalty program for existing customers is a smart strategy, promoting loyalty on the web does have its challenges. For example, establishing loyalty online tends to be more difficult given the nature of the web environment and its one-click access to competitors. So what is an online merchant to do? Best practices include speaking to shoppers' uniqueness, not requiring the user to jump through hoops to participate, and providing a simple reward structure and clear reward and value for information given.

SHOPPING BOTS

If you're an online business owner, you know that attracting qualified traffic—people who are already interested in buying your product or service—is fundamental to your success. That's why you should know about "shopping bots."

Shopping bots are like search engines except that instead of finding information, they're designed to help shoppers find the products or services they're looking for on the internet.

Shopping bot sites list specific product information so shoppers can compare features and prices. And this means that shopping bots can be an excellent way for your potential customers to find out exactly what you have to offer—and how to get it.

Best of all, shopping bots can be a great place for business owners struggling to stand out in competitive markets to capture the eyeballs of qualified potential customers—without spending more than they can afford for the more popular pay-per-click ads such as on a Yahoo! sponsored search. (For more on pay-per-click programs, see Chapter 14.)

Though shopping bot sites differ slightly from each other, registering your site and products with most of them is usually easy.

Lead sites include Froogle (http://froogle.google.com), PriceGrabber (www.price grabber.com), Shopping.com (www.shopping.com), Shopzilla (www.shopzilla.com), and Yahoo! Shopping (www.shopping.yahoo.com).

Using shopping bots is definitely a great way to beef up your web site traffic, bringing you qualified (i.e., interested) shoppers without costing you a lot of money. The most important thing to remember is that not every shopping bot site works in the same way. Choosing the one that suits your product or service will be crucial to the success of your ad.

And while shopping bots are an excellent source of cheap, qualified traffic, be sure you don't limit yourself to this one tool. Used properly, shopping bots can be a great addition to your online ad campaigns and can nicely complement your other marketing efforts.

Minority Report

Your web site already reaches the general public. But have you considered targeting specific ethnic groups to ring in additional sales?

Roughly 16.4 million Hispanics in the United States accessed the internet from home, work, or college in July, 2006, according to research from ComScore Media Metrix, a division of ComScore Networks Inc. In addition, 8.5 million African Americans and 2.4 million Asian Americans accessed the internet that month.

Many e-tailers and netpreneurs are taking notice and reaching out to these markets more aggressively. While doing so can potentially pay off for almost any kind of business, experts point to health and beauty, food, home, and wedding-related products as categories best suited for the strategy.

Before targeting ethnic groups on the internet, though, it's important to understand that such an undertaking requires time, effort, and money. Smaller e-tailers usually have a very small and specific marketing budget, and parsing it out among specific ethnic groups can be difficult.

Chapter 11 Summary
10 Things You Can Do Today

1. Remember that in order to keep your e-commerce business growing, you've got to get people to visit your site—and keep them coming back by using the right marketing techniques, such as smart e-mail marketing.

2. Use word processing tools to make sure your copy is up to snuff.

3. Always put your URL and a reason to visit your web site on your business cards.

4. Get active in the right online discussion groups and chats, and, where appropriate, give out your URL.

5. Always use online discussion etiquette when marketing via online discussion groups.

6. Try building traffic by posting items for sale on major auction sites, such as eBay, Yahoo!, and Amazon.

7. Closely monitor the results of any ad campaign you use and renew only the deals that are generating traffic to your site.

8. What's the best way to get people to respond to e-mail? Follow the law, and that means do not spam.

9. Make your site sticky by having good content, fast loading times, good copy, easy navigation, and loyalty programs.

10. Consider using a shopping bot to attract qualified traffic—people who are already interested in buying your product or service.

Cashing in on Affiliate Programs

*W*ANT TO GENERATE CASH, NOW, FROM YOUR web site? Even sites that aren't e-commerce-enabled—meaning they retail nothing—can put money in your pocket through the many affiliate programs now found on the web. From Amazon.com to Office Max.com, leading online retailers are eager to pay you for driving sales their way. How? By putting their link—such as a banner or text—on your site. For every click-through that results in a sale, you will earn a commission, anywhere from 1 to 10 percent for multichannel retailers, or 30 to 50 percent in the software sector. In some cases, you can get a commission on all sales that take place up to 10 days after you send someone to a site. For example, if a customer visits your site and clicks on the leading online company's banner ad and doesn't buy anything right away but purchases something a few days later, you still get credit for the sale.

In some cases, you are compensated even if the visitor doesn't buy anything, just for having driven traffic to the merchant's site. This is not as popular as the former examples, however. The affiliate's reward varies from merchant to merchant and program to program, depending on the terms of the merchant's offer.

It All Clicks

Supposedly, the idea for affiliate programs—where big merchants enlist small sites as a *de facto* sales force—got its start when a woman talking with Amazon.com founder Jeff Bezos at a cocktail party in 1996 asked how she might sell books about divorce on her web site. Bezos noodled the idea, and a lightbulb went on. He realized the opportunities for both parties to benefit were great, and the upshot was the launch of Amazon's affiliate program, one of the industry's most successful.

What's the appeal of affiliate programs? "The primary appeal lies in the fact that affiliate marketing is always tied to performance," says Wayne Porter, an editor of ReveNews.com, the leading blogging portal for affiliate marketing. "Marketers are not paying for relationships or placements that don't work. It is not without risk, nor is it always the most cost-effective in the long term, but dollar for dollar, it is usually a good investment."

How big is affiliate marketing? Although it's not as big a part of their overall sales and marketing programs as paid search or e-mail, affiliate marketing is an effective strategy to build broader brand awareness and drive motivated buyers to business-to-consumer (B2C) e-commerce sites, say web retailers participating in the latest *Internet Retailer* survey.

Most web retailers have already made a multiyear investment in affiliate marketing and count on a network of several thousand affiliates to drive visitor traffic, according to the magazine's survey.

For instance, 43.2 percent of web merchants taking part in the survey indicate that their affiliate marketing program is at least four years old, compared with 23.2 percent who say they've had a program in place for two to three years, and 10.5 percent say their programs are only about a year old.

For you, getting a share is simple. You put up a few links on your site (to any of the thousands of e-tailers that offer commissions to affiliates), and, as surfers click from your site into your affiliated site, you earn money. All this sounds so new, but think about it. Basically, you're getting paid for leads, a practice as old as selling that makes sense for everyone involved.

SMART TIP

Once you've pasted in an affiliate code, always preview the revised page before going live. Often the placement won't be where you'd thought it would be (centering a logo can be downright tricky—just use trial and error), and sometimes the link is dead (usually because a tiny bit of code got cut off during copying and pasting).

Google AdSense Makes Sense

Recently, one of the most significant changes in affiliate marketing has been the emergence of Google's AdSense (www.google.com/adsense). This service allows anyone who publishes online content to display text-based Google AdWords on their web site with a simple cut-and-paste format and receive a share of the pay-per-click payment. AdSense ads are similar to the AdWords ads you see on the right-hand side at Google. (For more on pay-per-click programs, see Chapter 14.)

There are many pluses to using AdSense. For example, proponents say AdSense is simple and free to join, you don't have to use different codes for various affiliate programs, and you can concentrate on providing good content because Google does the work of finding the best ads for your pages from 100,000 AdWords advertisers.

The payment you receive per click depends on how much advertisers are paying per click to advertise using Google's AdWords service.

Advertisers can pay as little as 5 cents per click and $10 or $12 in profitable niches, perhaps even more. You earn a share of that.

"Small affiliates now have a really easy way to monetize their real estate," says Porter. "I know stories of smaller affiliates who were making $2,000 a month using traditional affiliate marketing programs that shifted to the AdSense model and are making $15,000 per month."

A key reason for the success of AdSense is its revenue model: It is a cost-per-click model vs. a cost-per-action or cost-per-sale model. In other words, for affiliates to get paid, visitors to a site "just have to complete their click instead of having to complete a transaction," says Porter.

Yahoo! launched its own advertising option for small publishers in 2005 called Yahoo! Publisher Network (http://publisher.yahoo.com). Like Google's service, Yahoo!'s self-serve product displays text ads deemed relevant to the content of specific web pages. Advertisers pay only when a reader clicks on their ad. MSN may also start a service.

BEWARE

Never forget that a bad shopping experience at an affiliated site will tarnish your reputation, too. Choose affiliates cautiously, monitor them (check into their sites), and carefully heed any feedback you get from your visitors. Better still, shop at your affiliated merchants yourself and swiftly eliminate any that don't measure up. You simply can't afford links to bad affiliates.

Solid Links

AdSense aside, is it difficult to create an affiliate link? The job is simple, and you'll have it done within a minute or three. It works like this: You select the logo or link you want to show at your site (most e-tailers offer many choices, sometimes dozens, so you can get exactly the look you want). Click the logo you like, and the e-tailer will automatically generate HTML code that does two things: links to the e-tailer and includes your affiliate ID so you can earn commissions. Then you copy that code and, using any HTML editor (such as Microsoft's FrontPage), paste it into your site.

Doing all this is grunt work, not rocket science, and within a few minutes the link should look spiffy. Want to see this procedure in action? Head to Amazon's excellent resources for affiliates. For more information, visit www.amazon.com, and click on the "Associates" link.

Even sites with heavy traffic won't necessarily see big profits resulting from affiliate programs. To make money, you have to follow the rules:

- *Rule 1.* Don't make affiliate links your content. The advice seems obvious, but the web remains cluttered with pages that consist of nothing but banners from affiliates— nobody is apt to buy anything from these sites. That's why a basic element in setting up a thriving affiliation deal is to strictly limit the number of programs you join. You don't want a blizzard of banners on your site.
- *Rule 2.* "Do contextual placement; it's important," says Reve News.com's Porter. But be sparing—rarely should there be more than a single affiliate link on any page—and if you explain why you are endorsing this merchant and merchandise, you may just get visitors to check it out. A saloon owner, for instance, might recommend a cocktail recipe book; a web site design firm might endorse a web hosting service.

A TOUCH OF CLASS

Several years ago, the secret reason many small web sites slapped on a banner from, say, Amazon was to gain a kind of legitimacy. It was hoped that the hard-won (and expensively bought) credibility of Amazon would anoint a start-up with a certain classiness. Maybe it even worked—once. But if that's what you think affiliate programs will do for you now, forget it. With so many banners out there, people will think nothing more than that you took the time to copy and paste someone's HTML code into your web page.

This strategy may even backfire. Sites festooned with affiliate banners simply look cheesy, the very opposite of legitimate. The bottom line: The only valid reason to join affiliate programs is if they put cash in your pocket.

- *Rule 3.* Seek feedback from your site visitors. Do they find the links to affiliates useful? Distracting? Annoying? Pay attention to what they tell you—and if they are not clicking through to your affiliate merchants, that, too, tells you something. Put up different banners, or take them down altogether.

The Dark Side of Banners

You've digested the warning that, at a site with modest traffic, you're unlikely to see an affiliate check in this century, but there's more bad news to consider. For starters, whenever visitors clicks the affiliate link, they click away from your site. You may make the commission, but you'll lose the visitor. Is it worth it? That's your call, but this is an issue every site—no matter how heavy or light its traffic—has to ponder. Winning traffic just isn't easy in today's cluttered internet marketplace, and justifications have to be strong for you to willingly show a visitor the way off your site.

Keep in mind: The choice is difficult. An affiliate link might put money in your treasury, but would you make more money keeping the visitor at your site? Think hard on that.

If you choose to add a banner, remember that every banner you insert takes time to load, meaning your page will take that much longer to come into a visitor's view. Always check affiliate banners to make certain they load swiftly. Amazon banners usually pop rapidly into view, while those from lesser players sometimes can take many seconds. Ruthlessly delete slow-loading banners. You can't afford to waste your visitors' time.

And what if a site visitor clicks into an affiliated merchant and has a bad experience? Who do you blame when your pal Joe recommends his barber, and the haircut that barber gives you makes you look old, tubby, and poor? The barber, of course—but also Joe.

When affiliate programs work, they work, but when they don't, no web site owner should hesitate to take down the links and call it a noble but failed experiment. Look into affiliate programs, but don't be shy about pulling the plug if you're not seeing meaningful returns.

Want to discover more about affiliate programs? A site that offers speedy sign-up for multiple quality programs is LinkShare (www.link share.com), the wholly owned U.S. division of Rakuten Inc., the number-one portal in Japan for shopping, online finance and travel, and the seventh largest internet company in the world. LinkShare offers deals with Dell Computer, 1-800-Flowers.com Inc., Foot Locker, and more. Another leading company is Commission Junction, a ValueClick company (www.cj.com). While these programs may be on the pricey side, they are worth it.

Crave more obscure programs for your site? You'll find them at ClicksLink (www.clickslink.com), which provides a searchable directory

WORKING THE SYSTEM

Is joining an affiliate program an instant way to get yourself discounts on the stuff you intend to buy anyway? It might seem that way. Put up an Amazon logo and, bingo, whenever you buy a book, you get a 10 percent commission (or discount, since it's you shopping).

But affiliate program owners aren't that stupid. Read the fine print and, in most programs, there's a clause that says you won't get a commission on your own purchases. End of story? Maybe not: Whispers in the industry are that few affiliate program operators enforce that exclusion. Sources insist that although the program operators know it's you when you're buying—cookies make your identity known—they pay the commission anyway because they don't want to alienate affiliates and, furthermore, they are fearful of driving business to competitors.

Is that true? Try it for yourself when your next major purchase looms. Don't frivolously buy, say, a computer just to get that 3 percent discount—buy only because you need to—but if a check does come, pop a celebratory bottle of wine for us. Not only is the vino in effect free, but you've paid for this book, too. What a deal!

BEST PRACTICES

Want to follow some best practices when it comes to affiliate marketing? Then check out the Direct Marketing Association's (DMA) list of best practices for online advertising and affiliate marketing networks. The list is designed to assist marketers in protecting and growing their brands in the online environment and provides guidance to marketers employing affiliate marketing in their media plans.

According to the list, marketers using advertising and affiliate networks should:

- Obtain assurances that the online advertising and affiliate network is in full compliance with state law, federal law, and DMA's "Guidelines for Ethical Business Practice."

- Perform due diligence on prospective network advertising partners and make sure you are working with reputable firms. Additionally (if possible), obtain a sample list of current advertising clients. Due diligence should also include either asking for a full disclosure of eligible sites, or a review of processes to limit access to unwanted sites or channels. When partnering with an aggregate site online, advertising and affiliate networks should provide the marketer with a sampling of sites that are in their network. Due diligence should encompass the entire process from the marketer to the end consumer.

- Always use a written contract/agreement. This will provide you with the greatest possible control over your ad placement. This will also be the mechanism by which you devise and enforce formulas and/or guidelines for where and how online ads will be placed.

- Include specific parameters that must be employed to determine placement of your online ads in written agreements. Altering of an offer by an advertising or affiliate network is prohibited. If laws, guidelines, or set standards are violated, your contract with the violating advertising or affiliate network should be terminated.

- Develop a system to routinely monitor your ad placements as well as your contract with any online advertising or affiliate network.

To view the "Online Advertising and Affiliate Marketing Best Practices" document visit the DMA's web site at www.the-dma.org.

plus tools for signing up with everything from astrology vendors to watchmakers.

New Alliances

The old-fashioned approach to affiliate relationships—and still the web's most prevalent way—is to pop some HTML code onto one of your pages and hope that produces a ringing cash register for your affiliated merchant. But the drawbacks to doing e-commerce this way have prompted the creation of new styles of programs.

For example, some savvy merchants are giving private-label sites to their partners or finding more innovative ways to integrate them. Here are some examples, provided by Porter:

- RegNow's (www.regnow.com) affiliates can add targeted software products to their shopping carts and define style sheets so product purchases appear to be seamless on their sites.
- Smaller affiliate merchant systems such as My Affiliate Program (www.myaffiliateprogram.com) allow affiliates to pick up web pages or a web catalog with products and host them in their own databases.
- Flexible tools such as Website.Machine (www.w3M.com) allow merchants to produce private-label sites that can do not only commission splitting but also actual profit sharing.

Chapter 12 Summary
10 Things You Can Do Today

1. Think about experimenting with an affiliate program as a way to build broader brand awareness and drive motivated buyers to your site.

2. Check out Google's AdSense, which allows you to display text-based Google AdWords on your web site with a simple cut-and-paste format and receive a share of the pay-per-click payment.

3. Try the Yahoo! Publisher Network.

4. Don't make affiliate links to your content; make sure to do contextual placement, and seek feedback from your site visitors.

5. Choose your affiliates cautiously.

6. Make sure your site is not festooned with affiliate banners; these look cheesy.

7. Consider the dark side of affiliate programs: it might take a while to get your affiliate checks, and when visitors click an affiliate link on your site, he or she clicks away from the site.

8. Always check affiliate banners to make certain they load swiftly.

9. When affiliate programs work, they work, but when they don't, you shouldn't hesitate to take down the links.

10. Think about experimenting with quality affiliate programs such as those from Link-Share and Commission Junction.

e-Chat with eBags Inc.'s Peter Cobb

eBags Inc.
Peter Cobb, co-founder, senior vice president
of marketing and merchandising
Location: Greenwood Village, Colorado
Year started: 1998

Eliot and Peter Cobb, Frank Steed, and Andy Young joined Jon Nordmark in spring 1998 to build a major store for shoes and accessories out of bytes, not bricks, and boy, have they pulled it off. Currently, eBags (www.ebags .com) is the world's largest online retailer of bags and accessories for all lifestyles, and it has sold more than 4 million bags and accessories since the site launched in March 1999.

eBags has also grown 40 percent per month since its launch, and has launched eBags in the European Union and seen strong sales in the United Kingdom and Germany. Eliot Cobb, Steed, and Young are no longer involved in the business, but Peter Cobb and Nordmark are as active as ever.

The company now also has a footwear and accessory site called 6pm.com (www.6pm.com) that has more than 125 brands and 130,000 pairs of shoes and many of the same bag brands that are on eBags.

The site, formerly Shoedini.com, combines patent-pending guided navigation and search tools with some of the latest in web 2.0 technology to make shopping for shoes and bags participatory, community driven, and faster than ever before. This dynamic technology makes shopping for shoe and bag ensembles an interactive, fun experience and gives shoppers the power to make merchandising decisions.

Company owners say they are excited about the site because it allows for much more "ensemble merchandising" where eBags can show Stuart Weitzman shoes, for example, next to matching handbags or Allen Edmonds men's dress shoes with a Swiss Army laptop briefcase. In general, the company offers lots of fun opportunities to improve the shopping experience.

Steed was president of Samsonite USA and American Tourister prior to launching eBags. Peter Cobb, Young, and Nordmark were also top executives at Samsonsite. Each has product development, merchandising, and marketing experience with globally recognized consumer brands. Eliot Cobb was formerly the vice president/treasurer of The Wherehouse, a 350-store retail music chain on the West Coast. As a group, the Cobbs, Steed, Young, and Nordmark possess more than 60 years of bag and retail experience.

To start the company in early 1998, each of the five founders came up with a significant amount of cash and worked without pay for eight months. Then eBags raised $8 million from angels, friends, and family.

The company then decided it wanted to get venture capital funding, so it carved back its angel funding to $4 million and actually sent checks back to all its angels. In 1999, financial relief came from VC firm Benchmark Capital.

Other investors have followed, allowing eBags to continually invest in people and technology. To date, the company has raised a total of $30 million in VC funding yet has not raised VC money since 1999.

The company is doing well. In 2005, eBags had record holiday sales with an increase of 42 percent over 2004. In addition, 6pm.com has experienced exceptional growth, up 123 percent since its launch on November 14, 2005.

A key to the company's success? It does not overspend. For example, executives don't have golden parachutes or big bonuses. In fact, no one at the company, including its executives, makes a six-figure salary. And after 9/11, all employees, including the executives, took a 10 percent pay cut without complaint. This kind of frugal approach is one reason eBags.com is still around when so many other dotcoms aren't.

Another success secret? eBags maintains little or no inventory of its own. Instead, it relies on manufacturers to drop-ship products directly to customers. For example, 312 of the 330 brands eBags currently sells are sent by drop-shipping, including High Sierra Sport Company, Samsonite, and Kipling, a unit of VF Corp. The practice has turned eBags into a luggage "category killer," offering a selection of more than 15,000 stock keeping units (SKUs) that dwarfs the several hundred items carried by the average specialty baggage store. Company executives believe this lack of inventory is one of the primary reasons eBags has survived.

Here, Peter Cobb discusses some other secrets to eBags' success.

Melissa Campanelli: What made you decide to launch eBags.com?

Peter Cobb: In May 1998, we saw what was going on with people starting companies selling books and music online, and there was a product we knew and loved—bags—that we knew would be a great fit for the internet. We knew from our research that many people were buying bags through catalogs, so we knew that people didn't need to feel and touch the product to make a purchase decision. They were comfortable buying bags from Orvis, L.L. Bean, Lands' End, and Eddie Bauer catalogs. We knew bags and accessories weren't like clothes or shoes, where people really needed to see the color, the size, and the materials. Also, people don't really get excited about going to the mall Saturday afternoon to pick out some luggage or a backpack for their son. So with three, four, or five photographs nicely done for a product, you can really get the point across.

Another key reason we started was because the retail bag market was very fragmented. If you wanted luggage, you'd probably go to a travel goods specialty store. If you wanted a ladies' handbag, you'd probably go to a department store. And if you were looking for backpacks, you'd go to a sporting goods store. There was no "Bags R Us." Because of this fragmentation, we knew there'd be a great opportunity. And there happened to be nice margins on the product—markups [average] 50 percent.

The other important thing is that in the brick-and-mortar retail world, when inventory comes in, it's there for 180 days. If somebody buys a bag, the store orders another one. What's more, these stores are limited to about 250 products because of physical space.

Because we do business on the internet, however, we can offer more than 15,000 products, and when we take an order, we pass it on to Samsonite, for example, and Samsonite ships it to the customer. We get the sale and then, 30 to 120 days later, we pay the brand.

Campanelli: How long did it take to go from idea to funding to launch?

Cobb: Idea to funding was about eight months; idea to launch was ten months.

Campanelli: What's been the biggest surprise you've had in building eBags?

Cobb: There have been a few of them. The biggest surprise is how we've been able to gain such fantastic momentum. We've shipped 1.7 million bags.

Another one probably has been watching the flameout of all the e-tailers that took in many times more money than we did and somehow spent it all. It's been a huge surprise to see companies that I thought were pretty solid companies [fail]—like eToys [and] Garden.com sites I shopped on and had great shopping experiences with. What you don't know, however, is what is going on behind the scenes. These companies were spending tens of millions of dollars on inventory in their warehouses, which we didn't have to do. They were also spending money on television advertising, which we never really did. We have a saying at eBags: "Too much money makes you stupid." We just kept seeing that over and over again. We didn't raise nearly as much money as these guys did, and we always understood that the money we were dealing with was our money—money we put into the company with some investors' help. Every decision we made was "This is our money; how should we spend it?" as opposed to "Boy, we've got $80 million in the bank, so who cares if we spend $1 million on Super Bowl ads?"

Another surprise has been how much internet retailing has taken hold with a large percentage of the population. I think it has mainstreamed. I've heard numbers like 67 percent of the population bought something online during last year's holiday season and the growth of broadband has made online shopping faster and more enjoyable. I think that says good things for the future of internet retailing for those who are doing it right.

Campanelli: What's been your biggest challenge?

Cobb: I think the biggest challenge is managing your cash properly while continuing to grow.

Campanelli: How many VCs did you meet with before you got a funding commitment?

SMART TIP

Is there a niche out there that you are familiar with that isn't on the web yet—one you just know could be a perfect fit? Then what are you waiting for? As eBags's success shows, if you have the right niche product and you do e-tailing right, you will find success on the internet.

Cobb: We met with well over 100 VC firms.

Campanelli: What's your strategy in coming out ahead of competitors?

Cobb: Our competition is really brick-and-mortar stores. Online shopping isn't for everybody. Some people want to feel and touch and taste and smell before they buy a product, and that's OK. But a large majority of shoppers value convenience and selection, and that's why online shopping is experiencing explosive growth. Bags and accessories is a $30 billion market. Our strategy is just to continue to offer the ultimate shopping experience on eBags.com.

Chapter 13 Summary
10 Things You Can Do Today

1. Start your online venture based on a niche that you are familiar with.

2. Think about launching international sites.

3. Consider launching a satellite site that sells complementary products or services.

4. Improve your site with things such as guided navigation and search tools combined with the latest in web 2.0 technology to make your customers' shopping experience better and faster.

5. Make sure the shopping experience on your web site is fun for your consumers.

6. Try using a variety of sources to help fund your web site, such as angels, friends, and family. Then, think about moving on to venture capital funding.

7. If you go the VC route, be prepared to do the legwork. eBags met with more than 100 VC firms before it got a funding commitment.

---

8. Make sure to not overspend.

9. Think about using manufacturers to drop-ship products directly to your customers so you can maintain little or no inventory.

10. Find a way to manage your cash properly while continuing to grow.

Secrets of Search Engines

S EARCH ENGINES HAVE BECOME AN INCREASINGLY important part of the online experience of American internet users. According to a recent report from the Pew Internet & American Life Project—which produces reports that explore the impact of the internet—the number of American adults using search engines on an average day jumped from roughly 38 million in June 2004 to approximately 59 million in September 2005—an increase of about 55 percent.

"Most people think of the internet as a vast library, and they increasingly depend on search

SMART TIP

Usually, the "Add URL" or "Submit Your Site" button is at the bottom of the page, sometimes in tiny print. A few engines hide theirs. At Google, for instance, it's under "All About Google." Some engines don't offer this option and instead rely on their own spiders (search tools that automatically move from site to site, following all available links) to add listings. Find out more about spiders in "Spider Webs" on page 152. Keep in mind, however, that following Help links will usually bring up submission details.

engines to help them find everything from information about the people who interest them, to transactions they want to conduct, organizations they need to deal with, and interesting factoids that help them settle bar bets and backyard arguments," says Lee Rainie, director of the Pew Internet & American Life Project.

Search marketing is also a rapidly growing and profitable segment of the internet.

According to a 2006 study from JupiterResearch, a firm that tracks the impact of the internet and emerging consumer technologies on business, advertisers will continue to increase the share of total budgets spent online between 2006 and 2011, with the market reaching $25.9 billion or almost 9 percent of total U.S. advertising spending in 2011.

And according to the report, titled "U.S. Online Advertising Forecast, 2005 to 2011," paid search is the primary driver of growth in the online advertising market. Search advertising overtook display advertising in 2005 and will continue to be the largest online advertising component over the next five years.

"The large increase in search advertising is due to new clients experimenting with search and advertisers competing for keyword placement, which drives up prices," says Emily Riley, JupiterResearch analyst and lead author of the report. "Additionally, as search advertisers mature, they start using longer lists of keywords, increasing their overall budget."

Current online advertising spending is outperforming previous expectations, jumping 40 percent in 2005 and projected to grow 21 percent in 2006. In addition to paid search, large spending increases for online classifieds and rich media are fueling the market, which will continue to grow at a brisk pace over the next five years.

What's more, according to the Search Engine Marketing Professionals Organization (www.sempo.org) search engine marketing spending in North America was measured at $5.75 billion in 2005 and is estimated to be $11 billion in 2010.

While search engines are great marketing tools, getting your site listed where consumers are sure to see it isn't always easy. With more than three billion pages on the web, how do you win a high ranking in search engine results? The inside scoop is that many engines use algorithms—mathematical formulas—to rank sites. Not only do they all use different algorithms, but they don't reveal them, and, worse still, they change frequently. Should you just shrug your shoulders and give up? You can't. Experts agree that search engines have to figure largely in any web site's marketing plan because they are where users hunt for the information they want. So hunker down and follow these steps.

Which search engines are the most popular? Recent statistics from comScore Media Metrix—a division of market researcher comScore Networks, which provides internet audience measurement services that report details of online media usage, visitor demographics, and online buying power—show that Google was the most heavily used search engine in May 2006 (3.3 billion unique visitors), followed by Yahoo! Sites (2.1 billion unique visitors), MSN-Microsoft (963 million unique visitors), Time-Warner Network (499 million unique visitors), and Ask Jeeves/Ask Network (392 million unique visitors).

Do you use Dogpile (www.dogpile.com), which is owned and operated by InfoSpace Inc., or Mamma, the Mother of All Search Engines (www.mamma.com)? Don't try to list with them. These are "parallel engines" (also known as meta engines) that query various search engines with your question. They don't index sites; they aggregate information from other sites. Dogpile, for instance, queries the internet's top search engines, including Google, Yahoo! Search, MSN Search, Ask Jeeves, and About.com. These parallel engines are handy

BEWARE
While meta tags give web site owners the ability to control, to some degree, how their web pages are described by some search engines—and also offer the ability to prevent pages from being indexed at all—don't think they are a magic solution to get a top ranking in search engines. Don't assume, for example, that all you need to do is add a few magical "meta tags" to your web pages. Some folks think like this, and they are wrong.

to use when searching, but put them out of mind when seeking to get listed.

Getting Listed

The goal of search engines is to discover and index all of the content available on the web to provide the best possible search experience to users. In general, the Google and Yahoo! search indexes are more than 99 percent populated through the free crawl process.

However, you can submit your URLs to these indexes to make sure that they don't miss your site. In general, search engines do not add all submitted URLs to their indexes, and cannot make any predictions or

EXPRESS DELIVERY

You want a listing in Yahoo! now? Pay $299, and you'll qualify for Yahoo! Directy Submit. The hitch is, payment does not guarantee entry into the index. What the money buys is priority handling: Yahoo! guarantees you'll hear a verdict within seven business days of filing. Get more information at https://ecom.yahoo.com/dir/submit.intro.

Is this a good deal? If you get into the directory, yes, because you'll be weeks ahead of the game (in many cases, perfectly good sites simply get overlooked in the crush of applicants). But it's a risk—you may not get in and will have wasted the money.

You can also check out the Open Directory Project (http://dmoz.org). Like Yahoo! Directory Submit, this directory is compiled by human editors. Remember that good, relevant content and design are the secrets to getting listed in human-edited directories.

Try getting listed in these directories—just sign up, cross your fingers, and you may show up in one, as long as you meet stated guidelines. And, keep in mind: Getting listed in these directories provides important links that may help you rank better with crawlers.

guarantees about when or if they will appear. In addition, don't expect immediate results.

Rank and File

Getting listed is the easy part. Getting a high position in the search engines is another story, but that is also where the money gets made. It does little good to be the 212th business plan writer in Yahoo!'s search listings. Who will wade through 21 screens to find you? Nobody is likely to read that many pages of information. Most searchers only look at perhaps 30 results from a given search; in rare cases that number might be 50 to 100 if the query is proving elusive. Patience runs only so deep, and a surfer's attention span isn't infinite.

Can you do some of this yourself? You bet. The best way to score high in search engines is to have good, solid content, especially with regard to the terms that you want to be found for. Experts say it is also important to continually add new content to your site, and that good page titles are extremely helpful. As for meta tags, the experts recommend using the meta description tag as a way to help hint to search engines how you'd like to have your page listed. How to create a meta description tag is explained at http://searchenginewatch.com/webmasters/article.php/2167931.

Another good tip: If you have links on your site from good sites about topics you wish to be found for, that can help you rank better.

SMART TIP
Want to know more about search engines and rankings in general? Head to SearchEngine Watch.com (www.searchenginewatch.com), where all the ins and outs are explored. Another site worth a look includes Search Engine Showdown (http://searchengineshowdown.com).

Paid Inclusion, Paid Placement

What are paid inclusion and paid placement programs? In *paid inclusion*, you can pay a fee and submit your web site for guaranteed inclusion in a search engine's database of listings

SPIDER WEBS

Popular tools used by the engines in scoping out the lay of the web are spiders—also called crawlers—which meander from site to site, following links, and reporting findings back to the search engine.

Yahoo!'s spider is called Yahoo! Slurp. It collects documents from the web to build a searchable index for search services using the Yahoo! search engine. These documents are discovered and crawled because other web pages contain links directing to these documents.

Has your web site been spidered? Check your log file (see Chapter 8 for more on logs), and you'll easily see a spider's trail. A sure tip-off that a spider has come is when the log file reveals a request for the "robots.txt" file—a file that tells a visiting spider what parts of a web site are off limits.

As part of its crawling effort, the Yahoo! Slurp crawler takes robots.txt standards into account to ensure it does not crawl and index content from pages whose content someone does not want included in Yahoo! Search Technology. If a page is disallowed to be crawled by robots.txt standards, Yahoo! will not read or use the contents of that page. The URL of a protected page may be included in Yahoo! Search Technology as a "thin" document with no text content. Links and reference text from other public web pages provide identifiable information about a URL and may be indexed as part of web search coverage.

Do you need a robots.txt file? Some say no. Why? Because if you have nothing that's meant to be strictly private stored on your web site—and you shouldn't, because if a file is on the web, it's in the public domain—there's no need to tell a spider "hands off." What's more, a downside to having a robots.txt file is that a spider may miss key pages. If this happens, resubmit those pages to the search engine. Maybe the engine already knows them; maybe it doesn't. Either way, resubmitting is always a good policy.

for a set period of time. While paid inclusion guarantees indexing of submitted pages or sites in a search database, you're not guaranteed that the pages will rank well for particular queries. Of the major search engines, only Yahoo! does paid inclusion at the moment. This is different from services like Yahoo! Directory Submit (see page 150) because that service does not guarantee inclusion.

Paid placement—also known as sponsored search or pay-per-click—offers the ability to place your site in the top results of search engines for the terms you are interested in within a day or less. Basically, every major search engine accepts paid listings, and they are usually marked as "Sponsored Links" on the web sites.

In paid placement, you can guarantee a ranking in a search listing for the terms of your choice. The leaders in paid placement are Google, Yahoo!, Search Marketing, and MSN Search. These programs allow you to bid on the terms you wish to appear for, and you then agree to pay a certain amount each time someone clicks on your listing. Costs for pay-for-placement start at around a nickel a click and go up considerably based on how high you want your site to appear—and competition for keywords has the biggest bearing on that. For example, a bid on "web hosting" will result in payment of a few bucks a click if you want to get on the first page of results. But if you are promoting, say, lighthouse tours, you may be able to get on top by paying just a dime a click.

In the Google AdWords program, Google sells paid listings that appear above and to the side of its regular results, as well as on its partner sites. Since it may take time for a new site to appear within Google, these advertising opportunities offer a fast way to get listed with the service.

In the Google AdWords program, the cost of your campaigns really depends on you—how much you're willing to pay and how well you know your audience. It all boils down to knowing your own goals and letting Google know what they are.

There's a nominal one-time activation fee for Google AdWords of $5, and after that, Google will give the highest position to the advertiser with the highest bid for keywords and the highest click-through rate.

> **SMART TIP**
> Want to learn even more about Google AdWords? Then read Andrew Goodman's *Winning Results with Google AdWords* (McGraw Hill/Osborne Media). Goodman, a Google AdWords expert, shares tips, tricks, and strategies he's learned while working with clients on their Google AdWords campaigns.

SMALLER PAY-PER-CLICK CAMPAIGNS

Intense bidding for keywords on the major pay-per-click (PPC) search engines such as Google, Yahoo!, and MSN often leaves online marketers wondering if smaller PPC search engines—such as Miva (www.miva.com/us) and Kanoodle (www.kanooodle.com)—can still achieve a worthwhile return on investment.

So should you advertise with smaller PPC search engines? Here is a look at the pros and cons.

Pros

- *Name recognition.* Companies with a product they would like to market heavily may wish to be seen everywhere. As a result, it is a great idea to use many small PPC engines to get listed all over the internet.

- *Smaller fees.* In order to compete with large PPC search engines, the smaller PPC engines will offer lower start-up fees and lower minimum bids. This allows for more clicks for the dollar.

- *Easier to get to top.* Competition in smaller PPC engines for certain keywords is less than in larger engines so it easier and cheaper to receive a top billing.

Cons

- *Poor quality traffic.* Lesser search engines may have poor search match algorithms in place resulting in less qualified traffic.

- *Victim of click fraud.* Smaller engines don't usually employ IP tracking methods for keeping click-through tracking pure. So advertisers are charged multiple times for the same visitor.

- *Paid-to-click schemes.* Some small PPC engines pay visitors to click on products. This rarely results in quality sales or traffic for advertisers and is something advertisers should watch carefully for in smaller PPC engines.

- *Harder-to-get refunds.* Most PPC search engines will respond to requests by advertisers to refund moneys for click fraud. Smaller engines, however, are much more difficult to receive refunds from.

The MSN Search system called Microsoft adCenter is similar to Google AdWords in that all you need is $5 for a one-time signup fee, and the highest position will be given to the advertiser with the highest bid for keywords and the highest click-through rate.

Yahoo! Sponsored Search, a service offering from Yahoo! Search Marketing, allows you to bid on the keywords for which you wish to appear, and then pay a certain amount each time someone clicks on your listings. For example, if you wanted to appear in the top listings for "clocks," you might agree to pay a maximum of 25 cents per click. If no one agreed to pay more than this, then you would be in the number-one spot. If someone later decided to pay 26 cents, then you would fall into the number two position. You could then bid 27 cents and move back on top if you wanted to. In other words, the highest bid gets the highest position on Yahoo! Sponsored Search.

SMART TIP
Searching for some good examples of how to use search-engine marketing? Then see "e-Chat with Cashman Computer Associates d/b/a Moon River Pearls' Peter L. Cashman" and "e-Chat with Lessno.com LLC's Stanley Gyoshev and Assen Vassilev" in the Appendix.

Yahoo! Sponsored Search displays its listings on its own search results, in addition to MSN, InfoSpace, and many other partner sites.

There are two ways to create an account: Through a self-service online channel that requires a $5 deposit (this deposit will be applied to your click-throughs) or through a service called Fast Track, which has a one-time service fee of $199 and includes a custom proposal with suggested keywords, bidding recommendations, and more. Yahoo!'s minimum bid requirement is 10 cents. By carefully selecting targeted terms, you can stretch that money out for one or two months and get quality traffic.

Another smaller pay-per-click search engine to check out is from Miva Inc. (www.miva.com/us), formerly FindWhat.com, which was a major search player. (For more on this see the sidebar on page 154.)

While there are myriad choices out there and the concepts may seem confusing, many small businesses swear by paid search programs. As long as you plan your campaigns carefully, budget properly, and read the fine print, they can really help you improve your reach.

LOCAL SEARCH

Want local customers to find you? Then try local search engine advertising, which lets you target ads to a specific state, city, or even neighborhood. A growing number of small businesses are using local search. For example, a November 2005 survey by market research firm Yankee Group found that more than 30 percent of businesses with 20 to 99 employees and 40 percent of those with 2 to 19 staffers were using local search engine advertising. Those numbers are expected to increase substantially in 2006. Like other search engine advertising, the local variety lets you track your account closely to find out which keywords are most successful at drawing customers and how much you're spending each day.

As you can imagine, the major search engine companies offer local search options. To sign up with Yahoo! Search Marketing, for example, visit http://searchmarketing.yahoo.com/local. To sign up with Google, go to https://adwords.google.com/select, and to sign up with MSN, go to www.advertising.msn.com. In general, all of the programs follow a PPC model.

Chapter 14 Summary
10 Things You Can Do Today

1. Plan your search-engine marketing/optimization strategy. Now. It's that important.

2. When planning your e-business strategy, focus on being listed in the high-traffic engines.

3. Don't expect immediate results.

4. Think about signing up with Yahoo! Directory Submit if you want to be listed right away.

5. Get a high position in the search engines by having good, solid content, especially with regard to the terms that you want to be found for. And continue to add new content to your site.

6. Remember that good page titles are extremely helpful, as are meta tags. Also, plan to have links on your site from good sites about topics you wish to be found for; this can help you rank better.

7. Decide if you'd like to use the directories at Yahoo! or the Open Directory Project.

8. Research paid placement and paid inclusion programs, and figure out which would work the best for your business.

9. Decide if you will go with the bigger names when it comes to pay-for-placement programs, or smaller pay-per-click search engines.

10. Try local search-engine advertising if you want local customers to find you.

e-Chat with Newegg Inc.'s Howard Tong

Newegg Inc.
Howard Tong, vice president of marketing
Location: City of Industry, California
Year started: 2001

Have you ever heard of Newegg.com (www.new egg.com)? If you are interested at all in hardware or software products, you probably have.

Founded in 2001, Newegg Inc. is an online e-commerce company that has created a powerful channel for manufacturers of computer hardware and software, consumer electronics, and communications products to reach the do-it-yourselfers, hard-core gamers, students, small to medium-sized businesses, IT professionals, resellers, and consumers who desire a comprehensive digital lifestyle.

At the Newegg.com web site, consumers can find the latest technology parts and products, along with product information, pictures, how-to's, customer product reviews, and opportunities to interact with other members of the technology and game enthusiast community.

Newegg.com currently has more than 4.5 million registered customers and more than 1,100 employees globally.

Newegg.com is repeatedly cited as one of the best web sites out there by consumers. Why? Probably because it views every customer as a customer for life and instills this philosophy in its employees as well.

To get an inside look at Newegg.com—and to learn about how it has grown from a small player to one of the most well-known e-tailers around—we chatted with Howard Tong, vice president of marketing at the company.

Melissa Campanelli: Please tell me about Newegg. When was it started? Why?

Howard Tong: Newegg.com was founded by our CEO and chairman Fred Chang on January 1, 2001. I was fortunate to be one of the original executives who helped to create the business plan and model for Newegg based on my internet and e-commerce experience.

Before Newegg, there was ABS Computer Technologies Inc., a systems integrator making build-to-order PCs. ABS was founded by Fred in 1990 and specialized in high-end gaming PCs. During the late '90s, we started to recognize an emerging market in the DIY space. Since ABS had many customers from years past, many of them began to inquire if ABS could help them with upgrade parts for their existing systems. The answer was no, since ABS could only sell a complete system. Therefore, this is how we recognized this emerging market of tech savvy customers who were not afraid to crack open the case and upgrade or build their systems themselves. We called them the "do it yourselfers" or DIY and hence Newegg was "hatched" January 2001.

Campanelli: What were your start-up costs?

Tong: We started with only $100,000 and built Newegg to be just about a $1 billion-revenue company within four years.

Campanelli: What types of marketing do you do?

Tong: We have a fully integrated marketing plan which includes anything from print to online banners, search engine marketing, billboards, radio, and TV.

Campanelli: What was your goal when starting? Have you achieved that goal?

Tong: Our goal was to provide the best online shopping experience. In order to accomplish this, we needed to go above and beyond expectation of what a typical online shopping experience was. It is for this reason we created Newegg to stand on three pillars, each of which contribute to the overall product Newegg is today, and to the best customer experience.

Firstly, we needed to have the best selection and competitive pricing for our customers needs. But we didn't want to be just an e-tailer. Anybody can make a web site and sell products; we wanted to be an "e-marketer" being the most efficient solution between supply and demand. Newegg had to be the source on the internet to get all relevant content and information along with the products to purchase. By doing this we can not only serve the customer better, but also support the vendors to help reach the customer with education of their products. The result is a stronger partnership between Newegg and the vendors and resulting better support and pricing for the customer. Since IT was our background and expertise, we have one of the deepest selections of cutting-edge technology components with the best prices. This also meant stocking the products so we could assure quality of delivery.

That leads to the second pillar—logistics. In early 2001, it was apparent our sales orders were climbing quickly. The executive vice president at the time, Ken Lam, commissioned me to design and implement a state-of-the-art logistics center. I remember before Newegg was hatched, I would order from the internet and if the item was in stock, it would take several days to process the order. If it was not in stock, it may take weeks before they would ship. Then once the item would ship, it could take a week or more to arrive on my doorstep. Therefore, if you received your product in two weeks you were a happy camper. Our goal was to set a new standard in the online market; making sure we could ship same day and deliver next day. It was for this reason we needed to create our own custom state-of-the-art logistics systems; whether a customer buys one item like a piece of memory, or 30 different items to build a system from scratch, we would have it picked, packed, 100 percent accurate, and on the truck in 24 hours. That's how we ship 98 percent of our orders within 24 hours today. This speed of delivery without any extra premium was key to help grow Newegg in the early days.

Finally, the last pillar is that we decided for any online company, pristine reputation and customer service were a must. We wanted to be the Nordstrom of the web. Back in 1999–2000, online companies were notorious for having lousy customer service. This is especially important because for online companies, there is no face-to-face interaction. We had to have a customer-centric business model that started with the absolute best customer service. Newegg must earn all customers' trust and respect. Several years later it is paying off with Newegg's number-one customer satisfaction rating in the computer/electronics segment. When you're processing up to 30,000 orders per day, taking a few back to keep customers happy is easy.

Having the number-one customer satisfaction rating in our industry, fastest logistics, and best selection/pricing of products was part of what we needed to help accomplish our goal. There are many other factors like the web site function and features, but I would say we are happy with our accomplishments towards this goal, but never satisfied. We will continue to pursue the goal of providing the best online shopping experience.

Campanelli: Why have you decided to keep your company private? Have you thought about going public? Have you been approached to do so?

Tong: We are currently a private company but are contemplating an IPO in the future. We get many requests from customers and have been approached by the financial industry, but we will do so when the company is ready. We have many preparations under way so I think it is just a matter of time.

Campanelli: What advice do you have for entrepreneurs thinking about starting an online company today?

Tong: Always be customer-centric. Find out what the customer wants and provide it to them. The online world is dog-eat-dog. Anybody can make a web site and be an instant competitor. Therefore, it is crucial that you understand your customers and provide the added value to them. If you can't keep them loyal and retain them, there are open doors all over the internet for them to go through, and never return to you.

Campanelli: What are some best practices in online retailing in your opinion?

Tong: Being customer-centric is a must. But you need to have the proper tools to track online retailing. The beauty of the internet is that many aspects can be tracked and can be boiled down to a science. Best practices include having a good analytics tool to help generate the metrics and reports you need to make decisions. Also the best practices have to include the usability and effectiveness of the web site and e-mails. For example, for Newegg, we don't have brick-and-mortar locations—our

> **SMART TIP**
>
> Do you know your customers? Their likes and dislikes? How they like to communicate with you? If not, you'd better find out. And soon. As Howard Tong describes, being customer-centric is one of the main keys to success in today's competitive online world.

web site is the only interface we have with the customer—so you have to get that part right.

Campanelli: Who do you perceive as your biggest competitor today?

Tong: I would say our biggest competitors today would be players like Best Buy, Circuit City, Dell, Tiger Direct, and a host of other smaller online companies.

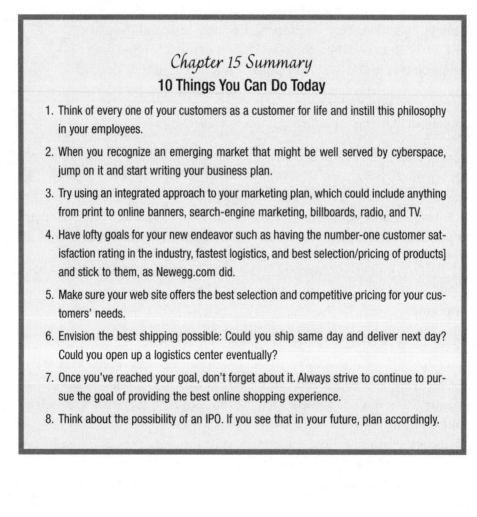

Chapter 15 Summary
10 Things You Can Do Today

1. Think of every one of your customers as a customer for life and instill this philosophy in your employees.

2. When you recognize an emerging market that might be well served by cyberspace, jump on it and start writing your business plan.

3. Try using an integrated approach to your marketing plan, which could include anything from print to online banners, search-engine marketing, billboards, radio, and TV.

4. Have lofty goals for your new endeavor such as having the number-one customer satisfaction rating in the industry, fastest logistics, and best selection/pricing of products] and stick to them, as Newegg.com did.

5. Make sure your web site offers the best selection and competitive pricing for your customers' needs.

6. Envision the best shipping possible: Could you ship same day and deliver next day? Could you open up a logistics center eventually?

7. Once you've reached your goal, don't forget about it. Always strive to continue to pursue the goal of providing the best online shopping experience.

8. Think about the possibility of an IPO. If you see that in your future, plan accordingly.

9. Plan to invest in a good analytics tool to help generate metrics and reports you need to make decisions.

10. Get to know your customers, their likes and dislikes, and how they like to communicate with you. Being customer-centric is one of the keys to success in today's competitive online world.

Tapping International Markets

ONE OF THE LURES OF THE WEB IS THAT ONCE your site is up, you are open for business around the world 24 hours a day. But don't be too quick to take the hype at face value. Yep, you are open 24/7, but international sales may prove elusive, and even when you land orders from abroad, you may wonder if they're worth the bother. Shocked?

There are excellent reasons for many e-commerce companies to aggressively pursue global business, but before you let yourself get dazzled by the upside, chew on the negatives. Then, once you have seen that foreign customers represent their own hassles but decided you still want them, you will find the information you need to grab plenty of international sales.

Foreign Affairs

Here's the root of the problem with selling internationally: Whenever you ship abroad, you enter into a complicated maze of the other country's laws. Let's assume you're in the United States. You know Uncle Sam's laws, and you know that one neat thing about doing business in the United States is that barriers against interstate commerce are few. For a Nevada e-tailer to ship to California is no more complicated than putting the gizmo in a box and dropping it off at the post office. With some exceptions, few e-tailers collect sales tax on interstate sales. (For more on internet sales tax, see Chapter 5.)

Sell abroad, however, and it's a quick step into a maze of complexities, including customs, for instance. Generally, it's up to the buyer (not you) to pay any customs owed, but make sure your buyers know that additional charges—imposed by their home countries and payable directly to them—may be owed. You can pick up the forms you'll need at any U.S. post office.

Some countries also charge a national sales tax, or a value-added tax (around 20 percent on many items in many European countries). Again, as a small foreign retailer, you probably don't need to worry about collecting these monies, but your buyers may (and probably will) be asked to pay, and they need to understand this is not a charge on your end.

Mailing costs, too, escalate for foreign shipments. Airmail is the best way to go for just about any package, and that gets pricey. A one-pound parcel-post shipment to Europe costs more than $10, for instance. Insurance, too, is a must for most shipments abroad, mainly because the more miles a package travels, the more chance there is that it will be damaged or lost. Costs are low (insuring a $100 item costs about $2.50 via

BEWARE

It's tempting: Declare that an item is an unsolicited gift, and the recipient often doesn't have to pay any customs charges. The amount that can be exempted varies from country to country; usually it's $50 to $100. But don't make that declaration even if a buyer asks (and savvy ones frequently will)—they are asking you to break the law.

the U.S. Postal Service), but they still add to the charges you've got to pass on to the customer. Add up the many fees—customs, value-added taxes, postage, insurance—and what might initially seem a bargain price to a buyer can easily be nudged into the stratosphere.

Getting authorization on foreign credit cards can also be time-consuming. Although many major U.S. cards are well-entrenched abroad (especially American Express and Diner's Club), and validating them for a foreign cardholder is frequently not difficult, this process is fraught with risks for the merchant, so be careful.

All Aboard

If you're still not discouraged, do one more reality check to make sure international sales make sense for you. Is what you are selling readily available outside your country? Will what you sell ship reasonably easily and at a favorable price? Even with the costs of shipping factored in, will buying from you rather than from domestic sellers be a benefit to your customers? If you pass these tests, you are ready to get down to business.

Step one in getting more global business is to make your site as friendly as possible to foreign customers. Does this mean you need to offer the site in multiple languages? For very large companies, yes (American Express, for instance, has more than 60 worldwide sites accessible at www.americanexpress.com, and many of them are written in different languages.) But the costs of doing a good translation are steep and, worse, whenever you modify pages—which ought to be regularly—you'll need to get the new material translated, too.

Small sites can usually get away with using English only and still be able to prosper abroad. Consider this: Search for homes for sale on Greek islands, and you'll find as many sites in English as in Greek. Why English? Because it's emerged as

SMART TIP

When is a foreign customer not a foreign customer? When he wants you to ship to a U.S. address (perhaps an Edinburgh father sending a birthday gift to his daughter at a Boston college) or when he is an American in the military or diplomatic corps (shipping to such an address is no different from mailing to a domestic address). Don't judge an e-mail address by its domain. The address may end in "it" (Italy) or "de" (Germany), but it can still be a U.S. order.

an international language. A merchant in Athens will probably know English because it lets him talk with French, German, Dutch, Turkish, and Italian customers. An English-only web site will find fluent readers in many nations. (But keep the English on your site as simple and as traditional as possible. The latest slang may not have made its way to English speakers in Istanbul or Tokyo.)

To make your site more friendly to foreign customers, put up a page—clearly marked—filled with tips especially for them. If you have the budget, get this one page translated into various key languages. (A local college student might do a one-page translation for around $20.) Use this space to explain the complexities involved in buying abroad. Cover many of the hassles we just discussed, but rephrase the material so that it looks at matters through the buyer's eyes. By all means, include the benefits, too, but don't leave anything out, because the more clear a customer's thinking before pressing the "Buy" button, the more likely he is to complete the transaction.

In the meantime, routinely scan your log files in a hunt for any patterns of international activity. If you notice that, say, Norway is producing a stream of visitors and no orders, that may prompt you to search for ways to coax Norwegians into buying. Try including a daily special "for Norwegian mailing addresses only" or perhaps running a poll directed at Norwegians.

Clues about foreign visitors will also help you select places to advertise your site. While an ad campaign on Yahoo! may be beyond your budget, it's entirely realistic to explore, say, ads on Yahoo! Sweden. If you notice an increase in visitors (or buyers!) from a specific country, explore the cost of mounting a marketing campaign that explicitly targets them.

At the end of the day, whether you reap substantial foreign orders or not is up to you. If you want them, they can be grabbed, because the promise of the web is true in the sense that it wipes out time zones, borders, and other barriers to commerce. That doesn't mean these transactions are easy—they can be challenging, as you've seen—but for the e-commerce entrepreneur determined to sell globally, there is no better tool than the web.

OH CANADA!

Although Canadians still lag a bit behind U.S. consumers when it comes to online shopping, that's starting to change. According to a June 2006 survey by J.C. Williams Group of 1,312 Canadians who had purchased online in the past six months, 32 percent made five or more purchases, and 68 percent made one to four purchases. Canadian e-commerce is growing substantially as well, with total e-commerce sales totaling $32.4 billion ($39.2 billion Canadian) in 2005, up 38.4 percent from 2004.

"U.S. retailers are looking for expansion possibilities internationally, and Canada is a friendly way to test systems and processes in an initial expansion strategy," says Maris Daugherty, senior consultant of multichannel practice at J.C. Williams Group in Chicago. "In addition, U.S. retailers are not too far from home, and there is untapped demand in Canada, and many Canadian retailers have not yet included e-commerce among their sales channels."

To design a web site that meets the needs of Canadians, use a single e-commerce platform that supports all countries. "The platform should have the ability to be centrally supported with localized content areas and processes defined by country, so the customer can choose their country of preference when they arrive, and it will then be customized by specific cultural options," Daugherty says. "In Canada, that would include language options in French or English, total pricing including sales tax and shipping charges represented in Canadian dollars, and customer service hours that reflect Canadian regions with availability to both English- and French-speaking agents."

Chapter 16 Summary
10 Things You Can Do Today

1. Decide whether you'd like to reach international markets.

2. Remember that whenever you ship abroad, you enter into a complicated maze of the other country's laws. And keep in mind that it's up to the buyer (not you) to pay any customs owed.

3. Remember that some countries charge a national sales tax, or a value-added tax, which your buyers may be asked to pay. For a general overview of VAT check out the following page on the European Commission's site: http://ec.europa.eu/taxation_customs/taxation/vat/how_vat_works/index_en.htm

4. Mailing costs escalate for foreign shipments, and getting authorization on foreign credit cards can also be time-consuming.

5. Another reality check to make sure international sales make sense for you: Is what you are selling readily available outside your country?

6. Make sure your site is as friendly as possible to foreign customers.

7. Don't worry about translating your entire site; English has emerged as an international language.

8. Make your site friendlier to foreign customers by putting up a page filled with tips especially for them. If you have the budget, get this one page translated into key languages.

9. Routinely scan your log files in a hunt for any patterns of international activity.

10. Plan to get your feet wet in the international market by targeting Canadians.

Customer Service
for Success

E-TAILERS USED TO BE INNOCENTS WHO THOUGHT
that with web-based retailing, all customer
service would be a thing of the past
because the entire sales and service process
would be neatly (and oh so inexpensively) automated. Ha! If there's a mantra for e-commerce
players—especially as you are growing and
managing your business—it's this: Customers
may be virtual, but their dollars are real.

Nowadays, consumers expect a high level of
service from online retailers. How can you use
customer service to your advantage? Just follow
the leaders:

- *Anticipate questions.* Many e-tailers anticipate questions and then answer them in their FAQs. This will save you and your customers time. Of course, sometimes customers will e-mail you with questions, and this can be a good thing. If you get lots of e-mail complaining about a certain feature that customers have misunderstood, or bemoaning the lack of a particular product that you know is in stock, then you are learning important things about how your site is failing to communicate to visitors. As e-mail comes in, don't ever look for how the e-mailers are wrong. Look for ways to reshape your site to eliminate user problems (even the ones they only imagine they have).

- *Stay in touch.* At Hewlett-Packard's e-commerce shopping site customers are asked if they would recommend www.shop pinghp.com to friends, and 88 percent say they would, according to chief operations manager Cindi Zelanis. But the small percentage who say "no" aren't forgotten. "We get back to these customers individually or through telephone surveys to ask how we can satisfy them," says Zelanis, who adds that this closed-loop approach is important: "Contacting them can win customers back and also generate ideas for new features on our site."

  Hewlett-Packard's way is cheap. Why aren't you doing likewise? A week or two after any order is filled, e-mail the customer and ask if they would recommend your shop. "No" answers will hurt, but follow up on every one because these are the people who will tell you what you need to do to build a winner of a web site. Given how powerful this simple tool is, it's stunning that more e-tailers haven't jumped on it. Don't make the same mistake!

- *Turn feedback into action.* HP's Zelanis says, "To win these 'no' customers, responding quickly is just one piece of the puzzle. We evaluate and prioritize the collected customer feedback to address key customer needs, and then implement new features to the web site that improve the online shopping experience for existing and new customers."

Others raise the bar higher still, with responses within four hours emerging as the new goal of many. What's right for you? With a smaller staff (and probably no staff during night hours), you might find a 24-hour standard to be enough of a challenge. But monitor customers. If they demand faster response, somehow you have to find a way to meet their needs.

- *Hold their hands.* "Online, not every customer knows how to shop, and you have to be ready to help them buy," says Anne Marie Blaire, former director of internet brand development at Limited Brands, where she ensured the successful launch of VictoriasSecret.com and the continued growth of the Victoria's Secret brand online. No brick-and-mortar retailer has to teach customers how to buy, but online, that remains a thorny problem. Every day, thousands of shoppers log on for the first time, and these newbies genuinely crave handholding as they make purchases. Understand that and be ready to help. Be patient, too. Only a very ignorant e-tailer complains about how stupid his newbie customers are. They can, in fact, become your best customers, because they will shop only where they feel comfortable—and if your site makes it on that shortlist, you will watch the orders tumble in.

- *Stay sensitive.* A worry with e-mail is that it's easy to seem cold and unresponsive in the formality of the written word. Read and reread your responses before they go out. You want to be—and appear—interested in the customer's issues and eager to find solutions.

- *Aim higher.* In the online space, the service bar is being lifted ever higher. "Good service is expected these days for online retailers," says Ken Young of 1-800-Flowers.com, a leading gift retailer and an online pioneer going back to 1992. "Only truly outstanding service will get your company noticed. And the term 'service' has been greatly expanded." At a minimum, you must have 24/7 phone support, as well as functionality like real-time chat and personalization that enables you to better meet your customers' needs."

Office Depot is another company that has gone beyond providing great customer service. For example, its web site (www.office depot.com) offers a free online "Business Resource Center" featuring expert advice, downloadable templates and forms, and a free online "Small Business Handbook" full of useful business information, including basic bookkeeping, recruiting and hiring, writing a business plan, and more.

In addition, OfficeDepot.com hosts a free online weekly "Web Cafe" seminar series featuring small business experts on topics such as marketing, using the web to build business, networking, and customer service. "One of our key goals is to help our small business customers to deal with an ever-changing business landscape by providing the products and services that help our customers grow and succeed," says Monica Luechtefeld, executive vice president for business development and information technology for Office Depot. "It's a combination of multichannel and customer-centric strategies that helps us to better understand our customers in each channel and tailor an online as well as multichannel shopping experience to their needs."

These steps will get you started delivering better customer service, but they are not enough. Successful entrepreneurs say that the only way to do online service right is to have the right attitude, really believe the customer is king, and make sure that every one of their customer service representatives knows it. Many fail on this score, but when you've made customer service your top and continuing priority, success is within reach. Don't get seduced by the notion that the web sites with the best technology will inevitably win. Usable, reliable technology is a must, but where the real e-tailing battlefield will be

SMART TIP

Take a tactic used by the slick catalog companies, and when you haven't heard from a customer in a while, drop him or her an e-mail: "Have we disappointed you in any way? We would really value your feedback." Maybe the customer is indeed irked with you; maybe not. Either way, this e-mail will remind the customer that you are a store that cares.

STELLAR CUSTOMER SERVICE:
DO YOU HAVE WHAT IT TAKES?

The great thing about the internet is that anyone can set up shop. Of course, that also means you now have to compete with the big guys—and customer service is no exception. "Customers today are very savvy," says Lauren Freedman, president of the e-tailing group inc., an e-commerce consulting firm in Chicago. "They expect best-of-breed customer service everywhere they shop on the web. They don't care if you are smaller."

Each year, Freedman's firm tracks the top 100 e-tailers on 11 criteria relative to customer service and communication. The most successful online businesses offer the following:

1. *A toll-free number.* "This is pretty critical today," says Freedman. "If a small business doesn't offer this now, it should think about it."

2. *Keyword search.* According to Freedman, "People today are used to searching for things online, and they want a seamless search experience on the web sites they are considering buying from."

3. *Timely answers to e-mail questions.* "A small e-tailer should probably strive for 48 hours," says Freedman, who adds it's important to personally address customer queries vs. sending automated responses.

4. *Four or fewer days to receive a package via ground shipping.* "A small e-tailer should try to strive for five business days," says Freedman. "And they should make it very clear—in all their communications with their customers—what their shipping policies are."

5. *Six or fewer clicks to checkout.*

6. *Inventory status.* While real-time status is best, "[Let] your customer know within 24 hours if the product they are ordering is in stock or is not in stock," says Freedman.

7. *Online shipping status.* "[Offer] a link to UPS or FedEx so they can check their orders on their sites," says Freedman.

8. *Order confirmation in the shopping cart.*

9. *An e-mail order confirmation with the order number included.*

10. *Recommendations for other products and features during the shopping process.* "This is a standard for the larger merchants, but something that small e-merchants should strive for," says Freedman, who adds doing so can help you increase order size.

11. *Clearly displayed customer service hours.* This is especially important if you have limited customer service hours, says Freedman.

is in service. That's the irony about e-tailing: At the end, what prevails online is what prevails off—and that's consistent, respectful, considerate service.

It's Your Call

You know how important good customer service is to the success of your web site, so why not take it up a notch with click-to-call technology? The feature, which has grown more affordable and popular thanks to voice over internet protocol (VoIP), gives customers real-time support, differentiates your site from the competition, and can boost sales, too.

Click-to-call makes it easy for customers to connect directly with a sales or customer service agent: They simply click an icon on your site and input their phone number. Within a few seconds, they receive a call from an agent, who can provide a guided online experience and even suggest complimentary items and relevant offers based on the caller's information.

Click-to-call providers include eStara (www.estara.com), LivePerson (www.liveperson.com), and LiveOffice (www.liveoffice.com); prices vary. LivePerson's click-to-call service, Live-Call, for example, offers live chat, e-mail management, and

SMART TIP

Want to meet an entrepreneur who really understands customer service? Then see "e-Chat with Headsets.com Inc.'s Mike Faith" in the Appendix.

FAQs and costs $150 per month. LiveOffice's service costs 10 cents per minute for each call completed. eStara's higher-end product charges a setup fee that costs several thousand dollars and a licensing fee based on call volume.

Chapter 17 Summary
10 Things You Can Do Today

1. Make sure your web site offers a high level of service. Nowadays, consumers expect it.

2. Anticipate questions and then answer them in their FAQs. This will save you and your customers time.

3. Keep track of any negative e-mails you receive, and don't ever look for how the e-mailers could be wrong. Instead, find ways to reshape your site to eliminate user problems.

4. A week or two after any order is filled, e-mail your customers and ask if they would recommend your shop. Then turn any negative feedback into action.

5. Respond to your e-mails as quickly as possible.

6. Hold your customers' hands and help them every step of the way on your site.

7. It's easy to seem cold and unresponsive in e-mails, so make sure to read and reread your responses before they go out.

8. In the online space, the service bar is being lifted ever higher, so always aim in that direction.

9. Offer great content, along with great customer service.

10. The only way to do online service right is to have the right attitude, really believe the customer is king, and make sure that every customer service representative knows it.

e-Chat with Netflix Inc.'s Reed Hastings

Netflix Inc.
Reed Hastings, founder and CEO
Location: Los Gatos, California
Year started: 1997

Netflix Inc. (www.netflix.com), the world's largest online DVD movie rental service, is a true e-business success story.

Founder and CEO Reed Hastings and his colleagues formed Netflix in 1997 and launched a subscription service in 1999 with the goal of becoming the world's largest and most influential movie supplier.

The company wanted to use the DVD format and the internet to make it easier for people to find and get movies they would appreciate. As a result, they could reliably discover and enjoy lesser-known titles and watch more films, and at the same time, filmmakers could reach a larger audience and produce more new films.

Hastings is no stranger to successful start-ups. He founded his first company, Pure Software, in 1991, took it public in 1995, completed several acquisitions, and made it one of the 50 largest public software companies in the world by 1997. Pure was acquired in 1997 by Rational Software.

Currently, Netflix has six monthly plans starting at $5.99 for two DVD rentals a month, with one rental out at a time. The most popular plan costs $17.99 a month and allows members to have three movies out at a time. And, in all cases, there are no late fees or due dates. This model has eliminated the hassle involved in choosing, renting, and returning movies. Netflix also has five other price plans, starting as low as $5.99 per month for a limit of two DVD rentals per month with one DVD out at a time.

Members enjoy free shipping both ways, and currently more than 90 percent of Netflix's members receive next-day service. Netflix also operates 40 shipping centers—a key to providing overnight delivery—and plans to open more throughout the country.

Members are encouraged to rate movies, allowing Netflix to customize its site based on a member's movie tastes. Netflix says this helps to make the more than 50,000 film titles it offers relevant and accessible. The company, which is now a cash-flow-positive public company traded on Nasdaq, had total revenues of $239.4 million in the second quarter of 2006, up 46 percent compared with $164.0 million for the second quarter of 2005. The all-important net income number for the second quarter of 2006 was $16.8 million, compared to $5.7 million for the second quarter of 2005. It also ended the second quarter of 2006 with 5.2 million subscribers, a 62 percent increase over the previous year.

The company has weathered competition from heavyweights. In the spring of 2005, Wal-Mart closed its online DVD rental business and, in a joint announcement with Netflix, referred its online customers to Netflix. Blockbuster has started an online DVD rental service but it has not impeded Netflix's growth.

Can Netflix stand up to the competition? Netflix thinks so. The company recently forecast subscriber growth of at least 6.3 million subscribers by the end of 2006. And, in an effort to expand its business, in January 2007, Netflix introduced a service to deliver movies and television shows directly to users PCs as streaming video. The service is free to Netflix subscribers and initially worked with a limited catalog of 1,000 movies and TV shows. Throughout 2007, the service is expected to expand.

Here, Hastings offers some secrets to his success.

Melissa Campanelli: Why did you decide to start an internet company focusing on DVD movie rentals?

Reed Hastings: It was a growth opportunity to improve the movie experience for consumers using the internet. An internet store can offer a very broad selection and free home delivery, and I believed there was a need for something like this—there was nothing else like this out there.

On a broad scale, the idea stemmed from the fact that consumers in general dislike the late fees, the due date, and the limited selection of the store-based video rental model.

The idea also stemmed partly from personal frustration. I had a very large late fee one day—approximately $40—and it was all my fault because I had not returned a movie that I had rented from a little independent movie rental store. After that experience, I started thinking that one could do video rental on a subscription basis with no late fee.

Campanelli: How was Netflix funded?

Hastings: We raised a little over $100 million in venture capital from Technology Crossover Ventures and Foundation Capital. We received our first round of funding in 1997.

Campanelli: In your opinion, what was it about your company that attracted that kind of cash from VCs?

Hastings: A lot of companies attracted that kind of cash back then, but it's not the case today. They saw great potential.

Campanelli: What is your marketing philosophy?

Hastings: Early on we had very lean marketing. We did a deal back in late 1997 with Sony and Toshiba where they put a "try Netflix for free" offer in their DVD players. We did some online banners, and we did the search listings—both paid and regular search—on Google. But our biggest source of marketing early on was word-of-mouth, which has grown over time as we've gotten a better reputation. We recently have expanded our marketing to include TV and radio advertising, direct mail, more online advertising, and events and promotions, but word-of-mouth continues to be extremely effective for us.

Campanelli: What's the biggest surprise you've had in building Netflix?

Hastings: How complicated the logistics are. We ship over one million packages a week, and it is very complicated dealing with large volumes. There are [many] things that can go wrong, such as performance issues, mail ability—just the complexity of the whole process.

Campanelli: What has been your biggest challenge?

Hastings: We've grown so rapidly. We've nearly doubled every year, so scaling our operations systems to be able to ship more and more movies has been very challenging.

Campanelli: Whom do you consider to be your competition? What's your strategy in coming out ahead of them?

SMART TIP

The essence of Netflix is both very simple and very complex. Its founder, Reed Hastings, realized that the web was the perfect tool for a no-hassle, subscription-based DVD movie rental service that charged no late fees and offered free delivery. Tomorrow's billionaires are likely to come from the ranks of creative thinkers who get out of the box and see new ways to put the web to use. What new ways can you think of?

Hastings: Blockbuster remains a competitor but Netflix has demonstrated its ability to grow in the face of tough competition.

Campanelli: What is your market objective over the next five years, and how will you go about reaching that goal?

Hastings: To get 20 million subscribers by continuing to improve our service and the web site. Just improve every aspect of the business.

Campanelli: What are your secrets to success?

Hastings: We focus on a simple, core proposition and doing that really well, and not getting distracted by 100 gimmicks or extensions on the business model. Instead, we focus on doing the core model very, very well.

Chapter 17 Summary
10 Things You Can Do Today

1. When putting together your e-business plan, focus on areas that appear to offer growth opportunities online as Netflix's Reed Hastings did.

2. Think about a problem that people may have brick-and-mortar stores and offer a solution through your e-store.

3. If you plan to go the venture capital route, keep in mind that cash does not flow as easily as it once did.

4. Focus on lean marketing, such as word of mouth.

5. Understand that the most complicated part of your business—if you are selling a product—will most likely be logistics, and plan accordingly.

6. Make sure you pace your growth; growing is not always a good thing, especially if you can't scale your operations to meet demand.

7. Know who your competitors are, and keep abreast of them.

8. Have a goal and stick to it.

9. Focus on a simple, core proposition and do that really well.

10. Think outside the box. Reed Hastings did, and it worked for him.

Identity Theft, Credit Card Fraud, and More Bad Stuff

*I*T SEEMS TOO SIMPLE: PUT UP A WEB SITE, AND you're on the road to riches. Guess what? There are plenty of potholes in that road. Experts are eager to acknowledge the dark side of the web—the many ways it is easy to go wrong, often before you even suspect there's a problem.

According to Wally Bock, an author and consultant on business in the digital age, "Today more than 70 percent of web sites are bad. They don't answer the questions or solve the problems that visitors have. They are hard to use, and many simply don't work the way they

GETTING TO THE CHECKOUT

How can you make your site one where people buy, not just look? Experts heatedly debate all aspects of site design, but the one area where there is clear agreement is that visitors will shop when the site is created with a firm intention to make it easy to shop. A role model is Amazon.com—everything is there to enhance and simplify the buying experience. You don't want your site to be a carbon copy, but if you are an e-tailer, ask yourself the following about every site feature: "Does this simplify buying?" When the answer is no, cut out that feature. It's that simple.

should." Keep talking to experts, and look at any statistics on the number of dotcom companies that have failed and the fact that so few are starting up, and it's pretty clear that many dotcom companies are doomed.

Fledgling e-tailers—as well as those who are successfully growing and running their businesses—need to know the problems this industry faces, from visitors who look but never buy, to wholesale theft of your most sensitive information. Keep reading, and you'll discover the obstacles e-businesses face on the way to the top.

Security

Some experts say that identity theft—access to personal account information that leads to fraud—is still a big issue today. How can that be, when most web browsers and e-business server computers use encryption technology that scrambles a customer's information when it's moving through the internet? One of the biggest problems is hackers who break into web sites' computers and steal credit card databases. The cure? Work with security experts. Usually, inexpensive solutions can be implemented that safeguard data.

Consumers today are also concerned about the misuse of their personal information. According to a November 2005 survey, while 78 percent of American internet users planned to conduct some holiday shopping online that year, 69 percent of those shoppers would limit their online purchasing because of fears associated with misuse of personal information.

The third annual online shopping study was conducted by TNS, the world's second largest marketing information company, and TRUSTe, an online privacy company. The 1,005 consumers surveyed also indicated that concerns about privacy issues would deter more than 40 percent of consumers from shopping at smaller online retailers.

The survey indicated that based on these concerns, 22 percent of shoppers would not make any purchases online and an additional 14 percent would substantially limit their online spending. Among those willing to use e-commerce, nearly 42 percent prefer using the large, well-known online brands they believe will keep them safer from privacy related threats.

"More than three out of four shoppers feel more comfortable purchasing at sites that display a privacy statement or privacy seal," says

SECURITY SEAL

Want to let people know your site is secure? Then display the Verisign seal, a security related trust-promoting seal on your web site. Your customers can click on the seal to verify in real time that your business has been approved by VeriSign to protect confidential information with industry leading Secure Socket Layer (SSL) encryption. Without SSL encryption, packets of information travel networks in full view. Imagine sending mail through the postal system in a clear envelope. Anyone with access to it can see the data. If it looks valuable, they might take it or change it.

David Stark, North America privacy officer of TNS. Among these consumers, two-thirds are more likely to stick with well-known brands because they fear that lesser known e-tailers might misuse their personal information." The data overwhelmingly shows that privacy concerns continue to hinder the growth of e-commerce.

The top five factors that shoppers said might limit or prevent them from buying online in the 2005 holiday season were, in order: identity theft (cited by 49 percent), spam resulting from online purchases (39 percent), credit card theft (39 percent), spyware (38 percent), and preference for the "touch and feel" of shopping in brick-and-mortar stores (35 percent).

But there is hope on the horizon. The 2006 Identity Fraud Survey Report—released by the Council of Better Business Bureaus and Javelin Strategy & Research—shows that despite growing fears the growth of identity fraud is contained and that data compromise through the internet is actually less severe, less costly, and not as widespread as previously thought.

Identity fraud victims as a percent of the U.S. adult population have declined slightly from 4.7 to 4.0 percent between 2003 and 2006. What's more, most data compromise—90 percent—takes place through traditional offline channels and not via the internet.

No Buyers

The startling news is that industry publications report a 70 percent average shopping cart abandonment rate for the majority of retailers. Because on average, web sites convert visitors-to-sales at a rate of 1 to 2 percent, 98 to 99 percent of the visitors to your web site leave without purchasing. In other words, fight hard to get traffic, and that might not matter at all. A web site can be jammed, but the cash register may never ring.

BUDGET WATCHER

Well-funded e-tailers install systemwide redundancy—if the whole Amazon.com setup were to collapse, for example, a carbon copy would be ready to stand in and do the job. You probably don't want to incur those expenses, but you need to back up all your files. No need to get fancy here. Backups on Zip disks that are kept off-site will do. Why off-site? Losing your backup files as well as your originals in a fire, flood, or hurricane is a nightmare you'll want to avoid. If off-site storage is too much of a hassle, use a fireproof and waterproof safe.

OUNCE OF PROTECTION

Online fraud rates are going down—but fraudsters are getting more sophisticated, keeping retailers on alert. These were the key findings from the Merchant Risk Council's fifth annual survey released in April 2006. The Austin, Texas, council consists of 7,500 merchants, vendors, financial institutions, and law enforcement agencies.

Card-present fraudulent chargeback rates are usually less than 0.1 percent of sales, and 48 percent of the online retailers surveyed said their chargebacks match that rate, a significant improvement over the previous year, when online fraud outpaced card-present fraud by as much as five times. "The numbers show a very positive trend, but fraud still requires vigilance from online retailers," says Julie Fergerson, co-chairwoman of the Merchant Risk Council. With that in mind, Fergerson offers the following tips:

- *Create metrics for your business.* "Keep track of how much fraud you are having, what your chargeback rate is, and what your review rate is," she says. "Measuring this information is the logical place to start."

- *Aim for a low fraud rate.* Based on chargebacks, it should be less than 0.2 percent.

- *Optimize your fraud screening tools.* In general, when merchants accept an order, they run it through their fraud screening tools to determine if it's suspicious or not and if they need to further review it manually. "Some merchants review 50 percent of their orders manually, which says they haven't optimized their fraud screening tools," Fergerson says. "And other merchants only review 1 percent, which says they may be letting a lot of fraud sneak through. You want to find that optimal area for your business, and in general, less than 10 percent is a good place to be."

- *Use a variety of fraud prevention tools.* The top three are Address Verification Systems, customer follow-up when the order looks suspicious, and Card Verification Codes. "A combination of all of these tools will help you lower your fraud rate," Fergerson says.

- *Stay a step ahead.* The velocity check across multiple fields is the hot new technology for online merchants. "Here you are looking at how many times you've seen a different credit card number with the same e-mail address or IP address," she says. "Tracking this is important because some fraudsters will get 100 different credit card numbers, but use the same e-mail address and order from the same computer. The velocity check allows merchants to track this in an automated fashion."

Outages

eBay has had them, and so have many of the online stock brokerages. The inevitable result is a flood of bad publicity as daily newspapers rush to slam a faltering web business. Sometimes outages are flukes—bugs that surface in software or during a site upgrade—but often the problem stems from poor planning at the beginning.

More troubling still is that outages often happen exactly when a web site begins to catch on. For example, a site that works fine when there are 100 visitors a day may show strains at 1,000 and go into meltdown at 10,000 visitors. Sites need to be built to scale as traffic increases and, frankly, doing that requires nothing more than planning. Always ask, "If traffic goes up tenfold, how will we handle it?" If you don't know the answer, make sure your technical consultants do. And if you can, address the issue before launch—because when a web site catches fire, it often becomes a wildfire.

Fraud

A dirty secret about the web is that crooks love it. What better place to use stolen credit cards than under the relative anonymity afforded by the internet? Most e-tailers flatly refuse to talk on the record about their losses from fraud, but know that every site has had to battle with crooks.

What are some things to look out for? Experts say you should watch out for orders with different "bill to" and "ship to" addresses, as well as orders coming from countries with high cyberfraud rates, such as Ukraine, Indonesia, Yugoslavia, Lithuania, Egypt, Romania, Bulgaria, Turkey, Russia, Pakistan, Malaysia, and Israel.

For a comprehensive list of things you can do to reduce credit card fraud, check out "Eight sure-fire strategies any business owner can use to reduce credit card fraud," at www.scambusters.org. Internet Scam-Busters is a web site and a free electronic newsletter designed to help people protect themselves from internet scams, misinformation, and hype.

Chapter 19 Summary
10 Things You Can Do Today

1. Be prepared for the potholes in that road to e-commerce success. There are many things that can go wrong, often before you suspect there's a problem. What can go wrong? Security breaches, misuse of customers' personal information, lack of buyers, outages, and fraud.

2. Visitors will shop when the site is created with a firm intention to make it easy to shop; so make sure to plan for this.

3. Work with security experts before launching your online business. Hackers can break into web sites' computers and steal credit card databases.

4. Want to let people know your site is secure? Then display the Verisign seal, a security related, trust-promoting seal on your web site.

5. Consumers today are concerned about the misuse of their personal information; so make sure you don't misuse it.

6. Find ways to mitigate one of the biggest problems in the online world today: shopping cart abandonment.

7. Try not to have outages—ever. Sometimes outages are flukes—bugs that surface in software or during a site upgrade—but often the problem stems from poor planning.

8. Make sure to back up all your files. It's easy, inexpensive, and could help if you do have any type of outage.

9. Watch out for fraudulent activity, such as orders with different "bill to" and "ship to" addresses, as well as orders coming from countries with high cyberfraud rates, such as Ukraine, Indonesia, Yugoslavia, Lithuania, Egypt, Romania, Bulgaria, Turkey, Russia, Pakistan, Malaysia, and Israel.

10. Follow these additional tips to stop fraud: Keep track of how much fraud you are having, aim for a low fraud rate (less than 0.2 percent), optimize your fraud screening tools, use a variety of fraud prevention tools, and do velocity checks to see how many times you've seen a different credit card number with the same e-mail address or IP address.

Time for an Upgrade?

WAIT, DIDN'T YOU JUST FINISH BUILDING your web site? And haven't we covered how to successfully grow and manage it? Yes, but the reality is, as your online business grows, you will most likely need to upgrade your web site sooner rather than later.

Upgrading: The Facts

In fact, in an effort to respond to customer demands, more and more web merchants are spending more and more money upgrading their e-commerce platforms.

According to a July 2006 survey titled "E-Commerce Technology Spending" from *Internet Retailer* magazine, 79.3 percent of all retailers, catalogers, and web-only merchants surveyed will purchase more hardware, software, and services this year over last. In addition, 14 percent of virtual merchants plan to spend as much as 50 percent more on upgrading their e-commerce platforms and digital marketing programs. E-tailers are also taking the plunge even though, in many cases, upgrading is not cheap.

There are many ways you can upgrade your site. For example, if you are using a hosted solution, you can upgrade to a higher level plan. Or you can move from a do-it-yourself solution to an outsourced solution. Or you can do it the other way around.

One company that decided to upgrade its site is Giggle, a New York-based retailer that sells upscale baby gear in four stores (two in New York and two in San Francisco) as well as through its web site Egiggle.com (www.egiggle.com). The 60-employee company, which expects to have revenues of more than $10 million by the end of 2006, was founded in 2003 by Ali Wing, and a small web site went up shortly thereafter. In April 2006, however, Giggle upgraded its web site, and it now has a fully scalable e-commerce platform.

"This site was a big change for us," says Wing. "We now have a platform in place that is fully scalable and that is a true retail channel for us. Going forward, lots of technical functionality will keep being released." For example, Wing says the company will continue to invest in "easy-shop tools such as checklists."

Wing says the company also invests a lot in photography. "That's the most expensive part of being online, because the costs involved with keeping product databases current and photos that translate really well online is not easy."

To launch the site, Giggle switched to a new web development partner. And instead of outsourcing the entire project to the firm, Giggle does some of it inhouse. Virid, an interactive services agency in Reston, Virginia, developed the new Egiggle.com site with Giggle based on Virid's Covella e-commerce platform.

"Basically we do the art and design and user interface," says Wing. "They make it work that way and host it." Wing says Giggle launched the new site like this because "we were ready to take the next step. Until now we didn't have the right platform that we thought could scale with the demands of our business."

For example, Giggle prides itself on its customer service, so the site had to meet its high standards. "Anybody who thinks the online piece is cheap and easy just hasn't done it a lot," says Wing. "It is 24 by 7 selling, which means that data has to always be right, product has to always be right, everything has to be current, the site always has to be updated, and you have to be able to respond to however people are reacting to you. From an infrastructure perspective—and also an organizational one—we didn't have a platform that could support the demand."

Unlike other e-tailers, Wing says upgrading the site didn't cost her any more money than her previous iteration. "To do what we were doing third-party was much more expensive for the results," says Wing. "What I am actually spending for the results I am getting now is at worst commensurate. I am not spending any more since we did this upgrade. I'm just spending it differently and more effectively."

Typical Upgrades

Sean Grove, vice president of sales at Solid Cactus Inc. (www.solidcac tus.com), a Wilkes-Barre Pennsylvania-based full service e-commerce company that specializes in online store development, says that when e-businesses upgrade their e-commerce platforms, typical back-end upgrades include:

- Switching to a database driven e-commerce platform, or one that does not require the entrepreneur or web programmer to create each page manually.
- Switching to an e-commerce platform that has application programming interfaces so that third party modules can be tied into it.

GO MICRO?

Instead of upgrading your site, you might want to launch a microsite that lets you focus on a specific purpose, such as selling clearance or discounted items, products to businesses (vs. consumers), new merchandise that's complementary to your core products, or even try out a whole new product line. Before building a microsite, however, consider the costs. It costs essentially the same as setting up a traditional web site—from $2,500 to $50,000 or more, depending on the sophistication. In addition, a microsite may require additional employees. Before launching one, consider whether the same results could be achieved using your current web infrastructure.

- Switching to an e-commerce platform that allows for full freedom of design layout and custom functionality.

Typical front-end upgrades, Grove says, include a professional and clean design, and navigation features such as advanced site search.

Front-end upgrades also usually include features that improve the shopping experience, such as multiple image views, account registration that allows custom or information to be prepopulated on the checkout page, or one location that offers personalized information such as gift registries, wishlists, and saved shopping carts.

A front-end upgrade could also allow bundling features, such as "buy this item, get this item 10 percent off," as well as features to sell the customer on the store and its products such as customer reviews and testimonials on every page.

Expanding Your Reach

After upgrading your site you might want to consider partnering with other major web sites to create maximum exposure.

Consider Benson Altman, CEO, president, and founder of Kosher.com in Brooklyn, New York. In 2006, he struck up a relationship with Amazon.com that enables him to sell his more than 20,000 kosher products—including everything from fresh kosher butcher meat to kosher cosmetics—on Amazon.com.

Kosher.com's products have been integrated into Amazon.com's catalog, so customers can seamlessly buy them. Kosher.com ships the products to customers, and Amazon.com handles everything else, such as first-level customer support and billing.

The benefits of working with Amazon.com in this kind of arrangement are many. "We expect that our sales will increase from 10 to 20 percent as

PARTNERING PAUSES

Could this type of arrangement be good for your business? Before you move forward, keep the following points in mind:

- *Consider the costs.* Integrating Kosher.com's back end with Amazon.com's cost about $25,000. What's more, Amazon.com gets a commission on every sale. Altman also hired four additional employees to keep up with the extra business.

- *Make sure you can handle large orders.* While partnering with a big company such as Amazon.com is exciting, before you sign on the dotted line, "make sure you've got the ability—and the inventory—to fulfill the orders," Altman says. "It's essential."

- *Get your technology up-to-speed.* "The back-end system required to deal with Amazom.com is extremely complex and not for the faint of heart," says Altman.

- *Realize that it's a major commitment.* "You have to devote a certain amount of time to [the partnership], and you have to have a certain amount of quality control," says Altman.

- *Run a good business.* In general, Altman says that for a relationship like this to work, you have to run a professional, sophisticated business. "Your packages have to be on time, your orders have to be correct, and your customer service has to be great," he says. "If customers have too many complaints about you, [Amazon.com] can drop you."

a result of this partnership," says Altman. It also offers Kosher.com opportunities to promote its brand—potentially to the millions of people who visit Amazon.com's web site every day. While Kosher.com isn't referenced on the site, customers still see the Kosher.com brand when they receive their merchandise. "The partnership will allow Kosher.com to get our name out there and make ourselves available to people who need us," says Altman.

Chapter 20 Summary
10 Things You Can Do Today

1. Start preparing to upgrade your web site, because it's something you will need to do as your online business grows.

2. There are many ways to upgrade: If you are using a hosted solution, you can upgrade to a higher level plan; you can move from a do-it-yourself solution to an outsourced solution; or you can do it the other way around.

3. Understand that upgrading is an ongoing effort.

4. Invest more in customer service, no matter what kind of upgrade you choose.

5. Be aware that it may not cost you more money to upgrade; you might just spend your money differently and more effectively.

6. Keep in mind some typical business upgrades, such as upgrading to a more professional and clean design and using more robust navigation features such as advanced site search.

7. Consider other business upgrades such as multiple image views, account registration so custom information is prepopulated on the checkout page, or personalized information such as gift registries, wishlists, and saved shopping carts all from within one location.

8. Other typical business upgrades could include allowing bundling features, such as "buy this item, get this item 10 percent off," as well as customer reviews and testimonials on every page.

---

9. Think about the pros and cons of launching a microsite versus upgrading your site.

10. Decide if you'd like to expand your reach by partnering with other major web sites to create maximum exposure.

A Tour of
the Web

S AM WALTON, THE LEGENDARY FOUNDER OF WAL-
Mart, loved to shop—especially in competitors' stores. He did not necessarily buy
anything, but he delighted in roaming the aisles,
noting prices, and observing unique, eye-catching
ways to display merchandise. Why? Every
shopping trip turned into an exercise in competitive intelligence, and whenever Walton caught
a competitor doing something right, he looked
for ways to do it better in his Wal-Mart stores.

You would be wise to do the same, and that
means routinely surfing the web, visiting pace-
setting e-tailers, and learning everything you

can about what people are doing right. Don't think of surfing as goofing off. When you are doing it so that you can become a better e-tailer, it's some of the best work you can do.

Here's a yardstick: You are doing valuable work when, after every surfing session, you have specific, concrete ideas for improving your site. If you're not getting ideas, you're surfing the wrong sites or not thinking hard enough. And neither will get you ahead in the competitive world of e-commerce.

Want to know how to look at web sites? On the following pages, many name-brand web sites are critiqued. Some win generous praise, but throughout, the emphasis is on what we can learn from these sites. And next time you put in a surfing session, ask yourself the kinds of questions you'll see in these site critiques.

River of Dreams

Amazon.com Inc.

www.amazon.com

Amazon founder Jeff Bezos named his web site "Amazon" because that river is bigger than any other river on earth. Or so the story goes. And Bezos' aim from the get-go was to build the web's biggest store.

Bezos came up with the idea when, as an employee of a New York financial firm, he was asked to run numbers on various possible web businesses. When he hit upon books, all the lights went on—he knew he had a winner. Just a couple of distributors stock nearly every book in print, and it seemed simple to set up a business that amounted to a web site with no inventory. As orders came in, books could be bought from distributors, and whoosh—profits would roll in. Bezos took the numbers to his bosses and asked them to join in funding a start-up, but the verdict was no way. So Bezos quit, moved out to Seattle, and began building what just may rank as the web's crowning e-tailing achievement.

In a July 2006 tally of the Top 50 Internet Properties—which tracks total unique web visitors—from comScore Media Metrix, Amazon sites, including its international sites, ranked eight. Why is Amazon.com so successful? In part because its pages and tools are brilliantly executed, and throughout the site the emphasis is on making it as easy as possible for the buyer to make a purchase.

Case in point: "1-Click" buying. Like a book? A registered Amazon user can, with a single mouse click, buy it. It's that fast and that simple (so much so that tests showed users didn't believe it could be so easy—so afterward a screen pops up that says the deal has been done). It doesn't work only on books, however. Anything Amazon sells can be bought with a single click, and nowadays that includes TV sets, videos, CDs, power saws, toys, and more. Doesn't Bezos risk diluting Amazon's message by expanding into so many diverse product lines? Remember the company's name—from the start Bezos envisioned expanding into other product lines.

Amazon also offers free shipping. While free shipping has been used as an online promotional tool since the internet's earliest days, the idea really picked up steam in 2002 when Amazon began experimenting with it as a full-time service. Initially, the company offered free shipping to customers whose purchases totaled $99 or more. The company lowered the minimum to $49 and then to $25, which it currently offers. (There are some exceptions to free shipping, however, including oversize items, e-books and e-documents, software downloads, music downloads, and gift certificates.) While it may be difficult for a small company to offer this promotion, it is something to think about.

What else is cool about Amazon.com? Notice how fast the home page loads. The look is fresh and clean but is primarily text-based, with plentiful use of white space to make the page easy on the eyes. With its treasury, Amazon could well afford to put up the glitziest tech tools imaginable, but it doesn't. Cool tools—Java applets, sound effects, and

BEWARE

Amazon has filed patents on various bits of its site operation, and although nobody is clear about what Amazon intends to do to assert its rights, wary site designers are treading softly when it comes to closely imitating Amazon. This will not likely be a worry for you, because your operation will be small and your technology will not be nearly as robust as Amazon's, but if you find yourself exactly duplicating the "1-Click" purchase tool, back up a few steps and try another approach.

so on—gobble up bandwidth and really bloat page-loading times. And Bezos from the start has put primacy on making it easy for a customer to buy what he or she needs, fast.

Keep looking at the home page, and you'll notice that if you've bought from Amazon in the past, the page is personalized in keeping with your prior purchases. Books, music, and videos are recommended in line with an educated guess about what you'll like. Although personalization is hard for a low-budget site builder to incorporate, any site builder can insert "Today's Deals," just as Amazon.com does. Amazon.com also offers a freebie on its front page—"Free e-Cards," says the button. Again, any site builder ought to find a useful freebie.

In Full Bloom

1-800-Flowers.com Inc.
www.1800flowers.com

1-800-Flowers.com Inc., a leading florist and multichannel retailer of thoughtful gifts for all occasions, is in bloom. For example, in August 2006, the company reported record revenues of $211.1 million for its fiscal fourth quarter ended July 2, 2006, representing an increase of 13.4 percent or $25 million, compared with revenues of $186.1 million in the prior-year period. This growth was driven by online revenues, which increased 14.6 percent, or $15.9 million, to $124.4 million. Also contributing to the revenue growth for the quarter were the company's retail and fulfillment operations, which increased 51 percent to $26.1 million.

One reason for its success? 1-800-Flowers.com seems to be on a mission to offer the perfect gift to shoppers. In the past few years, the company's product line has been extended by the merchandise sold through its subsidiaries, including 1-800-Baskets.com (www.1800baskets.com), gift baskets; Ambrosia (www.ambrosiawine.com), wines; Cheryl & Co.

(www.cherylandco.com), baked goods and cookies; Fannie May (www .fanniemay.com), chocolate and other confections; HearthSong (www.hearthsong.com) and Magic Cabin (www.magiccabin.com) creative children's products; Madison Place (www.madisonplace.com) home furnishings; Plow & Hearth (www.plowandhearth.com), home décor and garden merchandise; Problem Solvers (www.problem solvers.com), unique gifts; and The Popcorn Factory (www.popcornfac tory.com), popcorn and specialty foods.

Another advantage? It's a company that truly understands and embraces internet-based selling. It was also a pioneer: Its first electronic storefront opened on CompuServ in 1992, followed by an AOL store in '94. Its web site went live in 1995, which is early in internet time. 1-800-Flowers accomplished that by serving as a beta tester for what became Netscape's Commerce Server. While other leading businesses often stumbled when it came to jumping into the online world, 1-800-Flowers got it right from the start.

Does the site still work? Absolutely. And keep this in mind: Flowers are easier to sell on the visual web than they are by phone. Do you know what a "Memory Garden" bouquet looks like? Of course not. And even if you're told it has a half-dozen roses arranged along with floral favorites such as stock, alstroemeria, and waxflower, you may be clueless about its looks. But at the web site you see the arrangement, which can usually be magnified.

A fast-loading site that includes text and plenty of imagery to capture the visuals of the floral business, 1-800-Flowers aims to make the shopping experience easy. Flowers appropriate for an upcoming holiday are noted. Tabs offer gift suggestions for common events—birthday, get well, love, and romance. A "What's Hot" tab tells a visitor what the hottest trends are—as well as a variety of specials—so it's easy to get important information quickly.

SMART TIP

Always compare your site to competitors' sites, and do this ruthlessly and without an iota of favoritism. What do your competitors do better? If you cannot list a dozen things, go back and look at their sites more closely until you come up with a dozen. The only way to make your site the best it can be is to study competitors, see what they are doing well, and then do it better yourself.

The most impressive thing about 1-800-Flowers is it offers up lots of information on a page that nonetheless doesn't seem cluttered or overwhelming. That is exceptional page design, and it is a goal every site designer ought to aspire to.

Another plus: The site offers a "Find a Gift Fast" feature, which allows visitors to the site to enter the date that a gift should arrive, where it is going, and what the occasion is; then several gift ideas pop up on a new page. Pretty neat, huh?

Pushing the Envelopes
Staples Inc., Office Depot Inc., and OfficeMax Inc.
www.staples.com, www.officedepot.com, and www.officemax.com

The three office supplies chains—Staples, Office Depot, and OfficeMax— slug it out online every bit as vigorously as they do in the brick-and-mortar world. And think of the barriers to building a good office supplies site: The products are nonvisual (who wants to look at a ream of paper?) and inherently unexciting. Hardly anybody gets a tingle thinking about buying the month's toner, paper clips, and envelopes. This is boring stuff, and, as consumers, we want to get in and out as quickly as possible.

That's good news for office supplies site designers. With some kinds of retail, shoppers actually enjoy the physical shops (fine jewelers, for instance), but with office supplies, if we never have to step into a brick-and-mortar store again, it's likely we'll all toast our good fortune. The trick for a site designer is making it all work on the web so that it's easy to make the purchases we need.

Not surprisingly, all three of the office supplies giants take essentially the same route. In fact, Staples, OfficeMax, and Office Depot erect pages that are stunningly similar—heavily text-oriented, scant use of graphics, and an organization that revolves around imitating the aisles in a physical store.

Which site comes out on top? For my money, it's Staples, but only by a nose. Its site offers a downloadable Easy Button, that is a one-stop link you can download onto your desktop to check on new products, search inventory, make purchases, find a store, or sign up to be a Staples Rewards member. If you already are a member, the desktop Easy Button allows you to check all your rewards purchases, points, and earnings with one quick click.

It's in the Mail

Stamps.com Inc.

www.stamps.com

The biggest challenge in selling is convincing people to do something new, something they have never done before. Witness escargots. You've seen them on menus. Have you ever eaten snails? If you have, you either like them or you don't, and you know without further ado if you'll order them again. But if you have never ordered them—never tasted a snail—it's difficult to be persuaded to order one at a restaurant. A freebie may help, but probably not. What would tempt you? Tough question, with no easy answer.

What do snails have to do with the web? Quite a lot, actually. Just look at Stamps.com, a site that has been around for several years but offers a service many people may have never used before. Of course you understand postage, but the way it has always worked is that you've gone to the post office with money and walked out either with a sheet of paper stamps or with credits entered into a postage meter. Stamps.com wants to change all that.

Its aim is to entice you to buy postage on the internet from a company you have never heard of and—somehow—to affix this postage to your outgoing mail in ways you do not yet understand. How could you ever be enticed into taking this deal? Simple: Sign up with Stamps.com, and your account automatically starts with $5 free postage and a free Stamps.com Supplies Kit ($5 value). After your trial period, you will receive additional postage coupons ($20 value), plus a free Stamps.com

SMART TIP

How can you make your customers' shopping easier? Are there "ready made lists" you can create? How about lists of the most ordered items? Face it: No matter what any tech headie says, web shopping lacks the buzz and fun of a mall (although it has other strong advantages). Build in tools that make shopping go fast, and your customers will thank you by spending more money in your store.

SMART TIP

What can you give away? Stamps.com gives away free postage among other things—which is something visitors know the value of and will use. But if you use this tactic, keep close tabs on both your visitor counts and the numbers that take advantage of any freebies you are offering. If the visitor count dramatically exceeds the number of folks who go for the freebie, maybe you are trying to give away escargots—meaning visitors don't know if they actually want what you are offering. The remedy? Think hard about finding a way to position what you are offering as both valuable and desirable, and keep tinkering with this value proposition until a healthy percentage of visitors are jumping on your freebie.

digital scale ($50 value)—a total value worth $80. Because it's free, you just might try it out.

Look closely at Stamps.com's front page. Its highest goal isn't to sell to you; it's to tempt you to try out the service. For example, the first button on the page isn't "Sign Up Now"; it's "Learn More." Is that putting priorities in the wrong place? No, because you won't be sold into buying Stamps.com's service until you try it, and the smartest, fastest, best way to induce you to try it is to give it away.

Everything about this front page aims at achieving that goal, and that makes this a well-designed site. It's a lesson web site designers should absorb. Sometimes the web merely offers new ways to do old things (as, for instance, Amazon.com adds a cybertwist to book buying), but in other cases the web is about wholly new things to do, which is the case with Stamps.com. And the only way to get customers to plunge into uncharted waters is to tempt them with freebies.

The site also promotes its PhotoStamps product, which lets consumers and small businesses take their own images or photographs and turn them into real U.S. postage.

The jury is out on the viability of Stamps.com or any of its competitors, but for now the site wins applause for doing all the right things to persuade us to, at the very least, give this newfangled way of buying and affixing postage a whirl.

The Right Dose

Drugstore.com Inc.
www.drugstore.com

Who likes shopping for aspirin, soap, razor blades, prescription medicines, and the rest of the stuff that takes us to drugstores? Almost nobody, and that's why an early niche targeted by trailblazing e-tailers was the drugstore category. Imagine if you could save yourself a half-hour—maybe more—weekly by eliminating those shopping trips and instead clicking a mouse a few times.

That's the value proposition put forth by Drugstore.com, a leader in this category that has won a variety of awards and accolades over the years. For example, it was number 32 in *Internet Retailer* magazine's "Top 500 Guide to Retail Web Sites" in 2005. The publication ranks America's 500 largest retailers based on their internet retail sales volume each year.

What is the company's secret to success? Just visit the Drugstore.com site. There is much to admire: pages that load very fast, numerous tools for personalization ("Your List"), and a well-organized store directory where you can shop by category such as "vitamins," "beauty," and "top sellers." Special offers are highlighted on the front page, as are prescription offerings, which are an important part of Drugstore.com's business and important for many customers as well. The company also offers everyday free shipping on orders of $49 or more for most products. This is another great feature.

The other distinguishing feature about Drugstore.com is that it's leveraged upon joint marketing arrangements with well-known businesses—notably GNC (www.gnc.com), which for example, even has a Drugstore.com link at the bottom of its home page. When you click on it, you are sent right back to Drugstore.com. And, there is a link to GNC.com on Drugstore.com's homepage as well. GNC, and other Drugstore.com partners, have spent millions of dollars nurturing consumer awareness and comfort, and they rank high in their niches. Drugstore.com gets to parlay their investments into a powerful play for consumers' trust and shopping dollars.

That's a brilliant move because no matter how long a cyberstore-front spends trying to drive traffic to its pages, it still has to wrestle with consumer distrust. Nobody's "seen" it, nobody's been inside, nobody's touched the merchandise on its shelves. Those are high hurdles, but not

SMART TIP

With whom can you forge alliances? Which companies will dress up your pages and build higher levels of visitor trust in your business? Make up a list, and start knocking on doors. For an online start-up, these kinds of partnerships can spell the difference between a fast ramp-up into success or a swift plunge into failure. A few partnerships are plenty; put too many on your page, and you risk blurring your message and losing your identity.

the only ones faced by Drugstore.com. Its products touch a customer's body, and that's a field where trust is paramount. Lack trust, and selling is simply impossible. Drugstore.com wins cheers for its attempt to bridge the trust divide through strategic alliances. That simply is first-rate marketing smarts.

Riding the Wave

Yahoo! Inc.

www.yahoo.com

SMART TIP

Surf around and visit all the portal or gateway sites that in the past several years Yahoo! has trounced. Let's face it, Yahoo! is clearly a winner when it comes to portal or gateway sites. This should lead you to keep asking, "What does Yahoo! do better, and how can I adapt it to my site?" Odds are you can't duplicate the sophisticated programming or the high level of personalization offered by Yahoo!. But keep surfing, and you'll soon be jotting down concrete ideas for your site.

No web site comes close to Yahoo! in winning visitors. It was among the internet's first web sites, but remained a powerhouse. In the July 2006 count of the top 50 internet properties by visitor count from comScore Media Metrix, Yahoo! sites had more than 120 million visitors in that month, and the company was granted the number one spot that month. Yahoo!'s performance is simply amazing, especially since this is month-in, month-out leadership that has lasted for years.

Surf into Yahoo!, and what you find is a monument to an internet philosophy of less is more. Graphical elements are so few as to be almost not used at all, and the page is heavily text-based—but it somehow manages to remain both uncluttered and readable. This is as skilled as web site programming gets: Yahoo! programmers manage to make an extremely sophisticated site design somehow look simple.

Now notice how many services and options Yahoo! offers, from personalized stock quotes to e-mail options, auctions—even a customized "My Yahoo!" page where registered users can select exactly the information they want to see. It's a rich array of individualized information, and since it's free, smart users tap into it.

When compared with its main competitors, Yahoo! has a better-looking site. Learn from Yahoo! that less is definitely more, and information—useful, relevant information—is power. Give surfers facts, make the page load fast, and you are following in Yahoo!'s footsteps, which is an excellent path to take.

It Takes a Village
iVillage, a wholly-owned subsidiary of NBC Universal Inc.
www.ivillage.com

A site aimed at women, iVillage.com is one of the nation's most successful online destinations for women. It's so successful that in May 2006 it was acquired by NBC Universal Inc.

Why is it so well-regarded? Log into iVillage and see for yourself. It's evident that the site strives to be a portal for women, the kind of page it hopes users will set up as their start page. That's because the site offers a full range of services, everything from horoscopes to quizzes to free stuff (such as contests and sweepstakes for free merchandise, trips, and even cash). There are recipes, beauty tips, pointers for parents, and places to chat online, Whatever a person could want to find online is offered on this page somewhere.

The site is also well-designed and easy-to-read. For example, one of the first things a visitor sees is a list of categories—such as "Health & Well-Being," "Diet & Fitness," "Love & Sex, and "Pregnancy & Parenting"—to click on for more information.

The most impressive thing about iVillage is it knows its target audience and gears everything to those viewers. Many sites are unfocused or try to be all things to all people, and that never works. What does work is knowing who your viewers are and gearing everything on the site to them. In this respect, iVillage excels.

SMART TIP
Have you defined your target audience? The more you know about your viewers, the more closely you can match your site to their interests and needs. Get to know your viewers—run surveys, solicit e-mail feedback, and routinely seek to find out what's on people's minds—and that will make it easier for you to tailor content to them.

Keeping It Fresh
FreshDirect Inc.
www.freshdirect.com

The odds are certainly against it, but FreshDirect Inc. (www.fresh direct.com), a New York-based online fresh-food retailer, is actually succeeding.

What is making this company succeed when other cybergrocers—such as Webvan and Kozmo.com—became some of the most well-known dotcom flops? Well, for one thing, those companies were straightforward grocery distribution companies with hubs located all over the nation. FreshDirect, on the other hand, is a fresh food and meal solution company that just happens to deliver its products to New York customers.

The company, conceived three years ago by Joe Fedele (a New Yorker who has started gourmet supermarkets), shortens the supply chain by purchasing fresh foods direct from the source and processing orders in a manufacturing facility using batch-manufacturing processes. Then it delivers its products to customers in parts of New York and New Jersey.

Its food-friendly facility lets the company do much of its own food preparation, such as roasting its own green coffee beans, dry-aging its own prime beef, and baking its own breads and pastries. It also sells specialty foods and popular grocery brands. And because it doesn't have a retail location, it doesn't pay expensive rent for retail space. These factors help keep food fresh and costs low and allow the company to pass the savings on to its customers. As a result, FreshDirect says it can save customers up to 25 percent compared with local retail markets. The service is currently available in most of Manhattan, large parts of Brooklyn and Queens, Riverdale in the Bronx, and Jersey City and Hoboken in New Jersey.

FreshDirect customers can shop anytime from work or home, and the company brings everything directly to them in a FreshDirect refrig-erator/freezer truck so the food is protected all the way to their door. There is a $40 minimum total per order. Delivery costs range from $4.95 to $9.95—and tipping is at the customer's discretion. Customers are advised to tell FreshDirect where and when they want their delivery by choosing a convenient two-hour delivery window on weekday evenings and all day weekends.

The formula seems to be working: the company has currently attracted more than 250,000 customers. There are numerous reasons for the company's success. One is the concept itself—fresh food sold at low cost and delivered to your door. Another is its focus on providing a robust shopping experience for fresh foods and meal solutions. It makes it easy to get a great and healthy meal on the table.

But another reason for its success is its easy-to-use web site. FreshDirect's online store is a cinch to use and is loaded with great information. You can learn about what you're buying, compare products by price, nutrition, and flavor, and get recommendations for foods to suit your taste. When you come back, the company remembers what you ordered last time so that you can reorder in minutes.

When you visit the home page, you'll see that it highlights its delivery information, which is important, especially since it must get many calls and questions from people about this important part of its business model. It also asks you to find out if the company is delivering in your neighborhood. All you have to do is enter your zip code.

Departments such as "Fruit," Dairy," and "Meat" are clearly listed, and you can click on the word or a picture (for fruit, there is a picture of a few apples, for example) to enter that department. Once you are in each department, you are treated to more graphics and details so you can easily click on the exact item you'd like. Prices are clearly listed here as well, which is a plus. As you go along, you are treated to even more details about each item. When I clicked on "Fruit," and then "Apples," and finally "Granny Smith," I was greeted with the following description: "The tartness of a Granny Smith piques your palate, but then its deep sweetness comes out to balance the flavor." I was also shown the

SMART TIP
A key to FreshDirect's success is its graphics. It shows all its products in a clear and very appetizing way. Are you selling products that would benefit from appealing graphics? If so, spend the bucks, and make sure the graphics look good. It really makes a difference to consumers. The more appealing something looks, the more likely people are to buy it.

price again. Checking out is easy as well—almost every page has an icon that lets you view your shopping cart or check out. All in all, it's a great experience.

Tech Savvy

Dell Computer Corporation
www.dell.com

Michael S. Dell, chairman and CEO of Dell Computer Corp., founded the company in 1984 with $1,000 and an unprecedented idea in the computer industry: Sell computer systems directly to customers. Michael, who is also the longest-tenured CEO in the computer industry, knew what he was doing.

Under Michael's direction, Dell has established itself as a premier provider of products and services required for customers to build their information-technology and internet infrastructures.

Dell is also acknowledged as the largest online commercial seller of computer systems. The company is known for redefining the role of the web in delivering faster, better, and more convenient service to customers.

To see how well Dell is serving customers, take a look at its web site. Navigation is very user-friendly. On the front page, online shoppers are clearly presented with a photo of a notebook, desktop, server, printer, and TV set. When you click on any of the photos, another link appears that allows you to search in the following categories: "Home & Home Office," "Small Business," "Medium & Large Business," and "Government, Education, & Healthcare."

You can also click on any of those categories to find Dell solutions. And prominent on the home page is a "Support & Help" link—always a good thing for a web site.

An important thing to remember: While Dell may have an elaborate back-end infrastructure, most of the elements on the

SMART TIP

Navigation is key to a web site—can users find what they're looking for on yours in a glance? Heavily monied corporations actually test and time users as they poke around rough-draft web sites. You can do the same. Ask employees, friends, or neighbors to navigate your site, and listen to their feedback. It does no good if you hide your gems—they need to be readily visible, even to casual lookers.

site are pretty basic and could be done by a small e-tailer just starting out. In fact, the real beauty of the site is not anything flashy but how it's organized. It's user-friendly and shows that Dell really understands its customers. This is a basic—but important—concept that any e-tailer should think about before finalizing site design plans.

If the Shoe Fits

Shoebuy.com Inc.

www.shoebuy.com

Shoebuy.com is yet another e-tailer that has found success despite the dotcom bust. The company is the largest retailer on the internet focused on all categories of footwear and related apparel.

Shoebuy has partnerships with more than 250 manufacturers and represents more than 400,000 products from top brands including Adidas, Aerosoles, Allen-Edmonds, Bass, Bostonian, Brooks, Clarks England, Dexter, Dockers, Dr. Martens, ECCO, Fila, Florsheim, Franco Sarto, Hush Puppies, Johnston & Murphy, Keds, K-Swiss, Mephisto, Merrell, Naturalizer, New Balance, Reebok, Rockport, Samsonite, Sebago, Skechers, Timberland, and Tommy Hilfiger.

Simplicity is the guiding principle of the Shoebuy.com web site. There are several ways to find your shoes of choice quickly and easily, and they are clearly listed on the Shoebuy.com home page. You can browse departments for men, women, teens, children, or sale shoes; browse by collection—such as "boots" or "bridal shoes"—or browse by brand. A search button clearly identified at the top of the page allows users to search by brand, size, wide shoes, narrow shoes, or sale shoes. There is also an "Advanced Search" button.

Shoebuy.com also offers a 110 percent price guarantee. Here, if you find a product for a lower price on another web

BUDGET WATCHER

How can you give away shipping and not go broke? While FedEx and its competitors negotiate highly favorable rates with big shippers, they won't necessarily do the same with small businesses. But that doesn't mean only big-bucks options are left. Use UPS standard delivery or the post office. Both are cheap. If that gets you a buyer who becomes a repeat customer, isn't it some of the smartest money you've ever spent? Don't be too quick to say you can't afford to offer free shipping.

site, the company will refund you 110 percent of the difference between the lower price and Shoebuy's price. It will even refund the difference if it lowers the price at Shoebuy. Plus, the company has been offering free shipping on all its orders since January 2000, when its site was officially launched. This freebie is prominently displayed throughout the site.

The CEO and co-founder of the company, Scott Savitz, has said he didn't want to enter into this business if he couldn't sell a product that offered free shipping, because he believed it was part of the whole value proposition. He felt that just because Shoebuy.com was offering a product on the internet, that alone wasn't enough for somebody to make a purchase.

Film at 11

Netflix Inc.
www.netflix.com

Here's a novel idea: Launch a movie rental service with the goal of using the DVD format and the internet to make it easier for people to find and get movies they will appreciate. This is what the founders of Netflix had in mind when they formed Netflix.com in 1997, and the site is now a success. Today, Netflix is the world's largest online DVD movie rental service, offering 5 million members more than 70,000 movie titles. Its appeal and success are built on providing an expansive selection of DVDs, an easy way to choose movies, and fast, free delivery.

The concept is simple: members can rent DVDs and keep them as long as they want with no late fees. Netflix also provides free, prepaid return envelopes so members can just drop their movies in the mailbox to return them to the company. And more than 90 percent of Netflix members receive their DVDs in one day.

Currently, Netflix has six monthly plans starting at $5.99 for two DVD rentals a month, with one rental out at a time.

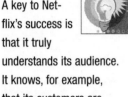

SMART TIP

A key to Netflix's success is that it truly understands its audience. It knows, for example, that its customers are films buffs, so it allows them to pick and choose films from genres that only true film buffs would understand and enjoy. What's more, it offers them fully personalized pages so they can rent DVDs the company believes they would like. While Netflix's personalization capabilities are at a level that many e-tailers might not be able to achieve, all e-tailers should still make an effort to get to know their customers and talk to them in their own language on their web sites. It's not rocket science, just pure business sense.

The most popular is three movies out at a time, with unlimited rentals, which is $17.99 a month.

The more you use Netflix, the more the site is tailored to your tastes. After you see a movie, for example, you can rate it by clicking on the stars that appear next to every movie's listing on the site, from one star if you hated it to five stars if you loved it. The more you rate, the more Netflix learns what you like, and it delivers personalized recommendations every time you log on. It also allows you to easily rent these DVDs by displaying a red "Rent" icon beside each movie description.

Besides highlighting picks especially for each member, the Netflix home page also allows you to search by genre ("Action Adventure," "Comedy," or "Documentary," for example).

Netflix is also expanding its business. In January, 2007, Netflix introduced a service to deliver movies and television shows directly to users PCS as streaming video. The service is free to Netflix subscribers and initially worked with a limited catalog of 1,000 movies and TV shows. Throughout 2007, the service is expected to expand.

The site clearly understands its audience—film lovers—and makes ordering DVDs a very pleasant experience.

Chapter 21 Summary
10 Things You Can Do Today

1. Watch your competitors and pace-setting e-tailers closely. When they are doing something right, do it better.

2. Strive for excellence, just as Amazon.com does. Have a fast-loading site with easy-to-read navigation. Offer great promotions that keep people coming back for more, as well as a personalized user experience.

3. Offer lots of information on your web pages without making them seem cluttered or overwhelming.

---

4. Build in tools that make shopping go fast. Your customers will thank you by spending more money in your store.

5. Offer consumers a deal to try a new product or service. Then watch the responses.

6. Think about forging alliances with other companies.

7. Define your target audience. The more you know about your viewers, the more closely you can match your site to their interests and needs.

8. It shows all its products in a clear and appealing way, and the better, more appealing something looks, the more likely people are to buy it. So, how does Fresh Direct do this? By using colorful, realistic-looking photos with descriptions that are easy and fun to read. The categories and layout also make sense.

9. Ask employees, friends, or neighbors to navigate your site, and listen to their feedback. If they can't find what they're looking for on yours in a glance, change it.

10. Experiment with offering free shipping. And don't be too quick to say you can't afford to offer it. Look into it.

eChat with Bruce Weinberg

WHERE IS E-COMMERCE HEADING? TOUGH topic, but to gain insight into the future, I asked Bruce Weinberg, an associate professor of marketing and e-commerce at the McCallum Graduate School of Business at Bentley College, for his thoughts.

A writer and thinker about the internet, with particular expertise in online shopping and online consumer behavior, Weinberg is both a tough critic of present-day e-tailing and a bona fide optimist about the role of e-commerce in tomorrow's retailing mix. You may not always agree with the opinionated Weinberg, but his thoughts are well worth pondering.

Melissa Campanelli: What's the best e-tailing site on the web?

Bruce Weinberg: The two most dominant online retailers are eBay and Amazon. Some key aspects of their approach to constructing and operating a business are:

- Enabling customers to develop high degrees of trust in the exchange process, which, theoretically and practically, is critical for long-term success in any business. As 1972 economics Nobel Laureate Ken Arrow said, trust reduces the friction in commerce.
- They each offer great value by making it easier for customers to find a wide variety of items through a one-stop shopping process. The notion of value in a one-stop shopping process in an online environment may sound strange given the ease with which you can switch from one web site to another. However, some factors at play that make this plausible are that time is relative and loyalty is an investment that keeps on giving.
- Time is relative. If I told you that you could be physically transported to the aisles of your favorite bookstore in five to ten seconds, you would be elated. Normally this could take on the order of five to 30 minutes. However, waiting five to ten seconds for a web page to download would drive you nuts (assuming the use of a high-speed internet connection). Normally, a web page loads in one to two seconds or less with a high-speed connection. In the physical world, one to two seconds is really fast; however, in the web world, one to two seconds is not so fast—it may even be annoyingly slow to some people. So time is relative. The few seconds it may take to type in another URL or search for another online store to visit may not be perceived as quick when operating in an online state of mind (with apologies to Billy Joel). One-stop shopping saves online consumers time.

- Loyalty is an investment that keeps on giving. On average, consumers continue to view shopping online as a very risky activity. This risk is reduced when consumers find a trustworthy and reliable merchant (or merchants, in the case of eBay). Consumers believe that the majority of online purveyors are untrustworthy, so when they find one they can trust, they are surprisingly likely to stick with it. One good experience after another increases customers' trust and loyalty. Consumers are investing their shopping hearts and minds in the online merchant. This results in a cycle that is difficult for a competitor to break. The loyal and invested customer is more likely to consider and value alternative offerings, such as those that could be offered in a one-stop shopping environment.

In general, a web site—and the processes set in motion based on customer interaction with a web site—should do the following six things:

1. Allow customers to perform some aspect of the buying process better than is possible through other means. If the purpose of the site is to provide information, then it should provide information either more effectively or more efficiently than was possible before the firm offered a web site. If the site allows customers to order products, then it should enable a better experience in some meaningful way. For example, catalog retailers should make the online ordering process either faster or more convenient than ordering via telephone.

2. Clearly describe a product so that consumers know exactly what they are considering (check out a camera review at www.DPReview, and you'll see an example of a site that leaves little to the imagination).

3. Put forth a sincere effort to truly understand a customer through communication and sincere interest, not exclusively based on click streams.

4. Provide full and accurate information upfront about what is being offered. For example, don't make customers go through the

checkout process in order to find out whether an item is in stock or to find out the full cost of an order (which includes the costs of the product, sales tax, and shipping).

5. Keep promises. Say what you mean and mean what you say. For example, deliver the next day when a customer pays for next-day service. And don't call something next-day service unless it means the product will be delivered to the customer on the next day.

6. Respect customers' privacy and security. Consumers have serious concerns about these issues. Once a person overcomes them to buy from you, do everything in your power to maintain the promised and expected levels of privacy and security.

Campanelli: Do you have a personal favorite web site?

Weinberg: My favorite sites tend to be the ones that help me *find* effective solutions to my problems. I'll mention two particular sites here, but I'll note a couple of experiences that speak to the general notion of a "favorite" web site that helps me find effective solutions. For online shopping, my most preferred site is eBay, the online auction site. At eBay, I almost always find what I want, when I want it, at a price that I find reasonable (as I play a role in setting the price when bidding in an auction). In addition, I get a thrill from shopping at eBay; it is an affect-rich shopping and buying experience. First, there is the excitement associated with finding an item that I thought I would never find anywhere (e.g., a Rolls-Royce key case, a brand new unit of an old version of a handheld solitaire game that was accidentally left on a boat while heading over to Nantucket). Next, there is the delight associated with interacting with other bidders (though some would call this the rush of competition). Then there is the agony of defeat or the thrill of victory (with apologies to the *Wide World of Sports*). Finally, I don't buy items on eBay; I win them. I love the feeling of getting a great deal when I win. But on eBay and other online auction sites, you should be careful of the winner's curse (in essence, paying too much for an item) and of the potential for addictively "chasing losses." Researchers at Harvard Medical School have observed some similarities between gambling and auction bidding with respect to human behaviors and emotions.

I also enjoy Google. In both my professional and personal life, I frequently find the need or desire to search for information online. Google typically leads me to information that will either solve [a problem now] or help me down the road in solving a problem. For example, I easily reconnected with a long-lost friend from Sweden by "Googling" him (i.e., entering his name into the search field—I typically place quotes around my search terms). His name appeared in a few web pages, one of which included his e-mail address.

Google has also helped me find web sites that addressed pressing problems for me. During the summer of 2005, for example, my central air-conditioning compressor unit stopped working. Most people would probably call an air-conditioning repair company. Well, I was not sufficiently confident that I would easily find one that would act mostly in my best interest (and pocketbook). A new unit could cost thousands of dollars! So I hit the internet looking for, and finding, a place where I could learn how to diagnose and, as it turns out, repair my central air-conditioning unit—visit the "Cozy Community" of CozyParts.com, a Lennox independent dealer in Oklahoma. Similarly, I recently had a problem in getting my radio to work in my 1993 Lexus LS400 after I had disconnected, and then reconnected, a battery cable after cleaning off some corrosion (i.e., entering my security code to bypass the anti-theft protection). I believe a Lexus dealer would have charged upward of hundreds of dollars to "help me out." In the end, I found a solution within a community of car owners at Carkb.com, which cost me a few minutes of my time in the end. My approach to resolving a problem may not be effective for everyone, as I can be a bit of a do-it-yourselfer type.

Campanelli: What's wrong with all—or virtually all—e-commerce sites today?

Weinberg: Tough question. I'll stop short of saying that certain problems are associated with all e-commerce sites. But I will highlight some areas where firms should seriously reconsider the status quo.

First, I believe many sites could benefit from a greater appreciation of the consumer buying decision process. The process has been the same for centuries, and it is unlikely to change in the foreseeable future. It details precisely what consumers do when engaged in the process of buying. They: 1) recognize a problem or need, 2) may search for information to reduce the risk associated with the buying decision to be made, 3) may evaluate alternatives and come to a decision about which one may be "best," 4) make the purchase, and 5) carry out a variety of post-purchase activities, such as consuming the product, spreading negative or positive word-of-mouth, returning the item, and so forth. For more details, see my report at www.InternetShopping247.com.

Second, firms should realize that humans engage in exchange and that the internet, the web, computers, and other technologies are exchange tools for humans—not the other way around. Model your approach for exchange based on this simple and important principle. eBay brings together buyers and sellers. Match.com brings together people who want companionship. EverQuest.com (http://everquest .station.sony.com), an online game with more than one million subscribers paying $13 per month to play] brings together people who like to interact through and explore fantasy worlds.

Third, scaling [growing your business] is a great way to garner more profits per dollar invested; however, scaling only works when a successful process remains a successful process in its scaled form. Don't assume that every business process that can be automated and scaled up in some way should be automated and scaled up. For example, using an FAQ section as a means for scaling the availability of customer service may not be enough. Sometimes the customer or the situation requires more assistance than that which is offered by a set of FAQs. Even mighty eBay learned this lesson, as they now offer real-time "live" help through online chat.

All this being said, there are situations where scaling online may be extremely effective. For example, consider the case of viral marketing, or getting others to pass along your message or some message that will bring customers to your door. The internet can be extremely effective in this regard. In addition, the web is a great way to scale the number of interactions with a person and the number of people with which you have an interaction—for example, through an electronic newsletter. The master in this domain is Michael Katz of www.BluePenguinDevelopment.com. This can effectively support a permission marketing program.

Campanelli: What business principles hold in e-commerce?

Weinberg: Tried-and-true business principles hold in e-commerce. If your value proposition is weak, then your appeal to customers will likely be weak. In addition, to survive in e-commerce, it is critical to have a clear vision and reasonable plan for success, determination and discipline in execution, and the ability to understand and satisfy consumers. You must not only have a great idea, but also be able to "make it happen." There is a long history of entrepreneurs who developed "greater mousetraps" that did not result in everyone beating a path to their door.

Campanelli: What niches have yet to be fully attacked by e-tailers?

Weinberg: I have observed many small businesses filling niches. I still see a lot of opportunity in luxury goods. Many long-established and premier luxury purveyors, such as Gucci, Tiffany, and Rolls-Royce Motor Cars, are online; however, their sites leave much to be desired. I see a great opportunity online for luxury providers who meet the expectations they set for their goods or services.

Several years ago I wrote that another great opportunity for online retailers was in the area of digital downloadable recorded music, that the record labels were scrambling to figure out a viable solution to this

SMART TIP

Where do eBay and Amazon excel? By enabling customers to develop high degrees of trust in the exchange process, offering great value by making it easier for customers to find a wide variety of items through a one-stop shopping process, keeping promises, and respecting their customers' privacy. Do you do these things? If so, you're on the right track to success.

BEWARE

Never count out brick-and-mortar retailers. Some of them may be dumb, but they aren't dead. And they do have money, domain experience, and deep supplier relationships. When a brick-and-mortar decides to make a move into a space, it can cause real pain to other e-tailers, so always assume that tomorrow you will be competing against them. Know ahead of time how you will prevail!

problem, and that I saw no reason why a new player could not devise a solution for this great opportunity. Well, Apple stepped up, and through its iPod [digitized music player] line and iTunes.com [digitized music web site] is extremely successful; many experts have said that this revitalized Apple. There have been rumors that the Recording Industry Association of America [RIAA] is going to make some potentially crazy decisions that could end up derailing the success of iTunes. That would be a shame for relevant industry players and consumers. I'm not convinced that the RIAA has figured out how to operate effectively in a digital world.

I currently see a lot of opportunity in online [video] games. Some massive multiplayer games have been successful, such as Everquest, and many have failed, such as The Sims Online. However, I see the stars aligning in terms of consumers' experience with mobile devices and relevant technological advances in wireless devices and service delivery, and game development. The line between physical reality and virtual reality is going to increasingly blur. Consumers will be doing more, and spending more money, in virtual/digital contexts.

Campanelli: What will the next-generation sites offer that today's sites don't?

Weinberg: Sites in the future will offer increases in speed, fidelity (e.g., the ability to feel items, speech recognition), ease of use, and access for the physically or psychologically challenged.

Campanelli: Why haven't brick-and-mortar retailers "gotten" the web? Will they?

Weinberg: The answer is pretty simple and age-old. They do not get it because they neither use it nor embrace it. I believe that most people realize success because they get immersed in their passions and work their tails off. If brick-and-mortar retailers want to get it, then they need to get everyone in their company online, using the internet, and shopping online. That being said, more retailers are beginning to "get it." Many have, in essence, outsourced with Amazon, e.g., Target. In addition, many are beginning to take a "multichannel" perspective on serving their customers. In short, multichannel marketing means you (i.e., the marketer/organization) see customers as individuals, rather than as members of a segment, you recognize that they (and you) may value a variety of means/channels for interacting (with you or other customers), and you see the internet is one conduit or channel among many that can be used to enhance the customer experience and profitability.

Campanelli: What are two bad e-commerce sites? Why?

Weinberg: Pick any two that make your blood boil or bring out frustration. The most common causes are grounded in content (e.g., limited product information, limited product availability), functionality (e.g., navigation, checkout, customer service), and privacy or security. A site that bothers me is that of Hermès, one of the world's leading luxury goods brands. The site provides an irritating shopping experience. Navigation is neither intuitive nor pleasant, and information is minimal.

Campanelli: What has fundamentally ailed the prevailing B2C web site business models?

Weinberg: I see many problems. Here are a few:

- Systems should be structured [according to how] consumers think and behave.
- Great ideas are wonderful things. They stimulate other great ideas. A great idea, however, is not enough to build a sustainable enterprise.
- Many firms got hung up on giving product to consumers. Some initial promotions effectively generated awareness and trial. At some point, however, these promotions should have stopped. Aside from credit card

SMART TIP
No, you don't have to be on the web, but if you've read this far, odds are high that you either are or you soon will be. If you still decide not to go online, good luck. You'll need it to compete in an age when consumers routinely look to the internet for the shopping information they need.

fraud, shipping charges are one of the most-mentioned [negatives] for those who have not shopped online (and even for some who have shopped online). If organizations were to provide free, or, alternatively, flat rate, shipping and drop the ridiculous promotions, I bet sales would do just fine and profits would be improved.

- Web sites lack personality; they can be sterile. Let's see some faces or caricatures on these sites. Provide cues that bring out human affect—we humans like emotion.
- Word-of-web is the most powerful and persuasive form of communication. Organizations should more actively look for ways to integrate this into their web sites. Allow customers to share their opinions/ratings and reviews, to read those of others, and to interact with one another. Sure, it means giving up some control, which can be frightening. But it can also be liberating and improve the customer experience and the bottom line!

Campanelli: If e-commerce is different in the near future, how will it be? How will it be the same?

Weinberg: I mentioned multichannel marketing before. Many aspects of e-commerce will be integrated into the ways business gets done and customers are served. It will no longer be perceived as a process that dominates the entire way a firm does business; rather, it will be considered an element in an overall business process. The government will play a greater role in regulating e-commerce and will more effectively enforce laws that are violated in an e-commerce context. Issues of privacy and security, particularly identity theft, will remain important. I expect to see a huge increase in the number of "digital" security companies. In the physical world, American life transitioned from a time where people left the front door open to one where you'd be crazy to leave your house or car without setting its alarm. I expect the same to hold in the virtual world. Digital security will become increasingly involving, complex, and lucrative as more aspects of our lives become "connected" online/electronically, such as the home, cars, and, yes, people. A variety of devices will begin to get connected via the internet. Think back to the 1967 movie *The Graduate* and say the word "wireless" instead of "plastic."

One big change I see is the powerful force of large players dominating various aspects of e-commerce and internet media. For example, just as ABC, NBC, and CBS were dominant when television broadcasting was emerging and maturing, I expect to see Google, Yahoo!, Microsoft, AOL, and, perhaps, in some shape or form, eBay, dominating internet information/functionality delivery. These sites, in many respects, have become one-stop "homes" for, or gateways to, all of one's internet needs, e.g., e-mail and other forms of communication such as voice-over-internet, search, geography mapping, shopping, etc. Many consumers will become accustomed to the "signature" look and feel of the various tools offered by a particular portal and will likely return most often to that portal for various internet needs, which, increasingly, is becoming most everything!

WIRELESS WONDERS

In the movie *The Graduate*, the future revolved around plastics, or so the young grad was told. Today, the future definitely revolves around wireless technologies. Find your niche in wireless, and you are on a fast track to success.

The wireless web soon will be in more hands than the conventional web is. Seem incredible? Well it's not. According to David Chamberlain, principal analyst, wireless, at In-Stat, a Scottsdale, Arizona company that tracks the communications industry, there are more than 60 million wireless data users in the United States. And, internet-ready phones have become so commonplace, the company no longer tracks them.

You can tap into this. Don't stop thinking until you've found six ways—then get busy implementing the best. Wireless is a wave that hasn't crested yet, but when it does, early in the 21st century, it will be a monster.

Chapter 21 Summary
10 Things You Can Do Today

1. According to Bruce Weinberg, in order to be successful, make sure your web site allows customers to perform some aspect of the buying process better than is possible through other means. Does your site do this?

2. Make sure your site clearly describes a product so that consumers know exactly what they are considering.

3. Put forth a sincere effort to truly understand your customers through communication and interest, and provide full and accurate information upfront about what is being offered.

4. Keep promises and respect customers' privacy and security.

5. Have a web site that offers effective solutions to consumer problems.

6. Make sure your site has a great appreciation for the consumer buying decision process, and understand that humans engage in exchange, that the internet is an exchange tool for humans—not the other way around—and that scaling your business is a great way to garner more profits per dollar invested.

7. Remember that tried-and-true business principles hold in e-commerce. For example, if your value proposition is weak, then your appeal to customers will likely be weak.

8. Make sure you can compete in the future by offering increases in speed, fidelity (such as speech recognition), ease of use, and access for the physically or psychologically challenged.

9. Change your site immediately if it has limited product information, limited product availability, poor navigation, poor checkout, or poor customer service, or if it is lacking in how it handles customer privacy or security?

10. Plan for the wireless web.

e-Chats

*H*ERE ARE SOME E-CHATS WITH SUCCESSFUL e-commerce entrepreneurs.

e-Chat with BlueSuitMom.com Inc.'s Maria Bailey

BlueSuitMom.com Inc.

Maria Bailey, president and founder

Location: Pompano Beach, Florida

Year started: 2000

It is amazing, the opportunities that still exist on the web. Ask Maria Bailey. A onetime marketing executive with AutoNation, she launched BlueSuitMom.com on Mother's Day 2000 with the aim of meeting the needs of executive working moms. Her take on the internet was that there were sites geared for working moms in general—but none aimed specifically at executives who also happen to be moms.

So she decided to build one, BlueSuitMom.com (www.bluesuitmom.com), which offers opportunities for networking, news geared for executive moms, and tips (how to manage time, for instance). In addition, what started as a single web site and a big dream has now grown into BSM Media, a full-service marketing firm specializing in marketing to moms. The team behind BlueSuitMom.com now produces "Mom Talk Radio," which can be heard on stations across America including KSL in Salt Lake City and WLVJ 1040 in South Florida, and BSM Media is currently working on nationally syndicating it. The team also wrote *Marketing to Moms: Getting Your Share of the Trillion-Dollar Market* (Prima Lifestyle), and *Trillion Dollar Moms: Marketing to a New Generation of Mothers* (Dearborn). Brilliant as the idea for BlueSuitMom may well prove to be, the ramp-up of Bailey's site wasn't smooth. Read on for her candid—and helpful—comments on building and growing an online business.

Melissa Campanelli: How much funding did you start with? Where was it raised?

Maria Bailey: We started with a commitment for $1 million from a former boss—but, unfortunately, the money did not become a reality. So we truly began with $100,000 raised from personal savings and a few friends.

Campanelli: What were the first big obstacles you encountered in building a web business?

Bailey: Our biggest obstacle has been getting interested investors to actually write the check. That stems from a historical obstacle: Career women have done such a good job at proving to the wealthy/powerful men they work with that they have obtained work and family balance that it is difficult to help my potential investors understand the needs of our market. And on top of it, these men are most likely not married to a woman who is a vice president or CEO. So you say "mother," and they envision their spouse, who is [usually] a stay-at-home mom.

There has been a bit of challenge in learning to manage the young technology pros you need to grow your site. There is little loyalty, and they convey an attitude that they have you by a leash, and without them you wouldn't be able to execute your business plan. They realize that their talents are in demand and are used to changing jobs often. Also, their confidence in technology has led many of them to believe that they also know how to run a business based on that technology. There is a short learning curve to adapt your management style to the new breed of employee you find in the web world.

Campanelli: How do you promote the business?

Bailey: We promote our business mainly by creating very strategic partnerships. For instance, we have a partnership with Stork Avenue, the largest retailer of birth announcements. They were willing to put our logo on five million catalogs in exchange for driving traffic to their site. We are relying too on the strong word-of-mouth network moms and businesswomen create and networking within women's professional organizations, HR departments, and parenting organizations. We have also been featured in the media, including *The Wall Street Journal* and *USA Today*. Also, we are sponsoring events such as parenting conferences and distributing our content to other web sites to build brand recognition, and we have been very lucky in creating great press.

Campanelli: What's the business's goal? What's the end game?

Bailey: Our exit strategy is not to go public. Our goal is to create a prequalified niche market that may be attractive to content aggregators,

SMART TIP

Building a web business is a road filled with ups and downs for any entrepreneur, but a wonderful thing about it is that it provides a space of genuinely equal opportunity. Color, race, gender, creed—none of it matters because all cybercitizens are created equal. Better still, whatever you are, if there are others like you, that's the basis for creating an internet community that just may become a profitable business.

such as iVillage, or a search engine. Because there is no one out there exclusively targeting our market, we feel we have a good shot at it. We monitor the women's market regularly and watch the internet strategies of others so that we can identify possible acquirers.

Campanelli: What unique advantages do you have vis-à-vis other web sites?

Bailey: We felt the best advantage we could have was to be the first to market—and we were. Because we are the first site aimed at executive working mothers, it has allowed us to create all the great press we've received. The other advantage we have is that anytime we are working with a woman to make deals or create partnerships, we almost always get what we need because the woman on the other side of the phone relates immediately to the elements of our site.

Campanelli: What's been your biggest surprise in building this business and your biggest disappointment?

Bailey: The biggest surprise has been how quickly the site and idea have grown. The response we have gotten from other internet companies and offline retailers, marketers, and associations has been overwhelming. We can't keep up with the people who want to do business with us. Also, the international response we have received has been incredible. We receive e-mails from women all over thanking us for our vision to create something that is valuable to them.

The biggest challenge is managing our growth. We have so much growth opportunity now. One of the biggest challenges is not going after every single opportunity, but selecting the smart opportunities.

• • •

e-Chat with CarMD.com Corp.'s Keith Andreasen

CarMD Corp.

Keith Andreasen, co-founder and CEO

Location: Fountain Valley, California

Year started: 2006

Meet Keith Andreasen, co-founder and CEO of CarMD.com Corp. (www.carmd.com), a company that empowers consumers by providing them with the tools and information they need to make better-educated decisions about their vehicle's health and maintenance.

The CarMD system is a combination of a handheld tool and an online repair database to solve the customer's vehicle problem.

CarMD.com's products and services are sold directly to consumers online and via an 800 number, which allows the company to offer a unique and much-needed product to drivers at a reasonable cost.

The vision for CarMD.com began in 1997. The company's technical development team saw a need for providing consumers with a solution for a vehicle's "Check Engine" light problem that would be as simple as checking tire pressure or oil levels.

With that goal in mind, the team began researching and developing a product that would give drivers safe, simple access to their vehicle's computer and the ability to diagnose and process that vehicle's health just like a mechanic with years of experience.

In 2003, the "CarMD" name was registered with the U.S. Patent and Trademark office, and the first of several U.S. patents on the tool were granted.

Meanwhile, with the increased popularity of the internet, the company's vision expanded to include an online resource with which consumers could quickly and easily learn more about their vehicles and car maintenance.

By 2004, a team of ASE-certified technicians, master technicians, computer software engineers, consultants, and associate repair shops were completing a database to "consumerize" the information that until then only mechanics could understand.

Today, the CarMD.com handheld tester and online database are reshaping the way consumers diagnose their vehicles' health and enabling them to extend the life and efficiency of their cars.

Read on to learn more about Andreasen and CarMD.com.

Melissa Campanelli: How is the site different from your competitor's sites?

Keith Andreasen: Honestly, CarMD.com Corp. doesn't have any true competitors. We are the first and only company to offer an affordable easy-to-use tool combined with an online, repair-solutions-database web site exclusively for consumer automotive diagnosis and repair use. There are a few companies that offer tools, but not both. These tool companies include SPX Corp. (www.spxcorp.com), Snap-On (www.snap on.com), and Innova Electronics Corp. (www.iEquus.com). However, these tools are all designed for do-it-yourself and professional automotive repair use. There are also companies that provide web-based diagnostics, including Identifix.com (www.Identifix.com) and eAutoRepair.net (www.eAutoRepair.net); however, these are designed for skilled professionals or do-it-yourselfers. The closest competitor to CarMD.com at this time is OnStar (www.OnStar.com); however, it is exclusively factory installed via wireless voice communications (not web-based). Of course, these and many other web sites offer great resources for drivers.

CarMD's goals for the future include offering a one-stop shop for drivers to get value-added information about everything related to their vehicles. We hope to someday be an online hub for everything from mechanic referral services to purchasing customized vehicles direct from manufacturers. We realize this will take time; for now, we are happy to provide drivers with a much-needed product and service.

Campanelli: Did you have a business plan? How did you go about writing it?

Andreasen: Yes. The CarMD.com business plan was first written in 1999 by our marketing director, with assistance from an outside market research consultant. However, product and internet technology was changing so fast that the CarMD.com business plan was rewritten several times between 1999 and 2006, when the product was launched.

In order to fully understand our target markets, we engaged an independent market research firm, MarketingBank, to conduct research. We chose to conduct our initial surveys online because much of the CarMD.com product/service would be driven by internet access, sales, and information. The following three surveys were conducted between January and March of 2004: 1) Features & Benefits, 2) Naming, and 3) Pricing. The surveys, which were distributed to a random sampling of the general U.S. online population, garnered results from more than 3,600 respondents. More than 87 percent of respondents were interested in learning more about a product that would provide them with "Check Engine" light error code information for their vehicle and nearly 50 percent were "very interested." According to Brad Peppard from MarketingBank [a marketing expert], this product "garnered one of the highest scores [we have] ever seen on a new product concept."

The CarMD.com business plan also included product and web site overviews, market penetration, marketing tactics, sales goals, distribution details, competitive strategies, SWOT analysis [strengths, weaknesses, opportunities, and threats], budget, and timeline. We formed an internal direct marketing team, which consisted of employees and consultants from a wide range of departments, including R&D, technical, marketing, and shipping. The team met semiweekly to review the business plan, product development, and overall progress. We also had the business plan reviewed by graduate and post-graduate students at some of the local universities. This was a very cost-effective way to fix holes in the business plan and bring new ideas to the table.

Campanelli: When did you start the site?

Andreasen: We issued an RFP [request for proposal] for the CarMD.com web site in October 2004 and hired two agencies in January 2005—one for the front end and a second company to handle the back end.

CarMD is such a unique product, in that its true consumer value comes from a very substantial database of real-life automotive problems, fixes, and associated costs. Irvine, California-based Metafuse was hired to handle the back end, which needed to leverage CarMD.com's vast knowledgebase to provide highly valuable information to customers by merging the physical tool with a PC and the internet.

However, because CarMD.com was to be sold direct to consumers via e-commerce transactions, the public portion of the web site needed to have strong consumer appeal and tie in with the overall marketing and advertising campaign. Full-service marketing communications firm, The Phelps Group, was hired to handle this.

Campanelli: What were your start-up costs? Where did you get your funding?

Andreasen: All of the start-up costs for CarMD.com, including product development marketing research, tool production, online repair database building, web site design, and initial direct marketing expenses, have been privately funded internally. Start-up costs have totaled approximately $6 million (at the rate of about $1 million per year). We expect to see a profit by year two.

Campanelli: How is selling a service on the web different from selling products?

Andreasen: We believe that selling a service is more like selling an experience—trying to satisfy each customer's expectation in a very short period of time and right on the spot. On the other hand, selling products relies on the products' performance and support in the long run, after the customer has left the web site.

Because CarMD.com sells both a product and a service, we have the added challenge of convincing consumers that we are a viable and reputable company that will continue to provide information and support in the future. We have found that posting positive customer testimonials and endorsements on the site helps. Also, we have found it beneficial to share the fact that CarMD.com is developed and manufactured by a company with nearly 30 years of experience in the automotive after-market industry—we're in it for the long haul.

Campanelli: Why is the internet a good place to sell services, specifically your services?

Andreasen: The CarMD.com system is a combination of a handheld tool and an online repair database to solve the customer's vehicle problem. Because our customers really need to have internet access to get the full value out of the product and service, it makes perfect sense to sell to people who are already on the internet.

Campanelli: Is this a do-it-yourself site, or did you hire a programmer/outside source to start it up?

Andreasen: We hired several outside programmers, software development companies, and web design consultants to develop the CarMD.com site.

Campanelli: What are your monthly revenues?

Andreasen: We are currently selling about $25,000 per month in product—but we are only a few months into our product launch. CarMD.com officially launched its web site in April 2006.

Campanelli: What are your monthly visitor counts?

Andreasen: Our average monthly visitor count is about 40,000. We are also averaging close to 500,000 hits to the site each month.

Campanelli: How do you attract visitors?

Andreasen: There are a lot of great ways to attract visitors to the web site. The secret is finding the most cost-effective way to reach those most likely to purchase your product. We are still testing various direct marketing tactics to determine which are the most efficient and effective. So far, hands down, the most successful strategy for CarMD.com has been

SMART TIP

Do you think your company—or the products or services you sell—would appeal to the press? If so, then do what CarMD.com Corp's. Keith Andreasen did—reach out to the media. In fact, he says the most successful marketing strategy so far for CarMD.com has been public relations. Print, television, radio, and online media across the board have shown interest in reviewing the product because it appeals to many genres from techno-gadgets to automotive to consumer advocacy. Andreasen said securing a positive endorsement from well-respected reporters and editors has really worked well for CarMD.com. Maybe it will work for you as well.

public relations. Print, television, radio, and online media across the board have shown interest in reviewing our product. It appeals to many genres from techno-gadgets to automotive to consumer advocacy. Securing a positive endorsement from well-respected reporters and editors has really worked well for CarMD.com. Other ways we attract visitors are through banner ads, online links, promotional sponsorships, and print ads in publications ranging from AAA member magazines to SkyMall.

Campanelli: How do you make money? Is it a subscription-based service?

Andreasen: CarMD.com makes money by selling our product at $89.99 (plus shipping and handling). Our customers receive free automotive diagnostic reports. Future plans call for selling additional vehicle information, which many customers have requested. For added revenue, our business plan calls for selling online ad space and links, which we will soon offer. We are also in talks with several reputable organizations to offer mechanic referral services, for which we will collect a pay-per-click fee from each participating shop to whom we refer a customer. Future plans also call for serving as a "toll-booth" to connect CarMD.com customers with third-party automotive products and services.

Campanelli: What are your secrets of success?

Andreasen: There are really no true secrets, rather life lessons. One of our company founders encourages us to ask ourselves the following, every time we make a decision: "Is this good for me? Is it good for the company? Is it good for our customers? Is it good for society?" If any one answer is a no, we just don't do it. If all answers are "yes," success will follow.

Campanelli: What were some challenges you had starting out?

Andreasen: We underestimated how long it would take to develop the product from beginning to end—particularly the web site portion. We may have jumped the gun in hiring outside marketing agencies. Our ramp-up period was so long that it left for a flat product launch. We chose to outsource most of our work so we could manage costs and ensure future success for each of our employees. If money were no object, it would have been preferable to have a few more core management positions filled prior to launch—particularly that of CIO and on-staff webmaster.

Campanelli: Have you run into any security/fraud issues?

Andreasen: Thankfully, we have not run into security or fraud issues with our web site, database, or financial transactions. We have been very careful to outsource payment transactions, web site back end, and the like, to reputable and knowledgeable companies. We also spent the extra time and money to have SAVVIS [an IT infrastructure services firm] conduct a security penetration test to ensure CarMD.com and customer data are secure from outside hackers, which I highly recommend doing.

Campanelli: How is the business growing?

Andreasen: Again, as we're only three months into the launch, growth has been steady, yet slow. We are approached every day by new opportunities. Our customer base is growing at about 40 percent per month, and we are learning new lessons and getting new ideas every day.

• • •

e-Chat with Cashman Computer Associates d/b/a Moon River Pearls' Peter L. Cashman

Cashman Computer Associates
Peter Cashman, chairman/CEO and co-founder (with son Bob Cashman and John Ekegren)
Location: Old Lyme, Connecticut
Year started: 2004

Want to learn some pearls of e-commerce wisdom? Then meet Peter L. Cashman, chairman/CEO of Cashman Computer Associates, which provides IT outsourcing and support for small to medium companies in New England. CCA also does business as Moon River Pearls. Its web site, www.moonriverpearls.com, is an online jewelry store selling classic and modern pearl jewelry.

Prior to CCA, Cashman was chairman and co-founder of Environmental Data Resources Inc., an e-commerce environmental information services company, and CEO of Sanborn Map Company, acquired by EDR in 1996. The enterprise was sold in 1999 to the Daily Mail and General Trust PLC, of London.

Having successfully sold EDR, and bored with retirement, Peter, in the spring of 2004, was introduced to the idea of e-commerce by his son Bob, who encouraged him to take a look at a new business model for Bob's company, Cashman Computer Associates, LLC.

Bob proposed that CCA put the company's internet technology talents and web hosting infrastructure to work creating e-commerce web sites in partnership with small, ongoing direct mail businesses and/or create a new business selling profitable specialty products on the internet.

"Not surprisingly, the e-commerce idea was the result of listening to our customers, something that we pride ourselves on as we go about our daily activities providing on-site IT consulting services," says Bob.

Bob says one of these customers had launched a successful teen clothing site in 2003 and a silver jewelry site in 2004. "I could see no reason that CCA, given our staff and IT focus, could not provide e-commerce services to existing sites or whole new businesses," he says.

Peter says the key to launching the new business was finding the right product. The criteria were straightforward: The product had to be appealing, have high margins, and, because of the need to ship worldwide, be lightweight.

With these criteria in mind, Peter began a series of lunches, phone calls, and meetings with a long list of friends, acquaintances, and former business associates he had met over the last 35 years.

His search ultimately led to John Ekegren. "I have known John, a graduate of West Point and a phenomenal mechanical engineer, for many years," Peter says. "I knew he had been involved with trade between the United States and China but I did not know that he served on the board of a Chinese manufacturing company and that he typically traveled to China at least four times a year."

"At lunch," Peter continues, "I learned that a Chinese businessman who served on a board with John had once told John that if he ever wanted to sell pearl jewelry in the States, he had a great source in China." One thing led to another and the future partners became very serious about this opportunity.

To assess the competition, CCA purchased pearls from the top ten pearl web sites and evaluated every aspect of their product, price, packaging, site design, guarantee, return policy, and service.

"That evaluation," Peter says, "convinced us we could be a successful niche player. We agreed that John's company, PTI, would supply the jewelry from China and provide shipping, handling, and customer service, and that CCA would build, maintain, own, and operate the e-commerce web store."

Bob says, "Our goal is to offer the best value in classic pearl jewelry available on the internet. We believe we have accomplished that objective."

Peter says that it took six months of heroic effort by the combined staff of PTI and CCA to be ready for business in December 2004.

The site offers a convenient, simple approach to buying great gifts for any occasion. Peter said that Moon River's jewelry sells for a fraction of the cost of retail, ships free via UPS, comes with a 30-day money-back guarantee, and arrives in an elegant gift box. In coming months the Cashmans plan to add Tahitian pearls, gemstone and silver jewelry from India, and unique designer items to the site. Read more about Cashman's success story.

Melissa Campanelli: What were your start-up costs?

SMART TIP

Peter Cashman says the key to launching a new business is finding the right product. For Cashman, that meant an appealing, lightweight product that had high margins. Pearls, of course. Remember, not every product is right for online selling. So before you decide to break into the world of e-commerce, make sure you have the right product to sell, and an ample supply of it. Hey, you never know, it could be the next big thing.

Peter Cashman: Nominal. We had all the programming staff and IT infrastructure in house. The learning curve was steep but we did add two new staff for this project at a total cost of roughly $150,000.

Campanelli: What are your monthly revenues?

Cashman: Annual revenues are growing at two times over last year and we anticipate sales in excess of $500,000 this year.

Campanelli: What are your monthly visitor counts?

Cashman: In excess of 20,000.

Campanelli: How do you attract visitors?

Cashman: Pay-per-click and a major effort to win the search engine battle, which is a big deal. Viral marketing is also huge for us. Twenty-five percent of our business comes from repeat buyers, which in the online jewelry business is fantastic. So getting folks to the site is job number one. Job two is converting them to customers. Once they experience our customer service they will come back!

Campanelli: What are your secrets of success?

Cashman: Smart people who work damn hard.

Campanelli: What were some of the most difficult challenges you had starting out?

Cashman: We underestimated how difficult search engine optimization could be, and it took time to get enough product on the site to be meaningful.

Campanelli: What advice would you give e-commerce entrepreneurs just starting out?

Cashman: If you don't have capital you can start small if you are patient, are willing to learn, and work 24 hours, seven days a week. Customer service is also a huge component of success, so remember that it will chew up a ton of time. Finally, it goes without saying you need a quality product offered at a compelling price.

• • •

e-Chat with Corporate Toners Inc.'s Kapil Juneja

Corporate Toners Inc.
Kapil Juneja, co-founder, COO, and CTO
Location: Canoga Park, California
Year started: 2002

Want to learn how a successful business-to-business (B2B) company works? Read on.

Corporate Toners Inc., which was founded in 2002 by Kapil Juneja and Mike Costache, prides itself on providing on its web site Corporatetoners.com (www.corporatetoners.com) the highest-quality inkjet cartridges, refill kits, remanufactured cartridges, and toner cartridges at the lowest possible prices. Its goal is to get these products to its customers as quickly as possible and in the most cost-effective manner. While the company sells its goods to individuals, a large majority of its sales are to businesses, organizations, and schools.

Melissa Campanelli: What's been your biggest surprise at Corporate Toners?

Kapil Juneja: We were astonished when we found ourselves struggling to get the banks to provide us with additional credit card processing capacity every third month as our company grew 100 percent month-on-month during the first year. We were a start-up company with a short track record, run by two fresh college graduates. It was a big challenge to convince the banks that we were a legitimate business with real growth. It was like doing everything right in starting a business just to find out that you can't collect money from the banks. Finally, the banks issued a bigger credit line, and since then we created a multimillion-dollar company in the last three years.

A booming business should be a cause for celebration, but at Corporate Toners, it was something of a mixed blessing. As sales increased sharply—from 150 orders per day in August 2004 to 300 per day by January 2005—we found that an old infrastructure was making it hard to manage new business. Customer records were incomplete, customer inquiries were not attended to on time, and business information was scattered across different databases. It was a less-than-ideal way to [do business and to grow a business].

With sales information stored on so many systems and so many login passwords to remember, it was hard to find customers' data when customers called us. We quickly adopted an all-in-one e-commerce, CRM, and back-end technology platform provided by a San Mateo, California-based company, NetSuite Inc. NetSuite offered everything we needed—from the ability to have all data in one central location to the ability to set up customized transactions for each of our sites so we could integrate all the processes in an online platform available to all our employees at different locations.

Campanelli: Did you approach investors?

Juneja: We sure did. We went to various seminars and events organized by the likes of the Los Angeles Venture Association (LAVA), The IndUS Enterpreneurs (TiE), a Washington, DC-based nonprofit global network of entrepreneurs and professionals established to foster entrepreneurship and nurture entrepreneurs, and the Larta Institute, a Los Angeles-based nonprofit group that connects technology start-ups with funding; and we networked with alumni from our school, Pepperdine University.

We actually met an interested investor at LAVA's annual Investment Capital Conference in early 2002, and the fact that he was an alumnus of Pepperdine and had a large accounting firm and the gray hair we needed made us think we found our ideal investor.

We talked to various [other] investors, but in 2002 nobody cared to finance a B2B start-up with no proprietary technology and no real competitive advantage. Every door we opened was shut with a nice, "Come back with something more tangible 'cause I like you guys, and I see your burning desire to be entrepreneurs." But we knew that we had something going for us: We were experts in getting on the top five results in search engines through organic search-engine optimization. This traffic cost us nothing since we understood how the search engines worked and reverse-engineered the process to beat their rules.

We were about to make a huge mistake by giving 33 percent of the company's equity for $35,000 in cash and office space for the first year in our investor/incubator's firm [the accounting company mentioned earlier]. Luckily for us, the investor kept prolonging the negotiations, knowing that we were two young guys out of college pressured for money. We decided to stop all negotiations since we realized that it was a really bad deal for us. That was probably the best decision we've made to date.

Campanelli: How is building a B2B site different from building a B2C site?

Juneja: It's a completely different mentality when servicing a $20,000 repeat order from a B2B customer than a $53 one-time order from John Doe with no loyalty to your product or service. During the early phases of running an e-business, we realized—and our research concluded the same—that businesses are the biggest consumers of printer supply products. They remain loyal as long as you consistently provide them with good products and excellent service.

So we built a professional-looking B2B web site while providing 100 percent quality products, money-back guarantees, and good customer service. We wanted the web site to be easy to navigate, quick to load, and have quality content to keep the trust and loyalty of our corporate customers. In the online B2B marketplace, you compete with the companies that might be 10 to 1,000 times larger than your company. The disadvantage of being a smaller company compared to the big sharks is

BEWARE

Juneja was smart: He had a bad feeling about an investor who was stringing the company along, so he decided to stop all negotiations. The moral of the story? When it comes to money, go with your gut.

overcome by employing the right back-end management and sales tools. We learned it the hard way when we lost a couple of our big corporate customers as we were not able to service them accurately on time. [That's when we integrated] Net-Suite. NetSuite gives us better organization of our sales data and more information on our customers, which boosts customer service and leads to customer retention and repeat business. NetSuite offers us the tools to provide a world-class service to our B2B customers.

Campanelli: Is there a potentially bigger payout in B2B? Why?

Juneja: B2B has a different cash flow model where customers want competitive pricing with payment terms compared to B2C credit card transactions, where the bank provides the money in three to five days from the transaction date. Selling to well-established businesses requires that you provide them with a high level of customer service (pre- and post-sale). Price is not always the key, but service is. An individual, one-time buyer is much more price-sensitive compared to a corporate client, who may remain your customer for life as long as you consistently provide them with good products and service. Higher sales volume, repeat business, and high retention rate are some of the major advantages when you deal with corporate clients. In the long run, B2B definitely is a bigger payout. As long as you keep your business customers happy, they will continue to give their business to you.

Campanelli: What advantage do you have over the many competitors in your space?

Juneja: We specialize in marketing our web site online on various search engines where we are able to get high ranking on thousands of keywords related to our products. Of course, customer service, quality products, and competitive prices all matter, but our margins are bigger than our competitors' because we have a very low cost of customer acquisition.

Technology is one of our key advantages that we have over our competitors. Using NetSuite's technology with our web sites, we have an all-in-one system to manage all our business processes compared to our competitors, who may use a virtual armada of stand-alone software packages: QuickBooks for accounting, GoldMine for sales calls, LivePerson for e-mail management, a customized online shopping cart, Microsoft Excel for reporting, GoToMyPC for remote access, and several proprietary databases for customer data.

NetSuite's CRM solution provides a robust system where all our customers' inquiries are logged in their respective customer records, so anytime a customer contacts us, we look up their record and provide them an immediate response. We not only save our time and customers' time, we are able to provide a superb customer service, which is a key when dealing with corporate customers.

Since our systems and web sites are based online, we also enjoy the advantages of running our inbound customer service and outbound telemarketing call center from New Delhi, India. The lower cost of running the operation in India combined with highly skilled English-speaking employees enables us to provide excellent service to our customers on time. Finally, we have better coordination between our warehouse and our sales office in Los Angeles, and our back-end customer service and support.

• • •

e-Chat with Fridgedoor Inc.'s Chris Gwynn

Fridgedoor Inc.

Chris Gwynn, president and founder

Location: Quincy, Massachusetts

Year started: 1997

Fridgedoor Inc.'s web site Fridgedoor.com (www.fridgedoor.com) has one primary goal: to be the single largest stop for all things magnetic—novelty magnets, custom magnets, and magnetic supplies.

The company, founded in May 1997 and located outside Boston, is a retailer of novelty magnets for consumers, custom magnets for businesses, and magnetic supplies for consumers and businesses. The items are purchased at wholesale from more than 100 suppliers around the world. The company stocks close to 2,000 items for immediate shipment. Visit www. fridgedoor.com and you're greeted by lists of dozens and dozens of magnets—everything from Elvis Presley magnets to U.S. Postal Service state stamp magnets. Products include humorous magnets set, such as the popular Cat Butts set, custom-imprinted business-card-size magnets, attractive magnetic bulletin boards, and sheets of magnet material.

Fridgedoor was founded and is operated by Chris Gwynn, whose online experience dates from early 1994 and encompasses marketing and e-commerce positions with Ziff-Davis's ZDNet, the AT&T Business Network, and Industry.net (an internet-based marketplace for industrial supplies that's now a part of Techsavvy.com) and as a business-to-business internet commerce analyst for the Yankee Group. Gwynn started Fridgedoor as a part-time endeavor in May 1997 while employed as the product marketing manager for Industry.net. Revenue had reached a point by the end of 1999 that Gwynn felt comfortable enough about the company's future to quit his day job.

Melissa Campanelli: What were your start-up costs?

Chris Gwynn: The start-up costs came to approximately $20,000. The most significant expenses were inventory and a software program to handle all back-end order processing, credit card payments, and inventory management functions. Smaller expenses, such as hosting fees, domain name registration, telephones, etc., collectively get expensive.

Campanelli: Is this do-it-yourself, or did you hire a programmer?

Gwynn: I created the site myself using a template-based store builder and hosting solution designed for nontechnical users like myself. I wanted to avoid a situation where I was beholden to a programmer to make changes and maintain the site. Creating a basic site took less than a day. The time-consuming part is determining the products you want to offer, and creating product images and descriptive copy. Creating the site is the easy part.

Campanelli: What are your monthly revenues?

Gwynn: Our monthly revenues are in the low six figures.

Campanelli: What are your monthly visitor counts?

Gwynn: Fridgedoor [has] approximately 125,000 unique visitors per month.

Campanelli: Where did you get the idea for the site?

Gwynn: I had always wanted to start my own businesses and thought the web was a unique opportunity for someone with a limited budget. I also felt I had an understanding of how people buy online that I developed by working in marketing for an online service and later at web-based companies. I looked for a "low touch" product that was easily displayed online, easy to ship, and relatively hard to find. I hit on magnets, which I personally like, and decided to give it a try. Luckily, it worked.

Campanelli: How do you attract visitors?

Gwynn: We rely heavily on search engines, word of mouth, and press [coverage]. Since we've been around for a while, we're extensively indexed by the search engines. Our market is very fragmented, making it difficult to profitably attract customers through traditional print advertising. Creating positive word of mouth by handling customers properly is our best advertisement.

•   •   •

BUDGET WATCHER
Do you make something unique or special? Put up a web site, submit the URL to all the main search engines, and see if traffic comes in. Chris Gwynn suggests building traffic on the cheap. His is not the kind of site that's likely to become a gazillion-dollar business, but it's a site that can easily generate a nice, steady cash flow, month in and month out.

e-Chat with Gift Services Inc. d/b/a GiftTree's Craig Bowen

Gift Services Inc.

Craig Bowen, CEO and co-founder (with wife, Esther Diez)

Location: Vancouver, Washington

Year started: 1997

Want to meet a successful e-tailer that has expanded into the world of mail order? Then meet Craig Bowen, CEO and co-founder (with Esther Diez) of Gift Services Inc., d/b/a GiftTree.

In business since 1997, GiftTree (www.gifttree.com) is a premier gift services provider. Its clients include many large multinational and U.S. corporations as well as consumers. Its products include handcrafted gift baskets, as well as new baby gifts, balloon bouquets, thank-you gifts, get-well gifts, wedding and business gifts.

In 2003, the online merchant decided to add a catalog to its e-tailing business. Why? Because catalogs keep e-tailers "top of mind" with customers and ultimately encourage those customers to come back for more, says Bowen. That catalog is now a key part of the company's marketing plan. Here's a closer look at Bowen's mail-order experience.

Melissa Campanelli: Tell me about your company. When was it founded?

Craig Bowen: Our company was started in 1997 by myself and my wife in our studio apartment in Key West, Florida. My wife is from Spain and our dream was to build an internet company, sell it, and move back to Spain (where we met). We're still working on the "move back to Spain" part.

Campanelli: Why did you decide to start the company?

Bowen: We felt the internet was the perfect medium for busy people to buy and send gifts. I really liked the idea of jumping into the internet "revolution" and seeing how I'd do running our own business.

Campanelli: When did you decide to add a mail order, or catalog component to your company?

Bowen: Our first catalog went out in 2003. It was sent to a small group of very specific clients during the holiday season and it worked very well. We even saw a lift in sales. We were encouraged by its success and began to grow our catalog distribution. We sent another during the holiday season in 2004, and then sent two out in 2005; one in the fall and one around holiday time. We are expanding our distribution to four catalogs in 2006.

Campanelli: How did you go about launching the catalog? How expensive was it?

Bowen: GiftTree decided to create and design its catalog inhouse. Employees took photographs of GiftTree's products in the company's own photo studio. The company hired a printer to print and manufacture the catalogs, and then mailed the catalogs through the U.S. Postal Service.

Since the catalog was launched in tandem with other fliers it printed—and since GiftTree used in-house employees for the work—it's hard for me to give an answer for how much the whole project cost. However, taking on this kind of project is definitely not cheap: it can cost at least $100,000 once you factor in the costs of hiring an agency to produce it, in addition to printing, mailing, and perhaps buying or renting a prospect list. Basically it is as expensive as you'd like it to be. Also, we have exceptional technological capability for a company our size, so most of these things are costing us far less than other companies our size.

Campanelli: What types of changes did you have to make on the back end to support the catalog?

Bowen: Initially, very few. Launching the catalog was a logical channel for GiftTree to explore. The company's fulfillment system was already in place, ready to take orders. And GiftTree had already collected the names and addresses of customers to whom it could send catalogs. Now that we are trying to gather more data and increase our catalog distribution, we are finding that we need to add or change technologies.

Campanelli: In general, was adding a mail order component to your company difficult to do?

Bowen: It's time-consuming and mistakes or missteps can be costly. There is a lot of knowledge available on the subject and time spent on research will make things easier, or at least, reduce some anxieties you might feel when creating your first catalog. For those who can afford it, a web site and a catalog make the perfect marriage. There's a reason people do catalogs: They work. If you make a very beautiful catalog, and it's got what consumers want in it when they see it, they are far more likely to order from you than if you didn't send them something.

Campanelli: What types of challenges did you face?

Bowen: Making our product "appear" more like a catalog product. There is a difference between web and print. Catalogs are not interactive and that was new for us. Print is also very unforgiving; once you make a decision, you can't "undo" it with a few keystrokes.

Campanelli: Has the catalog side of your business helped the growth of your company?

Bowen: Yes, and we expect it to add more as we move forward.

Campanelli: How successful is your company?

Bowen: I think we are very successful. We're still a bit of a diamond in the rough, but we've done most of the hard work already.

Campanelli: What are your secrets to success?

Bowen: Never give up. Never surrender.

•　　•　　•

e-Chat with Headsets.com Inc.'s Mike Faith

Headsets.com Inc.
Mike Faith, CEO and president
Location: San Francisco, California
Year started: 1998

Want to meet an entrepreneur who has built a successful online business—and is watching it grow every year? Then meet Mike Faith of Headsets.com Inc., a leading provider of headsets through its web site Headsets.com (www.headsets.com).

Melissa Campanelli: Please tell me about your background. Why did you start Headsets.com? When was it founded?

Mike Faith: I emigrated to the United States from England, where the business climate is so stifling that it felt like "entrepreneur" was a dirty word. I wanted the freedom to do business in a way that supported my creativity, and the United States seemed like the perfect place. So in 1990 I jumped on a plane, and never looked back. I started a few ventures, which were moderately successful. They taught me some of the fundamentals of running a business, and generated enough capital for me to start Headsets.com in 1998. Those early companies were call-center based, and so we used a lot of telephone headsets. Finding good quality units at a reasonable cost and with decent supplier support turned out to be harder than it should have been, impossible in fact, and that tripped my opportunity radar.

Campanelli: How much money did you start Headsets.com with? Did you get venture capital money? Was it self-funded?

Faith: Six weeks after realizing the opportunity, and with $40, 000 of my own money, we were in business selling headsets. It was 1998, and we had a single product. The simplicity and cost of our offering was an instant hit, and we quickly grew revenues to the point that I was comfortable putting up the shutters on my other businesses to concentrate on the opportunity. Two years later, in 2000, our competitors were slashing prices and their margins—we were losing our differentiator. We looked at our business, and the original opportunity, and realized we had only served two of the three needs of the market—a good product, at a low cost—we were missing that vital third part—service. So in 2000, as we incorporated from an LLC, we accepted a small round of funding, and that allowed us to fund a cultural shift in the organization, to deliver what we think is world-class customer service.

Campanelli: Where did you open up shop? Why?

Faith: My wife and I were living in San Francisco when I started the business, and so naturally that's where we opened up shop. The bay area is a wonderful region with a near-endless pool of world-class talent, and an attitude to business innovation that for me, at least, captures all the reasons I moved to the United States. Many times, over the years, people have questioned the premiums we pay running a call center in the middle of one of the most expensive cities in the country, but every time it comes up, we can't help but see it as a strength. If you want the best, you have to pay for it. We want the very best!

Campanelli: What's been the biggest challenge you've had in building your company?

Faith: The biggest challenge we've faced, I'm proud to admit, has been my own growth. I'm an entrepreneur, I make decisions like you'd expect me to, and I've had to learn to involve others, think longer term and more strategically, and deal with a lot more formality and "corporate stuff" than I'm used to. It took a while before I built a team that I could trust to share the load, to execute with my vision and my passion. Now we are just crossing that 50 employee threshold, and our challenges are to continue to build a strong, robust organization that is growing at 50 percent annually, without losing those things that made us successful— our adaptability, agility, and efficiency. It's a challenge I relish.

Campanelli: How have you broadened your offerings or diversified your company since starting out? Why is this important for e-tailers to do?

Faith: I'm going to give you an answer that perhaps will go against conventional wisdom. The world's greatest marketer, Al Ries, taught me about ruthless focus years ago—and it's been an invaluable lesson. We sell headsets and we only sell headsets. Because of this, we know more about selling headsets than anybody else, and we sell more headsets than anybody else. The more headsets we sell, the better we get at it. It's a wonderful virtuous cycle. I believe that other e-tailers would do well to stay focused, do less, do it better, and reach deeper into a narrower market.

Of course, we've been tempted to diversify—we have this fantastically efficient, high service model for selling business-to-business productivity tools. Why shouldn't we apply that to as many products that fit the mold as possible? Well, we dabbled in a few areas, but found that even trying to pick up incremental sales in similar categories like audio headphones and telephone conferencers complicated our business to the point that the whole became less than the sum of the parts—not more.

Many people warn us of disruptive technologies or saturated markets and we aren't cavalier or arrogant enough to believe that these risks aren't real—they are, but for us to tackle these risks through diversification means abandoning our core strengths, and that's just not an acceptable trade.

Campanelli: Who is your competition? Are they big guys? If so, how do you find your niche against them?

Faith: You can get headsets from lots of places, but it's almost always part of a diverse offering of products. A headset is still for the most part a consultative sale, despite their widespread adoption and the simplicity of the product relative to other things on the corporate desktop. So we make sure we remain

SMART TIP
You don't have to spend a lot of money on a big, traditional mass media advertising campaign to be successful. Look at Headsets.com: It sends out targeted, B2B direct mail catalogs and uses search engine marketing. Of course, it helps that it also has a memorable name (Headsets.com) and 800 number (800 Headsets) that say nearly everything you need to know about them.

true to our company tagline "America's Headset Specialists" and we serve the market's needs better than generic telecoms suppliers, or office equipment suppliers who try and bolster volume by slashing margins and the all-important expert knowledge and service. For the longest time we were the little guys, carving out a niche with the small companies and new headset users, while our big rivals squabbled over the large call-center market. But now we look around the competitive landscape and find the call-center market dwindling as it moves increasingly offshore, and new headset adoption in the small office sector driving all the growth in the industry, with us leading the charge and the historic big guns standing eerily silent. It's exhilarating.

Campanelli: Have you thought about going public? Why or why not?

Faith: I've often thought of taking Headsets.com public, but I usually talk myself out of it the same day. Then a month later, I'll think of it again. The shift to a public company would change our business, and our ability to compete on the terms that I know will win. Public companies maintain their stock price by focusing on growth. But like success and happiness, growth is a byproduct of doing something to the best of your ability. The pursuit of growth for growth itself will always come up short. As a private company we are free to focus on delivering what the customer wants: the best product at the best price, and with the best service. The irony is of course, by not focusing on growth, we are enjoying it in abundance, around 50 percent annually.

Campanelli: How do you market your site? What works? What hasn't?

Faith: We don't market our site specifically—our web site, as proud of it as we are, is nothing more than a way for our customers to place an order as quickly and efficiently as possible. We do market our products of course (which ultimately drives traffic to our web servers and our call center) and we do that through a pretty significant business-to-business direct mail program using a catalog and solo product offerings. We also

SECRETS TO SUCCESS

What is Headsets.com's secret weapon against some of the bigger companies that may sell headsets? For one, they are experts—headsets are all they sell. In addition, they offer great prices, unbeatable guarantees, a solid reputation, and free trial of products—all backed up by knowledgeable, smart, professional reps offering what Faith calls the "world's best customer service." These are all weapons any small e-tailer or online business owner can use to compete against the big guys—and win.

use pay-per-click online advertising and do phenomenally well in natural search rankings and have a lively affiliate program. Of course, it helps that our company name (Headsets.com) and 800 number (800 Headsets) say pretty much everything you need to know to find us and what we sell. But above all of our marketing efforts, we've found that we've reached a critical mass, with repeat and referral business now becoming our largest source.

Campanelli: How do you up your look-to-buy ratio?

Faith: We simply remove all the barriers to buying our products. I know that sounds trite, but it's true. We offer great prices, unbeatable guarantees, a solid reputation, free trial of our products, all backed up by knowledgeable, smart, professional reps offering the world's best customer service. I challenge anyone who needs a headset to *not* buy from us—why would you go anywhere else? Hey—even I want to buy a headset from us, and I'm a skeptic!

• • •

e-Chat with Lessno.com LLC's Stanley Gyoshev and Assen Vassilev

Lessno.com LLC

Stanley Gyoshev and Assen Vassilev, co-founders

Location: Long Island City, New York

Year started: 2006

Stanley Gyoshev and Assen Vassilev are two friends who were born and raised in Bulgaria and came to the United States to attend college. In 2002, when Vassilev was an undergraduate at Harvard College and Gyoshev was getting his Ph.D. at Drexel University, they set out to launch an easy-to-use discount travel reservation web site called Lessno.com.

In 2006, their dream became a reality, and today Lessno.com—which is short for less money, no hassle—is competing with the likes of Expedia, Orbitz, and Travelocity. Lessno.com (www.lessno.com) is designed to keep the best interest of the customer in mind by acting like a personal travel agent. It does this by using the most innovative new search technology and a friendlier interface.

Lessno.com cross-analyzes user preferences for destination, reason for travel, airline, and cost to generate a customized list of travel options. Unlike other travel web sites, Lessno.com works with both major and discount carriers to provide its users with the most comprehensive menu of flights and prices available anywhere. This is true of both domestic and international flights.

One of the web site's differentiating features is its "Vacation Planner" for leisure travelers looking for a great deal. Users can select a region to which they want to travel as well as a range of dates, and Lessno.com does all the work. The result is a customized selection of destination, date, and cost options designed to meet the users' needs. Lessno.com saves users not only money, but also the time and hassle of searching each destination and date range individually.

Lessno.com also provides an added advantage for frequent business travelers. Users can store all their frequent flyer numbers in their free personal profile, and Lessno.com will leverage them to ensure users get the most for their money. Users can see their account balances for all major frequent flyer programs through the Lessno.com "Account Aggregator" feature.

Another popular feature for both business and leisure travelers is Lessno.com's "Active Search." It lets users specify when and where they want to travel, as well as the price they would like to pay, and e-mails them deals that meet their parameters. Unlike Priceline and other web sites, Lessno.com gives users the difference between the price they set and the actual price of the fare.

Read on to learn more about Gyoshev, Vassilev, and Lessno.com.

Melissa Campanelli: Why did you decide to start Lessno.com? Where did you get the idea for the site?

Assen Vassilev: One rainy evening in November 2002, we finished playing bowling and decided to play bridge. On the way to a friend's place at the Harvard dorms, Stanley started complaining that there were different online travel agencies, which were supposed to make buying tickets easier, but were instead making it more complicated.

We discussed quite at length that all the information was available, but there were a lot of search problems. Travelers either had to specify two exact dates or had to check every airfare for availability. It was reminding me of the old Yahoo! directory search, when users were getting thousands of options and needed to spend a lot of time finding what they wanted.

At that point I had spent four years combing the online reservation systems to find some truly spectacular deals (the best one was a Boston-Miami for $97 including tax during spring break—cabs to and from the airports actually cost us more than the flight), but the process took about half a day and included a lot of hit and miss.

By the time we were done with the first game of bridge, we had the Lessno.com interface drawn on a napkin—I dusted off an old idea that I had worked on all the way back in 1999—and a decent idea of the type of artificial intelligence that could make it work, thanks to Stanley. We applied for a patent and went into business.

Our initial idea was to build an interface that can take into account the flexibility of a traveler, be it different dates or different airports, and help them find the best deal with a single search. However, several months later, as purchasing travel online became the norm, good old-fashioned travel agents started disappearing and there was no one left to help travelers make sense of the frequent flyer/airline alliance jungle or to pick up the phone when they had a problem. That made us expand the initial idea to include up-to-date frequent flyer information and readily available customer service that actually picks up the phone and tries to help.

As every good search engine and customer-centric company, Lessno.com is always changing and hopefully improving. We feel strongly that the purpose and future of any kind of search is using technology to provide the customer with the right mix of information so that they can make an educated choice. This requires not only market incentives but also a good grasp of the knowledge domain that allows the search engine to guide the customer along the way, not just throw back tons of data.

Campanelli: How is the site different from your competitors' sites?

Stanley Gyoshev: More travel options—including low-cost airlines and special negotiated prices—as well as friendly customer care that is actually available and helpful, and better interface and search technology.

Campanelli: Did you have a business plan? How did you go about writing it?

Vassilev: Initially, no. We had an idea how we could improve the current online travel search and buying experience. We had a few avenues that we wanted to examine in terms of monetizing the idea—from licensing it out to building our own online travel agency. Once we decided to go ahead and build the web site, we developed a business plan based on travel market research and knowledge and our cost estimates from RFPs [requests-for-proposals] we sent out to different software companies.

Campanelli: When did you start the site?

Gyuoshev: The beta version came out in December 2005. The official launch was in May 2006.

Campanelli: What were your start-up costs? Where did you get your funding?

Vassilev: $100,000. We did a joint venture with an existing travel agency, Smart Travel Network Inc. [Based in Long Island City, New York, Smart Travel Network Inc. is one of the largest Bulgarian-American travel service firms in the United States.]

Campanelli: How is selling a service on the web different from selling products?

Gyoshev: Support, support, support. When customers buy a camera or a book, they know exactly what they are getting. Selling travel is similar in some respects—customers are getting a seat on an airplane, but there are several important differences. Customers often have special needs and requests that need to be accommodated. Travel plans change and you need someone who can work with you to help you minimize the cost and time associated with rebooking all your tickets. Frequent flyer programs and a number of other deals are often too complicated, so customers need someone to help them make sense of the web of alliances and bonuses. For all of this, personal support is invaluable and can never be fully replaced by software.

Campanelli: Why is the internet a good place to sell services, specifically your services?

Vassilev: The internet is a global marketplace. Travel is a very local business where some companies have deals on specific regions. Taking those local deals and bringing them to each and every traveler on the internet is where true value is created.

Campanelli: Is this a do-it-yourself site, or did you hire a programmer/outside source to start it up?

Gyoshev: [We hire] programmers and outside help that were very carefully selected.

Campanelli: What are your monthly visitor counts?

Vassilev: We get over 500,000 visitors per month.

Campanelli: How do you attract visitors?

Gyoshev: Paid search, organic search, online advertising, public relations, word of mouth, and referrals.

Campanelli: How do you make money? Is it a subscription-based service?

Vassilev: Fees from selling tickets and commissions from the airlines. This is not a subscription-based service.

Campanelli: What are your secrets of success?

Gyoshev: Listening to customer feedback, having a positive attitude, and hard work.

Campanelli: What were some challenges you had starting out?

Vassilev: We naively believed that most of the providers we were working with would actually provide reasonable quality product—in our case, timely and accurate data feeds. Needless to say, that turned out to be wrong, so we had to spend quite some time and money compensating for—or sometimes actually fixing—other people's problems. Due diligence on suppliers can work wonders, and we are very careful in this respect now.

Campanelli: Have you run into any security/fraud issues?

Gyoshev: Yes. The travel business is notorious for credit card fraud, but we have very stringent credit card checks and procedures in place that have so far allowed us to identify and stop all fraudulent transactions.

Campanelli: How is the business growing?

Vassilev: 50 percent to 100 percent each month.

Campanelli: Do you have any tips for the readers about how to successfully run a business after starting it up?

Gyoshev: Put a small, good, and most important, dedicated team together. Make sure they listen to customer feedback and let them surprise you with their creativity. And always keep an eye on the P&L (profit and loss) statement.

Campanelli: Do you have tips about how to successfully grow a business after starting it up?

Vassilev: Marketing, public relations, alliances. And never, never underestimate word of mouth.

• • •

e-Chat with RedWagons.com's Tony Roeder

RedWagons.com
Tony Roeder, president and founder
Location: River Forest, Illinois
Year started: 1998

Tony Roeder is one of the internet's biggest success stories. In 1998, with virtually no experience, capital, or programming skills, he launched RedWagons.com (www.redwagons.com), a site that sells a full line of Radio Flyer wagons, accessories, and other products. The company, which has had steady growth over its first year, sells upward of 60 different products.

How did Roeder, a former handyman, get the idea to launch the site? In 1998, he was on a customer's porch assembling a Radio Flyer wagon when he was struck by the look and feel of the wagon. He had lots of memories of Radio Flyer products growing up and started thinking about what a great company Radio Flyer was. Says Roeder, "Radio Flyer has been a part of my earliest childhood memories—from the Radio Flyer wagon we had careening down our suburban driveway to the old rusty wagon I pulled my children around in at the time I was sitting on that porch."

He was also looking for another line of work and wondered about e-tailing, since he worked regularly with a hardware store that had started selling Weber grills online. Roeder realized there was a lot of opportunity in this arena.

Then, by chance, he ran into a person who worked for Radio Flyer and had a casual conversation with the employees about putting a wagon together for one of his customers. When he learned that Radio Flyer was not selling its products online—despite its online presence—he jumped at the chance to do just that, even though he had no internet experience at the time.

Here, Roeder offers his insights into starting a successful dotcom company.

Melissa Campanelli: How did you start your web site?

Tony Roeder: I first hired a web designer for $4,000 who worked for Radio Flyer's informational web site, but he had never done an e-commerce site before and basically could not get the site up in a reasonable [amount of time]. I had to fire him. I then contacted Yahoo! and built my site on the Yahoo! Store [now called Yahoo! Merchant Solutions] system. Their costs were pay as you go, and back then, it was about $200 or $300

SMART TIP

An opportunity to start a successful business can happen when you least expect it. For Tony Roeder, a chance meeting with someone from Radio Flyer, the red-wagon company, was the catalyst that prompted him to start his company, Red-Wagons.com. Always keep an open mind—you never know where or when a chance to start a business will pop up.

per month, which was less than what the designer was going to charge me for monthly maintenance.

Yahoo! made it possible for me to be my own web designer and store builder virtually overnight. The site went live in November 1998, just in time for the holiday season.

Campanelli: How do you handle fulfillment?

Roeder: Fulfillment is an ever-evolving process, but the key is that we make an effort to get products shipped out as soon as possible.

Campanelli: What are the secrets to your success?

Roeder: The combination of the Yahoo! exposure, good search-engine placement, and good links put us on the map. Technology has also been very important to our company. Most of our challenges have been met by judiciously applying technology to our processes.

Campanelli: What are your plans for the future? Your goals and objectives?

Roeder: In September 2003, we opened a brick-and-mortar store, which now sells Radio Flyer products and a full inventory of other toys and accessories as well. We'd been kicking around the idea for a while, because we knew we had to change our business model. The competitors who are coming on—expecting to do as well as we have done—are going after a model that worked five years ago, and they are getting a smaller and smaller piece of a very small pie. We still have the biggest piece, but our piece is getting smaller, and they are all getting little bites. Until now, we really didn't have the location to do it. We then learned that a space was available nearby in River Fort, Illinois, and it was perfect. It's in a shopping center and had the three elements needed: location, location, location.

In general, our objective is to maintain profitability and to be innovative. Our birth, growth, and explosion were due to being at the right place at the right time. Those types of opportunities don't exist today, but there may be some tomorrow. We are always alert to what is happening with them. We are also constantly refining our processes, our marketing, and our communication—and we try to always be aware of our competition so we can continue to grow as a company.

• • •

e-Chat with Thralow Inc.'s Daniel Thralow

Thralow Inc.
Daniel Thralow, CEO/Founder
Location: Proctor, Minnesota
Year started: 2001

Want to meet a passionate, successful online entrepreneur? Then meet Daniel Thralow, CEO/founder of Thralow Inc., which operates Binoculars.com (www.binoculars.com), Telescopes.com (www.telescopes.com), Peepers.com (www.peepers.com), Pans.com (www.pans.com), and 35 other niche retail and media sites. In 2005, Thralow's company topped $20 million in sales, and he expects to make $27 million by the end of 2006.

Thralow has come a long way since opening up a vintage clothing store in Grand Forks, North Dakota, in 1987.

One item that sold well in his store—even better than the clothes—was sunglasses, so Thralow got rid of the clothes and expanded the sunglasses selection.

Then, in 1990, Thralow started a company called Peepers Sunglasses and opened a brick-and-mortar store in a mall in Grand Forks.

Peepers did well: by 1993, Peepers had three stores, one in Grand Forks, one in Duluth, Minnesota, and one in downtown Minnepolis. (In 1994 he closed the Grand Forks store.)

In 1996, a contact of Thralow's built a web site for him for $100, and Thralow's first internet sale took place in December of that year (it was for a pair of Ray Ban round metal sunglasses). The domain for the site was www.digitialdiscounts.com/~peeperssunglasses.html. The name was so cumbersome because Thralow had no idea how to register a domain and that was the one selected for him.

Was that the last sale? Despite the cumbersome name, no way. In January 1997, Thralow sold two pairs of sunglasses on the internet, and by February, the dollar value of his online sales doubled.

Thralow was doing so well on the internet that he closed his retail stores in 1997 and put every spare penny he had into developing his web site. By 1998, sales on his site exploded to $1.5 million. Also, in 1998, Thralow tested selling binoculars on his web site. When the binoculars started to sell well and the business, in general, started to grow, he acquired the domain Binoculars.com in January 1999.

Why binoculars? Thralow said binoculars were complementary to sunglasses, and they were an attractive online item because unlike sunglasses, people didn't feel the need to try them on prior to buying.

In the spring of 1999, Thralow also acquired the domain name Peepers.com. That same year, when sales were on pace to reach $3.9 million, a publicly traded company that wanted to do a roll up of all the eyewear companies online approached Thralow. The company wanted to buy his online stores—Peepers.com and Binoculars.com—and other online eyewear stores, and have Thralow run the business out of his offices in Duluth, where he was based at the time.

Thralow said he thought the concept was a good idea because it would protect the margins in the sunglass category, "and I certainly couldn't afford to do that." He also was told he could keep his staff, receive a big check, and have the opportunity to pursue his dream. "I thought 'Where do I sign,'" said Thralow. "But the romance period lasted only six months . . . our trajectory of double and triple growth had ended, and sales were actually declining."

The reason? "I was declined the authority to run the company," says Thralow. "Had I actually been allowed to manage the company, the sales trajectory would have continued upward at its historical pace. I think this is proven by the more recent history that when I regained control of the company the exponential growth rate was regained."

In May 2000, Thralow resigned because after the sale of his company in 2001, "the new owners gradually stripped me of power and responsibility. I was not allowed to make the changes necessary to allow the company to continue to grow."

But the company owed him some money, and he used that money to reacquire all of the assets from his former company. On January 12, 2001, Thralow and eight employees of the 40 that were left started rebuilding what is now Thralow Inc. By the end of the year, sales reached $2.1 million.

Thralow said that in 2001, he put a lot more energy into Binoculars.com for several reasons. One was because his relationships with sunglasses manufacturers had been destroyed as a result of the conglomerate not paying them.

"Binoculars and Binoculars.com were less untainted," says Thralow. "There was a little bit of dirt that had splashed onto Binoculars.com, but not nearly as much dirt as had covered Peepers.com."

Then, in 2002, Thralow purchased the domain name Telescopes.com and entered the telescope space. Again, telescopes were a complementary item to binoculars, "and since Binoculars.com was doing so well, it made sense to follow that template," he says.

The following digs a little deeper into the world of Thralow Inc., and takes a look at how Thralow has built and grown his company.

Melissa Campanelli: Why did you expand into other areas besides binoculars, telescopes, and sunglasses?

Daniel Thralow: The sizes of the binoculars market and the telescope market are finite, and they are not growth-oriented. So if we are going to grow our company to be a big company, we have to branch out into other areas. And if we are going to branch out, we may as well branch out into the areas that present the highest potential for growth margins.

To select the categories we are moving into, we basically look at the amount of competition going into that category, as well as the amount of demand—and then choose a category. Then we either register domain names related to those categories or buy them from people who have already registered them, and then find vendors for merchandise.

Campanelli: How do you acquire merchandise?

Thralow: We do a number of things, including flying to China, Taiwan, and India for merchandise. In fact, we even have a guy whose only job is to find product.

Campanelli: Who are your competitors today?

Thralow: Amazon.com and eBay.com are two of our biggest competitors.

Campanelli: How do you beat the competition?

Thralow: The advantages that we have over Amazon.com and eBay.com are that we focus on specialty products and our web sites are true specialty stores; there is no better place in the world to buy a set of binoculars. We have the world's largest selection, we have all of the inventory inhouse, and our customer service is stellar. Try to find a telephone number on Amazon.com. You can't find one.

Campanelli: Tell me how you market your site. Do you use search engine marketing? Do your rely on word of mouth?

Thralow: We use many different methods to market the sites. Of course, a large percentage of our marketing budget goes to Google directly for keyword purchases or Google Adwords (the company's paid search engine marketing product). Probably one-third of our marketing budget goes to Google, and that makes me nervous. Anytime you have one method or company that you are reliant upon for large portion of sales makes me nervous—and I consider this one of our biggest potential weaknesses. So in the last year we have made an effort to diversify our marketing, by adding affiliate marketing and a blog.

Campanelli: Tell me about your blog.

Thralow: In February 2005, we started a blog called Birderblog.com (www.birderblog.com). Targeted at bird-watchers, the blog was designed and programmed inhouse. We use the blog to direct people to Binoculars.com (and vice versa). When binoculars are mentioned in the blog's text, the reference is hyperlinked to a page featuring the product on Binoculars.com.

We get many leads this way, and we know this because we measure click-through to the commerce site and sales that directly result from birderblog.com. There is no better qualified lead than someone who actually makes a purchase. The blog also includes banner ads promoting Binoculars.com.

Campanelli: How much does the blog cost?

SMART TIP

Want to start a blog? Go for it. But before you do, make sure to do your research and understand what you are getting yourself into. Blogs are fun, but can be demanding. A great resource is *The Weblog Handbook: Practical Advice on Creating and Maintaining Your Blog*, by Rebecca Blood (Perseus Books Group, 2002). The book is a very useful guide to weblogs: How to start one, how to grow an audience, how to deal with angry e-mail, and how to move up in technical sophistication.

Thralow: The blog costs $50,000 a year to maintain, but it cost about $60,000 to set up as a result of additional development costs in the first year.

The $50,000 goes to the salary of the blogger, the salary of tech staff to create and maintain the site, hosting costs for the site, and ancillary costs such as a digital camera, a computer for the blogger, and travel expenses.

Please note, however, that it absolutely does not have to cost as much as my company spends. If the passionate blogger is also the business owner, the labor could be free. While I am passionate about many things, I simply do not have time to maintain a blog. In addition, there are free "community blogs" out there with free or practically free hosting and software. Usually this requires the tradeoff of not controlling the advertising on the blog (usually Google AdWords). It was very important to me that our blog was pure and completely under our control. That is why it is much more expensive. For us, this is a long-term project and we do not expect to see return on investment (ROI) for at least a year, probably longer.

Campanelli: How do you advertise the blog?

Thralow: Our blog is promoted in several ways. First, we hired a passionate ornithologist. This gives us immense credibility. In addition, Laura is to birding as Julia Child is to cooking (no not dead—just famous). Among many other things, Laura does radio shows, leads tours, and speaks at many conferences. At each of these events, she usually has the opportunity to casually mention her blog (and, while we own the blog, it is her blog to run—it is important to not compromise her reputation). In addition to Laura's PR we have links on Binoculars.com to her blog.

Binoculars.com gets over 20,000 unique visitors every day, so this is great advertising. The blog is also promoted in newsgroups, on other birding blogs, and in e-mail newsletters. Then there are also those search engines.

Currently about 800 people per day visit the site compared to the more than 20,000 per day that visit Binoculars.com. However, the point is that it is continuing to grow. Birderblog.com is very young.

Campanelli: What are your secrets to success?

Thralow: I have 35 people working here, and my staff is very important to me. We share everything—we share all the financials. Letting the staff know as much as possible about what's going on in the company is a great motivator. They know that they can help it grow and that their input can really make a difference. We also work very hard to measure our marketing and make sure that it is effective.

Campanelli: What's next on the horizon?

Thralow: The online telescope and binoculars retail space can be a low-margin business. As a result, we are looking to expand and diversify.

As the next year approaches, we are looking more closely at expanding into other online shopping segments with potentially higher margins such as cooking and outdoor leisure, such as hammocks, where we already have a presence on the web.

•   •   •

e-Chat with Venture Point LLC's Karen Torbett

Venture Point LLC

Karen Torbett, president and founder

Location: Greenville, SC

Year started: 2005

Meet Karen Torbett, founder and president of Venture Point LLC (www.venturepointonline.com), an e-commerce web site that is a go-to resource for people seeking to buy or sell a business. For sellers, Venture Point maximizes potential for exposure through its multimedia advertising, opening them up to buyers all over the world. For buyers, Venture Point is a source of possibilities—a place to find something buyers may not even have known they were looking for. For attorneys, business brokers, and certified public accountants, Venture Point is a partner—an additional resource for them and their potential clients.

Torbett spent almost a decade running someone else's business. She was with a company during its early conception and later managed the company's sale to another party. Having worn a hat from nearly every department of the manufacturing facility, she compiled an immense amount of wisdom on the ins and outs of managing, running, and in the end, selling a business.

The inevitable stress of business management was contrasted by what Torbett was able to learn during this time—information she knew would benefit her when she eventually owned her own business, a dream and goal she'd been working toward all her life.

Though circumstances and responsibilities required her to take a different path at times, Torbett, a single mother of three, fed her entrepreneurial spirit by seeking out existing businesses for sale.

"At the time, a start-up was too risky for me," says Torbett. "I was interested in buying a business that was already established."

After looking on her own using different venues, such as newspapers, the internet, and brokers, Torbett was unable to find a business that was right for her. When the company she worked for went on the market, she handled the due diligence for its sale and realized that as long as a person had the time and determination, he or she could complete the process on their own. This insight motivated her to create Venture Point.

The purpose of Venture Point and its online service is to not only give people who may want to buy or sell a business on their own a venue through which to do it, but also to provide a "go-to" site for people to find information on buying and selling a business. It also offers a list of professionals, such as a business brokers, CPAs, and attorneys, that can help with the process.

"Owning a business—doing something I have always wanted to do—has given such purpose to my life," says Torbett.

In her spare time, Torbett volunteers in her church and local community and imagines ways to pass on her independent spirit to others, especially women, who have dreams of owning their own businesses. Unsurprisingly, she has also passed on her self-determination and confidence to her two daughters and son. "I've always stressed the importance of education and self-worth and have encouraged my children to *live* life, not just exist in it," says Torbett.

Want to learn more? Here is a closer look at Torbett and her business.

Melissa Campanelli: Why did you decide to start your company? Where did you get the idea for the site?

Karen Torbett: To be quite honest I never imagined owning an e-commerce web site. I was going between looking at pre-existing businesses for sale and starting one up. Most of my research was done on the internet. Many of the web sites that I went into that were selling businesses, I found to be overwhelming and would turn around and click back out of them. At first site they appeared to have a lot going on but taking a closer look I realized they were selling ad space, which is a revenue generator (probably some of it is ad exchange). I chose to forgo this type of revenue in order to have a clean, uncluttered, and professional-looking web site. I also wanted to give it a company or "bricks and mortar" feel. Not a cheesy web site that was thrown together overnight.

Campanelli: How is the site different from your competitor's sites?

Torbett: First of all, the advertising firm that I hired to build the web site researched and came to the same conclusion that I had—that there was no web site out there that was doing what I was trying to do. The difference being that I had a clean, uncluttered, ad-free, professional looking web site that was easy to navigate through. In addition, I wasn't just listing businesses for sale, but offering a complete resource with tips, ideas, and a "professional services" directory for those that may need help with the buying and selling process. I also had no confusing multi-level package plans, and all listings were considered "premium." Other sites, on the other hand, offered "standard," "deluxe," and "premium" listing plans, all at different price levels. I also beat their price rates and engaged in multimedia advertising, whereas most other web sites do little to no advertising outside of the internet.

Campanelli: Did you have a business plan? How did you go about writing it?

Torbett: A business plan is crucial in the success of a business; it shows the strategy of communication, management, and planning you intend to implement. Also, if a person plans on using a lending institution for funding of their business they will need to show a business plan. As the old saying goes, "if you fail to plan, you plan to fail."

Campanelli: When did you start the site?

Torbett: My idea came about in June of 2005. I hired an advertising firm a month later in July. The site was supposed to take approximately two months to build, but it took seven (the firm I hired had some internal issues). The site was officially operable by January 2006.

Campanelli: What were your start-up costs? Where did you get your funding?

Torbett: As with most start-up businesses the cost figured was not enough. The web site being five months overdue was a huge financial setback (I had only allotted for the web site to be one to two months overdue). I had allocated roughly $100,000 to $150,000. My funding was through a loan, mortgage line of credit, stocks, and savings.

Campanelli: How is selling a service on the web different from selling products?

Torbett: This has been my greatest obstacle to overcome. It is an intangible business. I'm not selling a product or meeting with people face-to-face. Any communication is done through e-mails. Even revenue generated is handled over the internet. Aside from advertising through various media forms, it is truly a virtual business.

Campanelli: Is this a do-it-yourself web site, or did you hire a programmer/outside source to start it up?

Torbett: This was not a do-it-yourself web site. It may have a simplistic look to it, but the internal operations are extremely technical. Also, I did not want a template-built site [which I felt would look too] generic. Instead, I was going for creative and original, and wanted to make sure that I had complete ownership of what was built. For this reason I sought out a company that had an inhouse programmer.

Campanelli: How do you attract visitors?

Torbett: From various forms of advertising—internet, news-papers, magazines, mailouts. As revenue is generated, it will continue to go into expanding the advertising.

SMART TIP

Karen Torbett's mantra might be "Make Lemonades out of Lemons." Why? Because instead of letting the stress of her former job keep her down, she took advantage of what was going on around her and learned information she knew would benefit her when she eventually owned her own business, a dream and goal she'd been working toward all her life. If you are currently in a stressful job, instead of getting stressed, take notes—you never know when you might learn something from the experience that you can apply when you start your own venture.

Campanelli: How do you make money? Is it a subscription-based service?

Torbett: It is a subscription-based service, although the web site is free for people seeking to buy a business or who need the help of a professional in their area of interest.

Campanelli: What were some challenges you had starting out?

Torbett: I was treading in unfamiliar territory. I had to get educated on the different types of web site designs and the building of one, as well as finding the right web site designer, merchant accounts/gate keepers, web hosting (whether to hire an outside source or carry it inhouse on my own server—I opted for an outside source), and the legalities for this type of site. Also, learning about all the different forms of internet advertising.

Campanelli: How is the business growing?

Torbett: Start-up businesses go through stages of development—concept or idea, start-up (business plan), first (operating and starting to take off—this is also the stage that investors like to come in on), second (asset and liabilities are forming), third (things are going well), and fourth (considering going public, selling, or merging). Venture Point is in the first stage of development. With the [young] age of the business, its growth is on target. It's starting to take off. I am still experimenting with what type of advertising works best. This is where the most trials, tribulations, and expense of a business lie. I am optimistic and excited about the direction Venture Point is going in.

• • •

Online Business
Resources

*H*ERE'S THE TRUTH ABOUT E-COMMERCE: Most of what you need to know will not be printed in books or even in magazines and newspapers. One medium that is successfully tracking the rapid developments online is the web itself. When you want to know more or need answers to questions, log on to the web and go searching. The information you crave is rarely more than a few mouse clicks away. Here you will find dozens of the sites that deserve tracking.

Competitive Intelligence

Fuld & Co.'s Internet Intelligence Index

www.fuld.com

Fuld & Co., a research and consulting firm in the field of business and competitive intelligence, has compiled this free index of information from a wide variety of public services. It contains links to more than 600 intelligence-related internet sites, covering everything from macroeconomic data to individual patent and stock quote information.

Hoover's

www.hoovers.com

The best content is available for a fee, but there is ample free content for anyone who surfs in. Research competitors, track stock market performance, and keep tabs on IPOs.

KnowX

www.knowx.com

The savvy engine ferrets through public records and reports on bankruptcies, liens, judgments, and such against individuals and businesses. Reports range from free to $24.95.

Thomas Register

www.thomasnet.com

This is the sourcebook on U.S. and Canadian companies; the book in print or on CD or DVD is free to companies in the United States and Canada, not including shipping and handling charges, and the content on the web is free as well.

Yahoo! Finance

http://finance.yahoo.com

This all-inclusive web site has everything from up-to-the-minute market summaries to stock research to financial news—and much of it is free.

Consumer Web Sites

BBBOnLine

www.bbbonline.org

The Better Business Bureau's entry into monitoring e-tailers.

Consumer Reports Web Watch

www.consumerwebwatch.com

A web site that aims to investigate, inform, and improve the quality of the information published on the web.

Federal Trade Commissions Consumer Web Site

www.ftc.gov/bcp/menu-internet.htm

Advice from the Federal Trade Commission that pinpoints common frauds.

How to Protect Yourself: Shopping on the Internet

http://myfloridalegal.com/consumer, then click on "Protecting Yourself from Consumer Fraud," and then "Internet Shopping"

Counsel from Florida's attorney general.

Internet ScamBusters

www.scambusters.org

This is a web site and a free electronic newsletter designed to help people protect themselves from internet scams, misinformation, and hype; much of the information focuses on internet merchants and consumers.

SafeShopping

www.safeshopping.org

Created by the American Bar Association, which bills it as "the place to stop before you shop."

WebAssured

www.webassured.com

An e-tailer evaluator.

Global Commerce

Going Shopping? Go Global! A Guide for E-Consumers

www.ftc.gov/bcp/conline/pubs/alerts/glblalrt.htm

A report from the FTC on online shopping overseas.

GlobalEDGE

http://globaledge.msu.edu/ibrd/ibrd.asp

Michigan State University's International Business Center's vast library of world trade resources that includes an outline of the business climate, political structure, history, and statistical data for more than 190 countries; a directory of international business resources categorized by specific orientation and content; and much more.

Planet Business

www.planetbiz.com

Business resources, arranged by country; a good place to look for foreign contacts, partners, and information.

Miscellaneous E-Commerce Information

All Domains

www.alldomains.com

There's more to web sites than ".net," ".com," and ".gov" domains. Find out about—and buy—international domains here as well.

ClicksLink

www.clickslink.com

For exploring offbeat affiliate programs—astrology, watch stores, and more.

Compare Web Hosts

www.comparewebhosts.com

This web site does just this—compares web hosting companies.

Constant Contact

www.constantcontact.com

A leading e-mail marketing service provider targeting small businesses; the company helps set up and run an e-mail list.

Keynote NetMechanic

www.netmechanic.com

For checking your site for bad code and broken links, free of charge.

LinkShare

www.linkshare.com

For signing up for affiliate status with name-brand e-tailers.

Microsoft Small Business Center

www.microsoft.com/smallbusiness/hub.mspx

A great resource for anyone starting a new business, with lots of information about Microsoft's products and services.

Network Solutions

www.networksolutions.com

A leading marketplace for registering U.S. domains.

Revenews.com

www.revenews.com

A leading blog that covers topics such as affiliate marketing, online marketing, contextual advertising, search marketing, online publishing, and spyware; the blog has very knowledgeable writers that offer commentary that is very current.

TopHosts

www.tophosts.com

Online and Offline Publications

Business 2.0
http://money.cnn.com/magazines/business

e-Commerce Times
www.ecommercetimes.com

Entrepreneur magazine
www.entrepreneur.com

Internet Retailer
www.internetretailer.com

MIT Technology Review
www.techreview.com

Wired
www.wired.com

Search Engines, Etc.

Ask
www.ask.com
Formerly known as Askjeeves.com, this site offers a robust search-engine technology.

Dogpile
www.dogpile.com
A meta search tool that is owned and operated by InfoSpace Inc., Dogpile simultaneously puts your query to the internet's top search engines.

Google
www.google.com
One of the best search engines out there, Google's is a serious hunting tool, even though its name is funny. Don't miss the "Cache" feature, where Google stores pages on its servers. If a site is down, the page may still be readable at Google.

Google AdWords
http://adwords.google.com/select
This site is devoted to Google AdWords, a leading sponsored search program from Google.

SearchEngineWatch.com
www.searchenginewatch.com
A great web site devoted to all things search.

Yahoo! Search
www.search.yahoo.com

Yahoo! Search Marketing
http://searchmarketing.yahoo.com
A leading sponsored search provider.

Shopping Bots

BidFind
www.bidfind.com/af
An auction bot.

BotSpot
www.botspot.com
An ambitious roundup of bots.

BottomDollar.com
www.bottomdollar.com

Froogle
http://froogle.google.com

mySimon
www.mysimon.com

PriceGrabber.com
www.pricegrabber.com

Shopping.com
www.shopping.com

Yahoo! Shopping
http://shopping.yahoo.com

Software

Dreamweaver 8
www.adobe.com/products/dreamweaver
The new version of the popular, higher-end web design software.

Microsoft Expression Web
www.microsoft.com
The web design software that takes over where FrontPage left off.

Interland
www.interland.com
A full suite of tools for building and hosting a complete e-commerce storefront.

WebExpress
www.mvd.com/webexpress
Robust, powerful software with a free trial available.

Zy
www.zy.com
Web-based tools for creating your own site; results can be first-rate.

Statistics and More

ClickZ Stats
Net-related stats in a readable format.
www.clickz.com/stats

eMarketer
www.emarketer.com
A great news source with an e-commerce focus and lots of stats.

Shop.org
www.shop.org/learn/stats.asp
An association of online retailers that devotes a section of its web site to the latest industry stats, compiled from more than 200 industry sources.

Traffic Reports and Ratings

comScore Media Metrix
www.comscore.com
The audience measurement division of comScore Networks offers an internet audience measurement service that reports on web site usage.

Internet Traffic Report
www.internettrafficreport.com
Measures router volume at various points around the world.

Nielsen//NetRatings
www.nielsen-netratings.com
A leader in internet media and market research.

Venture Capital Information

The Center for Venture Research at Whittemore School of Business and Economics at the University of New Hampshire
http://wsbe.unh.edu/Centers_CVR/about_us.cfm

The center has created a nationwide list of venture capital resources to help entrepreneurs find early-stage capital. You can order the list online for $40.

Kauffman eVenturing

www.eventuring.org

A web site from the well-known Ewing Marion Kauffman Foundation that can be tapped for timely, practical information on how to start, manage, and expand your business.

MoneyHunt

www.moneyhunt.com

The home page for the popular TV show that helps entrepreneurs link with VCs and angels.

National Venture Capital Association

www.nvca.org

This association's web site contains industry statistics and lists of venture capital organizations and preferred industry service providers.

vFinance Inc.

www.vfinance.com

A directory of venture capital resources and related services; a good site for getting info on who's who in the VC world and how deals get cut.

Web Site Building

Download.com

www.download.com

Allows users to download trial versions and full versions of software.

Webdeveloper.com

www.webdeveloper.com

One-stop shopping for advice and tools for building better web sites.

Web Site Design No-Nos

How to Build Lame Web Sites

www.webdevelopersjournal.com/columns/perpend1.html

An insightful—and sometimes funny—look at bad site design.

Jakob Nielsen's Web Site

www.useit.com

The guru of web usability, Nielsen particularly revels in pinpointing the "must nots" of web site architecture. If Nielsen says don't do it, don't do it.

Web Site Tools

123 Webmaster

www.123webmaster.com

Links to thousands of tools, from JavaScripts to web templates.

1NetCentral

www.1netcentral.com

Offers links to free stuff, such as a free web hosting directory and a free graphics directory.

Bravenet

www.bravenet.com

Free web site and free web tools.

Web Site Resource

www.wsresource.com

Links to free webmaster resources, tools, and tutorials.

Webmaster Tools Inc.

www.webmastertools.com

A site that offers tools to help build, maintain, promote, and market a web site.

Wireless Web

Open Mobile Alliance

www.openmobilealliance.org

This organization is designed to be the center of mobile service standardization work, helping the creation of interoperable services across countries, operators, and mobile terminals that will meet the needs of users.

TagTag

http://tagtag.com/site/index.php3

A free tool that will help you make your site wireless and web-ready.

Wap Catalog

www.wapcatalog.com

A directory of wireless web sites.

The Wireless FAQ

www.thewirelessfaq.com

A site where programmers for wireless devices share information.

Glossary

Angel: someone who invests his or her money in a start-up.

Beta site: a test site, usually erected in the authoring phase of a web site.

Bot: a robot, or program, that automatically does specified tasks.

Brick-and-mortar: a term describing traditional businesses with a physical storefront rather than a cyberbusiness.

Business to business (B2B): companies that seek businesses, not consumers, as customers.

Business to consumer (B2C): companies that market to consumers.

Common Gateway Interface (CGI) script: a simple program that runs on the internet; guest books, for instance, often are CGI scripts.

Clip art: off-the-shelf images anyone can use; web site authoring programs usually include lots of clip art.

Cookie: data created by a web server that's stored on a user's computer to identify that user on return visits to the web site.

Domain: the domain name is what comes before the ".com," ".net," or ".edu," all of which are known as top-level domains.

File transfer protocol (FTP): the system used to transfer files over the net; you FTP files to your web host.

First-mover advantage: the built-in advantage of being the first business in a particular category.

Host: a company that provides space for storing (hosting) a web site.

Hyperlink: a connection between one object and another; also known as a link.

Hypertext markup language (HTML): a code that creates web pages.

Internet service provider (ISP): the company that provides a telephone connection that lets a user connect to the internet.

Link: a connection between one object and another; also known as a hyperlink.

Log: a record of all visits to a web site; a log usually gives a click-by-click report on a visitor.

Look-to-buy ratio: a common measurement used in analyzing the effectiveness of an e-tailer; ideally a 1-to-1 ratio—one looker produces one buyer; look-to-buy ratios of less than 10-to-1 are desirable.

Meta tag: an HTML expression that defines a web site's content, to be read by search engines and crawlers.

Mind share: consumer awareness and loyalty.

Newsgroup: an internet message board or bulletin board.

Portal: a web "supersite" that offers links to substantial amounts of information and often to other sites; Yahoo! is the premier portal.

Search engine: a web site that exists to help users find other web sites; Google (www.google.com) is one of the best search engines.

Spam: unwanted, unsolicited commercial e-mail.

Spider: spiders (also known as crawlers) search the web for information; search engines use spiders to find web pages.

Template: a predesigned document; a web page template, for instance, requires the user to simply fill in some blanks to produce a publishable document.

Term sheet commitment: a written offer from a venture capitalist that sets out how much money the firm will invest in a start-up in return for what percentage of ownership.

URL: universal resource locator, or, more simply, a web page's address.

Venture capitalist (VC): a professional money lender who seeks out high-potential start-ups to fund.

Webmaster: a person skilled in creating and maintaining web pages

Wireless Application Protocol (WAP): the standard underlying programs that run on cell phones.

Wireless Markup Language (WML): the underlying computer code that produces pages that display on the wireless web.

Index